A RE-INTRODUCTION TO
THOMAS NEWBERRY
VOLUME 1

A Re-Introduction
to
Thomas Newberry
VOLUME 1

TYPES OF THE
LEVITICAL OFFERINGS

TYPES OF THE TABERNACLE

SOLOMON'S TEMPLE
AND ITS TEACHING

JOHN RITCHIE LTD
CHRISTIAN PUBLICATIONS

40 Beansburn, Kilmarnock, Scotland

ISBN-13: 978 1 904064 81 7
ISBN-10: 1 904064 81 7

Copyright © 2009 by John Ritchie Ltd.
40 Beansburn, Kilmarnock, Scotland

www.ritchiechristianmedia.co.uk

The *Classic Reprint Series* is derived from facsimile copies of the originally published material.

At times the quality of print and typeface may have been compromised as a result of either inferior original copy or the facsimile process itself.

We are confident, however, that the vast majority of the printed content is of reasonable quality and most importantly is legible.

Typeset by John Ritchie Ltd., Kilmarnock
Printed by Bell & Bain Ltd., Glasgow

TYPES OF
THE LEVITICAL OFFERINGS

Types of the Levitical Offerings

THOMAS NEWBERRY

CONTENTS.

TYPES

OF THE

LEVITICAL OFFERINGS

Introduction.

GOD, who knows our frame and remembers that we are dust, has, in His fatherly condescension, from the earliest times, instructed the children of faith by means of pictures, or object lessons. It is so difficult for man, who is a complex being, composed of body, soul, and spirit, to form purely abstract or spiritual ideas; they need, more or less, to be clothed in a material form.

Beginning with the first victim offered in Paradise, in the skin of which our first parents were clothed by the hand of God, onward by Abel's offering, and the long succession of sacrifices through the following ages, the Father was making known by type and symbol the deep things of God, and the precious things of Christ, which could only be spiritually apprehended by the teaching of the Holy Ghost.   Sight is threefold —physical, mental, and spiritual.

The eye gazes on the type, reason may form its conclusions, but the Holy Ghost alone can communicate the mind of God concerning the truths contained in it. In these types we have the embodiment of the thoughts of God concerning the person, work, and offices of the Lord Jesus Christ.

But as the spirit of man alone knows the inward thoughts of man, so these deep and wondrous thoughts of God can only be communicated to us by the Spirit of God Himself (1 Cor. ii. 11).

Moreover, as the Word of God endureth for ever, and the heavens and earth may pass sooner than one jot or tittle of the law may fail, we have in these types, in all their minuteness of detail, a record for eternity, imprinted by the Spirit of God on the pages of the eternal Word, for the instruction of the inhabitants of heaven and the universe, throughout the countless ages of eternity, concerning the incarnation, sufferings, atoning death, and priestly office of the Lord Jesus Christ.

The Offerings

(Leviticus i.).

Verses 1, 2. "And Jehovah called unto Moses, and spake unto him out of the tent of the congregation, saying, Speak unto the children of Israel, and say unto them, If any man of you bring an offering unto Jehovah, ye shall bring your offering of the cattle, even of the herd, and of the flock."

THE law was given from Mount Sinai. The patterns of things in the heavens having a shadow of good things to come were shown to Moses on the mount, when he was there with Jehovah forty days and forty nights. When the tabernacle was pitched, and everything arranged according to the commandment of God, "then the cloud covered the tent of the congregation, and the glory of Jehovah filled the tabernacle. And Moses was not able to enter into the tent of the congregation, because the cloud abode thereon, and the glory of Jehovah filled the tabernacle" (Ex. xl. 34, 35).

Leviticus i. is a continuation of Exodus xl. 35, informing us that Jehovah called to Moses out of the tent of the congregation. In Numbers vii. 89 we read, "And when Moses was gone into the tabernacle [tent] of the congregation to speak with Him, then he heard the voice of One speaking unto him from off the mercy-seat [propitiatory] that was upon the ark of testimony, from between the two cherubims : and He spake unto him."

9

From this we learn that whether Moses was standing without, or, as subsequently, entered within the tent, the voice which spake with him was the voice of sovereign grace speaking from off the mercy-seat—that is, speaking in grace—founded on redemption, showing on what terms the unworthy sinner might draw nigh to a righteous and holy God, and find acceptance with Him.

1. Man is a guilty transgressor, and needs forgiveness. Leviticus, chap. v. THE TRESPASS OFFERING.

2. He is a sinner, and needs an atoning sacrifice. Leviticus, chap. iv. THE SIN OFFERING.

3. He is in heart alienated from God, and needs reconciliation. Leviticus, chap. iii. THE PEACE OFFERING.

4. He is fallen and depraved in nature, and needs as a substitute One who is holy, harmless, undefiled, and separate from sinners. Leviticus, chap. ii. THE MEAT, or GIFT OFFERING.

5. He is utterly unworthy in himself, without anything of his own to recommend him to God; he needs, therefore, to be identified with One who is altogether worthy, and an object of Divine favour, that he might be accepted in God's Beloved. Leviticus, chap. i. THE BURNT or ASCENDING OFFERING.

The Burnt or Ascending Offering
(Leviticus i.).

IN the earlier chapters of Leviticus the provisions of Divine grace, meeting the requirements of man in these five particulars, are stated in their inverse order. In chapter i. it is the voice of love and mercy speaking from off the propitiatory. The ground of acceptance is stated, as shown in the BURNT or ASCENDING OFFERING.

COMMUNION WITH GOD.

Father, we come into Thy presence now,
And in the Saviour's name before Thee bow;
We gather round the person of Thy Son
And His supremacy would gladly own.

We meet dependent on Thy Spirit's power,
To lift our souls above in this blest hour;
To bring us into fellowship with Thee,
To feel Thy presence, and Thy glory see.

We want to hear Thee speaking in Thy Word,
O let Thy voice therein be clearly heard;
That it may not in letter only come,
But to each heart in living power speak home.

Grant us to realize our Saviour's grace,
To gaze upon our heavenly Father's face;
Communion with the Comforter to know,
Imparting heavenly joys to hearts below.

T. NEWBERRY.

11

Provision is here made for the individual's approach with acceptance before God : whether that individual be the sinner on his first approach, or the believer in his constant intercourse with God.

The word here rendered "offering" is *Korban*, from *Kahrab*, to draw nigh, hence styled the approach offering. In coming to the Cross as sinners for pardon and salvation, it is quite right to say,

"Nothing in my hand I bring" ;

but in drawing nigh to God, the Object of worship, the Divine statute is, "None shall appear before Me empty" (Ex. xxiii. 15).

In ourselves we are utterly unworthy; it is through Christ we have boldness and access with confidence before God by the faith of Him (Eph. iii. 12).

"For through Him we both [Jew and Gentile] have access by one Spirit unto the Father" (Eph. ii. 18).

The threefold division of this chapter is—from the HERD, from the FLOCK, and from the FOWLS.

The first is of the herd, and for a burnt or an ascending offering, so called because the victim, entirely consumed by fire, ascended as incense or perfume, a sweet savour, or savour of rest, unto God. The Hebrew word rendered "burnt offering" is *Holah*, from the root *Hahlah*, to ascend. The word rendered "offer" does not mean *burn on the altar*, but *let him bring,* or BRING NEAR; this is the offerer's part, the priest laid it on the altar.

The male offering from the herd represents Christ in His life of active and personal service, and obedience altogether perfect, even unto death itself—the death of the cross.

The context shows that instead of "He shall offer it of his own voluntary will," it is better to render it, "He shall bring it for his acceptance," for the word here employed is the same as in verse 4, and there rendered, "It shall be accepted for him."

The expression, which is correct, "The entrance of the tent of the congregation," refers to the space in front of the tabernacle where stood the brazen altar, and the laver, the appointed place of communion between God and His people (see Ex. xxix. 42, 43). It is here the question of drawing nigh to God, hence he brings his offering "before Jehovah."

The laying of the hand on the head of the victim is not so much expressive of the transfer of guilt as in the case of the sin offering (Lev. iv. 29), though that may be included; it is rather the identification of the offerer with the victim presented, whether accepted or refused. So Jacob sent his offering to Esau, whom he had offended.

This principle is well understood in other countries in the present day. If a gift sent to a chief is accepted, the offerer may reckon on a favourable reception; if it be rejected, it is his policy to retire as quickly as possible. Cain and Abel both presented their offerings to God. Abel's was accepted, but Cain's was refused. "By faith Abel offered unto God a more excellent sacrifice than Cain, by which he obtained witness that he was righteous, God testifying of his gifts : and by it he being dead yet speaketh" (Heb. xi. 4)

Notice, the promise is not he—the offerer—shall be accepted because of the offering, though that is true; it is even stronger—IT, THE OFFERING, shall be accepted for him. The offering being presented according to the appointment of God, and perfectly meeting all His requirements, could not be otherwise than accepted; and God has shown His acceptance of the offering of Christ by raising Him from the dead; and the believer in Christ who draws nigh through Him is accepted in God's beloved (Eph. i. 6).

Sooner or later the question of sin must be settled, and provision is made for this here; the victim was not only to be without blemish, but its blood was to be shed, and "without shedding of blood is no remission" of sin. So God has not only made the believer "accepted in the Beloved," that is, in Christ, but in Him "we have redemption through His blood, even the forgiveness of sins" (Eph. i. 6, 7); that is, we are accepted, not only on the ground of His perfect obedience, but in the value of His atoning blood.

Verses 3, 4. "If his offering [approach offering] be a BURNT SACRIFICE.[or ascending offering] of the herd, let him offer [or bring near] a male without blemish: he shall offer [bring it near] IT of his own voluntary will [or for his acceptance] at the door [or entrance] of the tent of the congregation before Jehovah. And he shall put his hand upon the head of the burnt offering [ascending offering]; and it SHALL be accepted for him to make atonement for him."

In the expression "It SHALL be accepted" the word "SHALL" in the original is not in the future tense, but it is in the *short* or *aorist* tense, expressive of decision and certainty; for "all the promises of God in Christ are yea and amen, to the glory of God by us." We have God's answer in the resurrection of Christ.

The assurance of acceptance comes from the throne of God, on which the Risen One is seated. In that acceptance the believer is included. "For He made Him to be sin for us, who knew no sin; that we might become the righteousness of God in Him" (2 Cor. v. 21).

Verse 5. "And he shall kill the bullock [son of the herd] before Jehovah: and the priests, Aaron's sons, shall bring the blood, and sprinkle the blood round about upon the altar that is by the door of the tent of the congregation."

The BULLOCK, as we have seen, is typical of the Lord Jesus Christ in His life of perfect SERVICE, as well as in His atoning death.

The bullock ploughed the land, brought home the sheaves from the harvest field, trod out the corn for the household—type of Him who was the pattern Evangelist, Pastor, and Teacher.

"Son of the herd." One in outward appearance made like unto His brethren, yet without sin, and set apart both for service and sacrifice to Jehovah.

It is the offerer who slays the victim; it is an act done by him, not for him, and this teaches an important truth. In drawing nigh to God, on the ground of the atoning sacrifice of Christ, it is well to realize, not only that He died for our sins, but that it was our sins and our transgressions that were the guilty causes of His death : for had we not sinned, He had not died. This is beautifully expressed in the well-known hymn by John Newton, beginning—

<blockquote>"In evil long I took delight."</blockquote>

And the victim was to be slain before Jehovah : faith not only apprehending that the eye of God rested on our sins, but that the same eye rests on the sacrifice for sin. So that the enormity of the transgression was met by the value of the sacrifice; thus—

<blockquote>"The very spear that pierced His side
Drew forth the blood to save."</blockquote>

The sprinkling of the blood was a priestly act; the place was the entrance of the tent of the congregation, where stood the brazen altar, and the laver filled with water from the smitten rock.

Here God promised to meet with the children of Israel, and to sanctify the meeting-place with His glory.

The blood was to be sprinkled round about upon the altar : on every side—east, west, north, and south.

It pleads to God on every account, and has a voice of invitation to sinners of every clime.   But it not only speaks to earth, but also to heaven—

> "Jesu's blood through earth and skies,
> Mercy, free boundless mercy, cries."

God, through the blood of Christ's cross, has reconciled all things unto Himself, not only things on earth, but things in heaven (Col. i. 20).

Defilement had entered into the heavens above, through the fall of angels, before it had entered into the earth through the fall of man.

The work of atonement is not only the ground on which God can forgive sinners, but it lies at the foundation of universal security.

The question of sin and creature responsibility has been settled for ever at the cross.   He who descended first into the lower parts of the earth has also ascended up far above all heavens, that He might fill all things.

His atoning work is not only the basis of stability below, but the keystone of universal security above, throughout all ages.   God "having made known unto us the mystery of His will, according to His good pleasure which He hath purposed in Himself : that in the dispensation of the fulness of times He might gather together in one [head up] all things in Christ, both which are in the heavens, and which are on earth; even in Him (Eph. i. 9, 10).

Verse 6. "And he shall flay the burnt offering [ascending offering], and cut IT into his pieces."

The offerer was to do this. He first removed the outward skin, and thus showed that there was no defect nor blemish beneath the surface; and he then cut the victim into its various parts, laying open its internal perfectness. First, he satisfied himself that the offering he brought was faultless and perfect, and then laying all naked and opened before the eye of God with whom he had to do (Heb. iv. 13).

Thus it is that our confidence in the sacrifice of Christ depends on the depth of our acquaintance with His perfections made known to us by the Word of God, which is as the dissecting knife.

Verse 7. "And the sons of Aaron the priest shall put fire upon the altar, and lay the wood in order upon the fire."

Observe the action of the offerer and of the priest alternatés. The priest is priest by virtue of the anointing. It is as having "an unction from the Holy One" that we act as priests and apprehend the spiritual truths here set forth.

The fire is emblematic of the righteousness and holiness of God. " For our God is a consuming fire" (Heb. xii. 29). The fire of the altar came originally from God, and was ever to be kept burning on it; it was never to go out (Lev. vi. 13). By the priest putting fire on the altar, therefore, we may understand his spreading the burning embers over that portion of the altar on which the victim was to be laid.

The wood is emblematical of sin, which provokes the righteous indignation of God. The priest laying the wood in order upon the fire typifies the setting forth of sin in the presence of a holy and a righteous God, as expressed in that word of the Psalmist: "Thou hast set our iniquities before Thee, our secret sins in the light of Thy countenance" (Ps. xc. 8).

Verse 8. "And the priests, Aaron's sons, shall lay the parts, the head, and the fat, in order upon the wood that is on the fire which is upon the altar."

Thus the sin of the offerer, in all its variety and detail, is met also in detail by the value and excellency of the offering; the parts, the head, and the fat, being symbolic of the perfectness of Christ, both in His person, and in the internal purity and preciousness of every thought and feeling, as He presented Himself without spot to God.

The fire was the fire of the altar, the wood was laid upon the fire, and the sacrifice was laid upon the wood. This symbolized the holiness of God, dealing with sin on the ground of redemption, and satisfied by the perfect sacrifice of Christ.

Verse 9. "But his inwards and his legs shall he wash in water."

The offerer was to do this. And by this washing is set forth the internal purity of the thoughts, affections, and desires of the Lord Jesus, and also the sinlessness of His ways and walk through a defiled and defiling world, in His whole progress from the manger to the cross. Without this twofold washing the victim would not have been a fit type of Him who was in all points holy, harmless, undefiled, and separate from sinners.

As a ray of sunlight remains pure, whatever objects it might shine upon, so the pathway of the Lord Jesus was unsullied by any of the scenes through which He passed.

"And the priest shall burn [burn as incense] all on the altar, to be a burnt sacrifice [ascending offering], an offering made by fire, of a sweet savour [savour of rest] unto Jehovah."

It is important to notice that in Hebrew there are three or four words which signify to BURN.

First, SAHRAPH, to "consume by burning" as in the sin offering, outside the camp (Lev. iv. 12).

Second, MOKDAH, "to consume by slow process," as the ascending offering was burning all night until the morning upon the altar (Lev. vi. 9).

Third, HIKTEER, "to convert by fire into incense," from Kahtar, to burn incense, which is the word here employed. This, again, is a priestly act, and by this is symbolized that Christ, in His entire service, person, experience, and walk, tested by the infinite holiness and righteousness of God, was found perfect and acceptable, a sweet savour unto God; and not only so, but also a savour of rest, for so the Hebrew word implies, being that on which God could rest with full satisfaction and delight, every attribute and perfection having been manifested, harmonized, and glorified thereby. To all this God has set His seal by raising Him from the dead, and setting Him on His own right hand. Thus the so-called burnt sacrifice is, properly speaking, the ascending offering, as it sets forth Christ, not only in life and death, but in resurrection and ascension. And in Hebrews iii. and iv. the Spirit of God invites the believer to have fellowship with God in His sabbatic rest.

Verse 10. "And if his offering [approach offering] be of the flocks, namely, of the sheep, or of the goats, for a burnt sacrifice [ascending offering]; he shall bring [bring near] it a male without blemish [perfect]."

In the offerings from the FLOCK, Christ as the Son of God is presented especially in the excellency and perfection of His CHARACTER. First, as the LAMB of God without blemish and without spot, holy, harmless, undefiled, and separate from sinners, the meek and the lowly One; or, secondly, under the figure of a GOAT, according to Romans viii. 3, in the likeness of sinful flesh, though Himself sinless—that is, made in all points like unto His brethren, yet without sin.

The offerer or worshipper, in drawing nigh to God, conscious of his own imperfection in character and

conduct, approaches Him in the name of One in whom
every human virtue and excellence was seen in full
perfection, the chiefest among ten thousand, and the
altogether lovely. To be accepted in the sweet savour
of what Christ was in the estimate òf God His Father,
in the perfection of His life as well as in the value of
His atoning death, this is signified by the offering of
a SHEEP.

Under the figure of a GOAT for a burnt offering
Christ is presented in another aspect, and as meeting
a deeper need. The offerer in the apprehension of the
sinfulness of his nature, his innate depravity, and that
in him—that is, in his flesh—dwells no good thing,
approaches God on the ground of the sacrifice of One
in whom, though Himself sinless, God "condemned
sin in the flesh" (Rom. viii. 3). For not only was sin
laid upon Him as the spotless Lamb, but, under the
emblem of a goat, sin was imputed to Him so that on
the cross, whilst He bare and put away the iniquity
of our outward transgressions, He also met our deeper
need in atoning, not simply for what we have done,
but for what we are; or, as Scripture expresses it, "He
made HIM sin for us, who knew no sin; that we might
become the righteousness of God in Him" (2 Cor. v:
21).

Verse 11. "And he shall kill IT on the side of the altar
    northward before Jehovah: and the priests, Aaron's
    sons, shall sprinkle his blood round about upon the
    altar."

The offerer slays the victim on the NORTH side of
the altar, the side of judgment, as meeting the requirements of Divine justice.

And in the presence of Jehovah, for the question is not so much am I satisfied, but is God? Angels gazed on Christ at Calvary, but the most interested spectator was the Father when Christ through the eternal Spirit offered Himself without spot to God. The sprinkling of the blood is a priestly act, as setting forth the ground on which alone we can draw near to a righteous and holy God.

Verse 12. "And he shall cut IT into his pieces, with his head and his fat: and the priest shall lay THEM in order on the wood that is on the fire which is upon the altar."

The internal perfectness and excellency of the victim are thus by the offerer laid open before the eye of God. The fire on the altar was to be for ever burning. Fresh wood was added from time to time. The pieces were laid upon the wood by the officiating priest; beautifully setting forth how the righteousness of God in redemption, dealing with man's sin, is met and satisfied by the perfect and precious sacrifice of Christ. God's holy priesthood, by virtue of the anointing—that is, by the teaching of the Spirit of God—are enabled to apprehend and set forth this.

Verse 13. "But he shall wash the inwards and the legs with water: and the priest shall bring it all, and burn [burn with incense] it upon the altar: IT is a burnt sacrifice [an ascending offering], an offering made by fire, of a sweet savour [savour of rest] unto Jehovah."

The washing of the INWARDS and the LEGS by the offerer sets forth the INTERNAL purity of the THOUGHTS, and the EXTERNAL purity of the WALK, of the Lord Jesus whilst He was here on earth.

The whole victim was burnt as incense by the priest upon the altar.

Verse 14. "And if the burnt sacrifice [ascending offering] for his offering [approach offering] to Jehovah be of fowls, then he shall bring his offering [approach offering] of turtledoves, or of young pigeons."

In the turtledove or young pigeon Christ is foreshadowed in His internal thoughts, affections, and desires. When at His baptism the Holy Ghost descended on Him, it was in a bodily shape like a dove (Luke iii. 22), and this dove-like spirit pervaded every thought, feeling, and desire. In our approaches to God, when conscious of our own imperfections in thought, purpose, and desire Godward, it is blessed to realize our acceptance in One who was divinely perfect in every internal feeling.

Verse 15. "And the priest shall bring it unto the altar, and wring off his head, and burn [burn as incense] it on the altar; and the blood thereof shall be wrung out at the side of the altar."

The priest brought it to the altar; so Christ, through the eternal Spirit, offered Himself without spot to God, and we, through Christ by the Spirit, draw nigh to God. The wringing off the head, and the wringing out of the blood, foreshadow the death and blood-shedding of Jesus on the cross.

Verse 16. "And he shall pluck away his crop with his feathers, and cast IT beside the altar on the east part, by the place of the ashes."

This was the action of the offerer, and corresponds with the washing of the inwards and legs of the other offerings, thus constituting the victim a fit emblem of Christ in His external and internal purity.

Verse 17. "And he shall cleave IT with the wings thereof, but shall not divide it asunder."

The thoughts, purposes, and desires of Christ, both in their substance and outgoing, though surrendered, were undivided. He served His Father with unswerving fidelity; it was His meat and drink to do His will and finish His work. His love to His Father was pure and undivided, and admitted no rival. In thought, purpose, and desire He was single and undistracted, there was nothing of a double mind in Him.

"And the priest shall burn [burn as incense] IT upon the altar, upon the wood that is upon the fire: IT is a burnt sacrifice [an ascending offering], an offering made by fire, of a sweet savour [savour of rest] unto Jehovah."

When our secret thoughts, purposes, and desires are seen in the light of God's countenance, and tested by His searching holiness, we may well say, "Woe is me! for I am undone"; but we draw nigh to God through One whose offering was found in every respect an offering and a sacrifice to God of a sweet-smelling savour, on which God could rest with perfect satisfaction and delight.

The Meat or Gift Offering

(Leviticus ii.).

Verse 1. "And when any will offer [bring] a meat offering [an approach offering of a gift offering] unto
Jehovah, his offering shall be of fine flour; and he shall
pour oil upon it, and put frankincense thereon."

THE so-called MEAT offering is, properly speaking,
a "GIFT offering," the Hebrew word *minkhah*
being derived from a root signifying to give.
It is a beautiful type, similar to that of the manna,
representing Christ as the GIFT of God in a threefold
point of view.

First, as the gift of the FATHER. "For God so loved
the world, that He gave His only begotten Son" (John
iii. 16).; again, "My Father giveth you the true bread
from heaven" (John vi. 32).

Secondly, as CHRIST'S gift for the Church, for
"Christ also loved the Church, and gave Himself for
it" (Eph. v. 25).

Thirdly, the gift of the HOLY GHOST, for He takes
of the things of Christ and reveals them unto us; Ex.

makes Christ ours, so that the individual believer can say, "He loved me, and gave Himself for me" (Gal. ii. 20). "Thanks be unto God for His unspeakable gift" (2 Cor. ix. 15). When we approach God in the name of Christ, presenting Him as the ground of acceptance, we may say with David, "Of Thine own have we given Thee " (1 Chron. xxix. 14), the gift of God's providing, faith presents before Him.

The FINE FLOUR is an emblem of the pure, perfect, sinless humanity of the Lord Jesus—the woman's seed, the Virgin's Son.

The OIL poured upon it represents Him as the Messiah, the Anointed One, according to the word of Isaiah (lxi. 1), quoted by Christ in the synagogue of Nazareth, "The Spirit of Jehovah is upon Me, because He hath anointed Me" (Luke iv. 18).

The Hebrew word for FRANKINCENSE signifies WHITE, conveying the idea of purity. The whole of Christ's spotless life was a sweet savour to God. To this the Father beareth witness again and again, "Thou art My beloved Son, in whom I am well pleased."

Verse 2. "And he shall bring it to Aaron's sons the priests: and he shall take thereout his handful of the flour thereof, and of the oil thereof, with all the frankincense thereof; and the priest shall burn [burn as incense] the memorial of it upon the altar, to be an offering made by fire, of a sweet savour [savour of rest] unto Jehovah."

As an offerer the believer draws nigh to God on the ground of the perfectness and preciousness of Christ; and as a priest he presents his offering on God's altar.

The offerer takes a handful of fine flour, and of the oil, with all the frankincense. This represents the believer by faith apprehending to the utmost of his capacity the purity, spirituality, and perfect acceptability of Christ before God, the soul's grasp of the truth concerning Christ. As a priest by virtue of the anointing, he apprehends that everything connected with Christ, as subjected to the searching holiness of God, is infinitely well pleasing to God, and that on which He can rest with Divine complacency and delight. It is faith's memorial before God of all that Jesus was in the days of His flesh, as well as of what He now is in the presence of God for us, for He is "the same yesterday, to-day, and for ever."

Verse 3. "And the remnant [remainder] of the meat [gift] offering shall be Aaron's and his sons': it is a thing most holy [holy of holies] of the offerings of Jehovah made by fire."

Fellowship in feeding together on Christ. The offerer, representing the believer, takes his handful of the gift offering : this is faith's portion. The memorial burnt upon the altar is God's portion. Aaron also and his sons, representing Christ as High Priest, and the priestly family as a holy and royal priesthood (1 Peter ii. 5-9), have their portion also ; for Christ "shall see of the travail of His soul, and shall be satisfied" (Isa. liii. 11), and in this satisfaction His believing people join.

The humanity of Christ, that holy thing that was born of the virgin (Luke i. 35), tested by the righteousness and holiness of God, was found to be "holy of holies," of all holy things most holy; purity and excellency of the highest order in the estimate of God is found there.

Verse 4. "And if thou bring an oblation of a gift offering baken in the oven, it shall be unleavened cakes [pierced cakes] of fine flour mingled with oil, or unleavened wafers anointed with oil."

This is faith's memorial of Christ on Calvary, when drawing nigh to God in the value of His sacrifice and work. It is the realization of Christ's sufferings on the cross in their most solemn aspect.

The sufferings of Jesus in accomplishing His atoning work were from three different sources.

First, FROM GOD. In the secret experience of His soul, shut in with God, an experience unrecognized by outward sight. This is symbolized by the gift offering BAKEN IN THE OVEN. This inward experience is expressed in Psalm xxii. 1-5, especially during those three solemn hours of awful darkness. Then the sun was darkened and became invisible, not only throughout the whole land, but it may be, as a telegraphic signal, flashed from star to star, and from world to world, throughout the universe, as the sign that then was being accomplished the most stupendous event in the annals of eternity. This was redemption through the blood of the Lamb, thus making provision at once for the putting away of sin, and laying the foundation for peace and security to the whole creation of God for time and for eternity (Col. i. 20).

As the appearance of the star in the East was the sign of the birth of Immanuel, so the disappearance of the sun at noonday was the signal of His death.

This darkness continued from the sixth to the ninth hour, and about the ninth hour the pent-up feelings of Immanuel gave vent in those impassioned accents, "My God, My God, why didst Thou forsake Me?"

The "fine flour" is emblematic of the pure, holy humanity of the Son of man, the woman's seed, the virgin's Son.

"Unleavened," for, though made in all points like unto His brethren, and "in the likeness of sinful flesh," He was perfectly without sin—"holy, harmless, undefiled, and separate from sinners."

The Hebrew word here rendered "cakes" is from a root which signifies to PIERCE, to WOUND, to AFFLICT. It points to Christ as the "Man of sorrows, and acquainted with grief"; "His visage was so marred more than any man, and His form more than the sons of men."

"Mingled with oil." This was expressed by the angel in those words concerning His virgin mother, "That which is conceived in her is of the Holy Ghost" (Matt. i. 20); and again, in his words to Mary, "The Holy Ghost shall come upon thee, and the power of the

Highest shall overshadow thee : therefore also that holy thing which shall be born of thee shall be called the Son of God (Luke i. 35). As every particle of the fine flour was saturated with oil, so every thought, every feeling, of the Man Christ Jesus was pervaded by the Holy Ghost. He was in every respect TRULY human, but in no one respect was He MERELY human : it was, if we may so express it, a spiritualized humanity. He was full of the Holy Ghost even from His infancy, and as He increased in years we read, "And the child grew, and waxed strong in spirit, filled with wisdom : and the grace of God was upon Him" (Luke ii. 40).

The root of the Hebrew word for "wafer" signifies EMPTY. This typifies Jesus, who, though He was in the form of God, and thought it not robbery to be equal with God, yet EMPTIED Himself when He took upon Him the form of a servant (Phil. ii. 6, 7); so that He could truly say, "I can of Mine own self do nothing"; "My doctrine is not Mine, but His that sent Me"; "The words that I speak unto you I speak not of Myself : the Father that dwelleth in Me, He doeth the works."

But while thus dependent on the Father's will, and upon the Spirit's power, He could say, and did say, "The Spirit of Jehovah is upon Me, because He anointed Me" (Luke iv. 18, 19). Thus He was truly the Messiah, the Christ, the Anointed One, as His name both in Hebrew and Greek signifies. In His title "Jesus Christ," the name "Jesus"—that is, Jehovah the Saviour—connects Him with the Triune God

Jehovah, and especially with the Father.   The title "Christ" identifies Him with the Holy Ghost.

The manhood which the Son of God took when He became incarnate was a manhood which was subservient to the will of God, and dependent on the wisdom and power of the Spirit of God.

But this very *Kenosis,* or emptying of Himself as Son of Man, made way for the bringing in of the will of the Father who sent Him, so that it became His meat and drink to do it; and it also made way for the wisdom and power of the Holy Ghost, in whose energy He taught and acted.

Herein He was an example for us, according to His own words, "As the living Father sent Me, and I live by the Father: so he that eateth Me, even he shall live by Me" (John vi. 57).   Jesus thus lived a life of dependence on His heavenly Father, so the believer is called to live a life of dependence on the Son of God.   Our truest wisdom is to say with Paul, "I live; yet not I, but Christ liveth in Me: and the life which I now live in the flesh I live by the faith of the Son of God" (Gal. ii. 20).   So that, whilst we are empty and insufficient in ourselves, we are complete in Him, whose grace is sufficient for us, and whose strength is made perfect in weakness.

Verse 5.   "And if thy oblation be a meat [gift] offering baken in a pan [the flat plate], it shall be of fine flour unleavened, mingled with oil."

In drawing nigh to God in the remembrance and apprehension of Christ as God's gift, and the One through whom we have boldness of access to God, we·

may contemplate Him, especially in His atoning sacrifice and sufferings on Calvary's cross. These sufferings were from various sources. GOD laid on Him the iniquity of us all, and hid His face from Him, as typified by the offering BAKEN IN THE OVEN (v 4);·He also suffered FROM MAN, for His crucifixion was a public spectacle. He was exposed to the gaze, taunts, and reviling of the multitude. The superscription over His cross was in Hebrew, Greek, and Latin; and priests, scribes, people, and Roman soldiers united in their cruel scoffings. This was typified by the gift offering BAKEN ON THE FLAT PLATE, exposed to open view. This also was the prophetic testimony of Psalm xxii. 6-18 :."They gaped upon me with their mouths.
. . . I am poured out like water : . . . My heart is like wax; it is melted in the midst of my bowels. My strength is dried up like a potsherd; and my tongue cleaveth to my jaws. . . . I may tell all my bones : they look and stare upon me." It was by the wicked hands of man He was crucified and slain; they pierced His hands and His feet, and cast lots upon His vesture. But it was the sinless One that they crucified, for the gift offering was to be of "fine flour unleavened"; it was He who knew no sin that was made sin for us; it was the just One who there suffered for the unjust, that He might bring us to God. He was the Christ, the holy One of God; for the fine unleavened flour was "mingled with oil."

Verse 6. "Thou shalt part IT in pieces, and pour oil thereon: it is a meat [gift] offering."

There is a beautiful significancy in this act of parting in pieces the unleavened cake, or unleavened wafer. The action of the Lord Jesus on the night of His betrayal throws a clear and instructive light on this, when He took the bread and brake it, and gave it to the disciples, and said, "Take, eat; this is My body" (Matt. xxvi. 26). And the truth which is foreshadowed by the oil poured upon the broken pieces, is explained by Heb. ix. 14. concerning the Lord Jesus, "Who through the eternal Spirit offered Himself without spot to God." We recognize the eternal Spirit in the conception and birth of Immanuel, and also in His anointing for living testimony and service. But do we equally realize the presence, grace, and actings of the eternal Spirit in the solemn scenes of the crucifixion? It was by the Holy Spirit that Jesus lived, and served, and testified; it was no less through Him that He offered Himself a sacrifice on the altar of the cross, for a sweet-smelling savour (Eph. v. 2), as the expression before the world and the universe of His love and obedience to His God and Father (John xiv. 31).

The Lord Jesus in incarnation was God's GIFT to man, "For God so loved the world, that He gave His only begotten Son, that whosoever believeth in Him should not perish, but have everlasting life" (John iii. 16).

Verse 7. "And if thy oblation be a meat [gift] offering baken in the frying-pan, it shall be made of fine flour with oil."

That which is baken in the OVEN is concealed from sight; that on the FLAT PLATE is entirely open to view;

whereas on the FRYING-PAN it is partly concealed and
partly open. We have the THIRD .aspect of Christ's
sufferings on the cross, in which the wrath of God, the
malice of man and the enmity of Satan were combined.
This is expressed in Psalm xxii. 19-21—"But be not
Thou far from me, O Jehovah : O my strength, haste
Thee to help me. Deliver my soul from the sword;
my darling [only one] from the power [paw] of the
dog. Save me from the lion's mouth "—wherein the
Lord Jesus prays to be delivered from the overwhelming confluence of evil—from the swcrd of Jehovah
(Zech. xiii. 7), from the power of profane and wicked
men, and from Satan, the roaring lion (1 Peter v. 8).
The gift offering, made of fine flour with oil, is typical
of the sinless humanity of the Lord Jesus as begotten
of the Holy Ghost.

Verses 8-10. "And thou shalt bring the meat [gift] offering that is made of these things unto Jehovah; and
when it is presented unto the priest, he shall bring it
unto the altar. And the priest shall take from the
meat [gift] offering a memorial [memorial portion]
thereof, and shall burn [burn as incense] it upon the
altar : it is an offering made by fire of a sweet savour
[savour of rest] unto Jehovah. And that which is left
of the meat [gift] offering shall be Aaron's and his
sons' : it is a thing most holy [holy of holies] of the
offerings of Jehovah made by fire."

The believer, in his priestly character, when drawing
nigh before Jehovah in worship, presents before Him
by faith the memorial of what Jesus experienced on
the cross, as thus typified. All that Jesus was in
person, character, experience, and atoning sufferings,
being tested by the holiness and righteousness of God,

is found to be most holy and acceptable, and such on which every divine perfection can feed with infinite satisfaction and delight.

In this holy fellowship the believer also, in his priest-ly character, through the fellowship of the Holy Spirit, has his share; he, too, can feed, and triumph, and repose. The priestly family, in fellowship with the High Priest of their profession, Christ Jesus, through the communion of the Holy Spirit, thus partake to-gether with the eternal Father in this holy feast of love divine.

Verse 11. "No meat [gift] offering, which ye shall bring unto Jehovah, shall be made with leaven: for ye shall burn [burn as incense] no leaven, nor any honey, in any offering of [to] Jehovah made by fire."

LEAVEN is the emblem of malice, wickedness, and falsehood (1 Cor. v. 6-8), in perfect contrast to the nature and character of God, who is loving, holy, and true.   It is absolutely necessary, therefore, in drawing nigh to God, through faith in the Lord Jesus Christ, that we should present Him our gift offering as perfectly without sin, holy, harmless, undefiled, even in His very humanity, that, though He was truly and properly man, yet He was sinless.

That which was burnt as incense upon the altar was subject to the testing fire of the altar, emblematic of the holiness and righteousness of God.   Nothing, therefore, which could not stand that test might be offered there.

HONEY appears to represent that sweetness and amiability of disposition which might be simply natural affection; but this sweetness—precious and excellent as it is in its place—will not bear the test of divine holiness in any individual born after the flesh. That human excellency which was manifested in Christ, and constituted Him the chiefest among ten thousand and altogether lovely, was not merely human, it was also spiritual and divine. In Him divine affections were manifested in human form. As every atom of the fine flour in the gift offering was permeated with oil—emblem of the eternal Spirit—so all that was natural in Christ was also spiritual.

Verse 12. "As for the oblation [approach-offering] of the firstfruits, ye shall offer [bring] THEM unto Jehovah: but they shall not be burnt on the altar for a sweet savour [savour of rest]."

The oblation of firstfruits here referred to is that mentioned in Lev. xxiii. 17, "Ye shall bring out of your habitations two wave loaves of two tenth deals : they shall be of fine flour; they shall be baken with leaven; *they are the* firstfruits unto Jehovah." This Pentecostal offering is typical of the Church of the present dispensation. It is composed of Jews and Gentiles, by nature sinful, though redeemed to God by sacrifice (chap. xxiii. 18, 19), and dwelt in by the Holy Ghost. It comprises all believers from the coming of the Comforter to the return of the Lord Jesus to receive His Church to Himself, who, being "a kind of firstfruits of God's creatures" (James i. 18), constitute "the church of the firstborn written in heaven " (Heb. xii. 23). These, in their own nature, cannot bear the test of divine holiness. In the estimate of God they can lay no claim to perfection in the flesh. The language of each one, as taught by the Spirit, will be, "Enter not into judgment with Thy servant: for in Thy sight shall no man living be justified" (Psalm cxliii. 2).

> **Verse 13.** "And every oblation [approach offering] of thy meat [gift] offering shalt thou season with salt; neither shalt thou suffer the salt of the covenant of thy God to be lacking from thy meat [gift] offering: with all thine offerings thou shalt offer [bring] salt."

Salt is the emblem of incorruption and perpetuity. In our estimate of the humanity of Christ, both these truths are to be borne in mind. Death and corruption are the results of sin, and although Christ was made a sin offering and suffered death for us, yet, being in nature sinless, God did not suffer His Holy One to see corruption (Psalm xvi. 10); and as the omer of manna in the golden pot was laid up in the holiest for a memorial, so also "the Lamb as it had been slain, in the midst of the throne" (Rev. v. 6) will ever occupy its centre position, as the lasting memorial of that sinless humanity in which Jesus lived, died, and rose again, and ever lives, whilst the ceaseless song from His ransomed ones goes up, "Salvation unto our God which sitteth upon the throne, and to the Lamb."

On the other hand, there is a solemn truth suggested in Mark ix. 47-49 respecting those bodies that shall be cast into Gehenna, into the fire which shall never be quenched, "where their worm dieth not, and the fire is not quenched," that "every one shall be salted with fire," which seems to imply that those bodies shall be so attempered to the action of fire as to continue unconsumed and unconsumable, even as the resurrection bodies of the redeemed shall be fitted for an eternity of ceaseless service and unending joy (see Rom. ix. 22-24). "What if God, willing to show *His* wrath, and to make His power known, endured with much longsuffering *the* vessels of wrath fitted to destruction; and that He might make known the riches of His glory on *the* vessels of mercy which He *had* afore prepared unto glory, even us, whom He *hath* called, not of *the* Jews only, but also of the Gentiles?"

Verse 14. "And if thou offer [bring near] a meat [gift] offering of thy firstfruits unto Jehovah, thou shalt offer [bring near] for the meat [gift] offering of thy first-fruits green ears of corn dried by the fire, even corn beaten out of full ears."

"Who shall lay anything to the charge of God's elect? It is God that justifieth. Who is he that condemneth? It is Christ that died, yea rather, that is risen again, who is even at the right hand of God" (Rom. viii. 33, 34). This is the attitude that faith takes in drawing nigh to God according to this type, presenting and pleading Christ in resurrection as the first-fruits of them that slept, and as the first-begotten from the dead. There is at the same time a full remembrance of what He suffered, even unto death : it is corn dried by the fire; the Lamb in the midst of the throne appears as it had been slain, the memorials of His past sufferings still there; and "green. ears," for though "His visage was more marred than any man, and His form than the sons of men," yet He Himself was sinless, as Christ Himself intimates in these words : " If they do these things in the green tree, what shall be done in the dry?"

" Even corn beaten out of full ears." "For He was cut off out of the land of the living" whilst in the prime of life.

Verse 15. "And thou shalt put oil upon it, and lay frankincense thereon: IT IS a meat [gift] offering."

Christ was not only anointed by the Holy Ghost for testimony and service here on earth, but in resurrection also, "being by the right hand of God exalted," He has received the fulness of the Spirit, for His heavenly priesthood, and for His Melchisedec kingship.

"And lay frankincense thereon."   Not only was Jesus well pleasing to God the Father whilst here on earth—His beloved Son in whom His soul delighted —but in resurrection also Christ will be His everlasting joy.

" It is a gift offering."   As He was to us God's gift in humiliation to meet our earthly need, even so He will be God's gift to the redeemed in resurrection glory for their eternal blessing.

Verse 16. "And the priest shall burn [burn as incense] the memorial [memorial portion] of it, part of the beaten corn thereof, and part of the oil thereof, with all the frankincense thereof: it is an offering made by fire unto Jehovah."

The believer, in his priestly character by virtue of the anointing—that is, by the teaching—of the Holy Ghost, realizes and keeps in remembrance the perfectness and preciousness of Christ in life and death and resurrection, as tested by the infinite righteousness and holiness of God. He is taught to realize the fact that God so estimates the person and work of Christ, thus furnishing the ground for unbounded confidence in drawing nigh to God; and, as all the frankincense was burnt, he is instructed to give God all the glory.

The Peace Offering

(Leviticus iii.).

Verse 1. "And if his oblation [approach offering] be a sacrifice of peace offering, if HE offer [bring] it of the herd; whether it be a male or female, he shall offer [bring] it without blemish [perfect] before Jehovah."

IT is still a question of APPROACH with confidence before Jehovah, and the ground on which a sinful man can draw near with boldness unto God. The name JEHOVAH is a title expressive of everlastingness, and it always combines the three persons in the ever-blessed Trinity—the everlasting Father, which implies the ever-lasting Son, and the eternal Spirit—in one undivided Godhead.

In chapter i. it is a question of ACCEPTANCE, here it is a question of PEACE; there can be no approach to God by sinful man apart from sacrifice, hence it is the sacrifice of peace offering—and " peace " is in the plural in the Hebrew—for in this near approach with confidence before God the mind, heart, and conscience must be in perfect repose : the blood of Jesus Christ, God's Son, is ever speaking, ever proclaiming, PEACE, PEACE, PEACE, and God will keep him in perfect peace whose mind is stayed on Him.

The sacrifice of the HERD, or BULLOCK, is that which represents Christ in His perfect SERVICE and obedience both in life and death. In the consciousness of our own imperfectness and shortcoming in our service to God, we need to realize in His presence the ground for confidence and peace which this sacrifice affords. The offering might be male or female, as typical of the active and passive obedience of Christ as meeting our need, both in the path of practical obedience or in passive subjection to the divine will.

The law of God concerning that which was offered —or, literally, "brought near"—before Him was, "It shall be perfect to be accepted" (Lev. xxii. 21) ; but as none of our services can be of this character, it is well for us that we can plead before the throne of grace the perfect service of Him who in obedience and suffering active and passive, was without a blemish and without a spot.

Verse 2. "And he shall lay his hand upon the head of his offering [approach offering], and kill it at the door [entrance] of the tabernacle [tent] of the congregation."

Christ is our peace. God proclaims peace through Jesus Christ. Christ has made peace not only between Jew and Gentile, but between God and man. The believer, in drawing nigh to God through faith, apprehends this, realizes it, and identifies himself with Christ as our peace. This is signified by the laying on of the hand of the offerer upon the head of the peace offering. But this peace with God is not secured by the living obedience of Christ only, something more than this was needed. He "made peace through the blood of His cross" (Col. i. 20); hence the offerer kills the victim before the door of the tent of the congregation, the appointed place of meeting and communion with God (Ex. xxix. 42, 43), thus confessing that it was his own sinfulness which caused the death of the innocent sufferer, and it was only on the ground of the atoning sacrifice of Christ that he could have peace with God, or draw near with acceptance before Him.

"And Aaron's sons the priests shall sprinkle the blood upon the altar round about."

This is a priestly act, and may be regarded as setting forth the action of the believer, in his priestly character, pleading that blood before God; or as setting forth that blood as the ground of approach to God, "preaching peace through Jesus Christ."

Verses 3, 4. "And he shall offer [bring] of the sacrifice of the peace offering an offering made by fire unto Jehovah; the fat that covereth the inwards, and all the fat that is upon the inwards, and the two.kidneys [reins], and the fat that is on them, which is by the flanks, and the caul above the liver, with the kidneys, it shall he take away."

"We which have believed do enter into rest"—God's REST—and have fellowship with God in that perfect

repose wherein He is resting; even so it is with PEACE.
Through faith in Christ we enter into God's peace; not
only peace with God, but the peace of God which
passeth all understanding. The sacrifice of Christ in
its internal excellency, having been tested by the
righteousness and holiness of God, has given Him
entire satisfaction. The words employed in Hebrew
to designate these inwards parts are beautifully significant. The word "fat" expresses that which is most
excellent, and is sometimes rendered BEST. The Hebrew word for "kidneys" signifies PERFECTION; and
the word for "flanks" expresses CONFIDENCES; while
the words "the caul above the liver" may be rendered
THE SUPERABUNDANCE OF THE GLORY. These inwards of
the victim, which were taken away and burnt as incense upon the altar, represent the internal thoughts,
feelings, affections, purposes, and desires of Christ,
whilst making peace with God for us on Calvary's
cross. Every inward thought and feeling, tested by
the infinite purity of a holy God, was all found a sweet
savour, or savour of rest to God.

Verse 5. "And Aaron's sons shall burn [burn as incense]
IT on the altar upon the burnt sacrifice [ascending
offering], which is upon the wood that is on the fire:
it is an offering made by fire, of a sweet savour
[savour of rest] unto Jehovah."

The fire was ever burning on God's altar. The wood
was ever consuming upon it, but the sweet savour of
the daily burnt offering was ever ascending up, and it
was upon this burnt, or ascending offering, that the

fat of the peace offering was laid; for Christ not only
presented Himself as the ground of our acceptance,
but as the foundation of our perfect peace with God.

Verses 6, 7. "And if his offering [approach offering] for
a sacrifice of peace offering unto Jehovah be of the
flock, male or female, he shall offer [bring] it without
blemish [perfect]. If HE offer [bring] a lamb for
his offering [approach offering], then shall he offer
[bring] IT before Jehovah."

In the sacrifice of peace offering before Jehovah of
the flock, male or female, provision is made for perfect
peace in drawing nigh to God, not only with regard to
SERVICE, as represented by the BULLOCK, but also as
to CHARACTER, as by the LAMB. Conscious as we must
be of our imperfections in character, active and passive, in our spirit, temper, and disposition, it is well
for us that we can present and plead for our acceptance
the name of Him who was altogether perfect—the
Lamb of God without a blemish and without a spot;
seeking meanwhile increasing conformity to Him, in
obedience to His gracious invitation, "Take My yoke
upon you, and learn of Me; for I am meek and lowly
in heart : and ye shall find rest unto your souls" (Matt.
xi. 29).

Verses 8-11. "And he shall lay his hand upon the head of
his offering [approach offering], and kill IT before
the tabernacle [tent] of the congregation: and Aaron's
sons shall sprinkle the blood thereof round about upon
the altar. And he shall offer [bring] of the sacrifice
of the peace offering an offering made by fire unto
Jehovah; the fat thereof, and the whole rump, it shall
he take off hard by the back bone; and the fat that

covereth the inwards, and all the fat that is upon the inwards, and the two kidneys, and the fat that is upon them, which is by the flanks, and the caul above the liver, with the kidneys, it shall he take away. And the priest shall burn [burn as incense] it upon the altar: it is the food of the offering made by fire unto Jehovah."

The blood of atonement was not only required to meet man's necessity as to outward transgression, it was equally needful to meet his inward condition as to feeling and disposition, for in heart he is alienated from God : the carnal mind is enmity against God ; it is not subject to His law, neither indeed can be. But the sacrifice of the Lamb which God has provided for a peace offering furnishes the basis for perfect, lasting, and eternal peace. For it was when we were ENEMIES that we were reconciled to God by the death of His Son (Rom. v. 10).

When we contemplate the scenes of the judgment hall and of Calvary we gaze on the exterior, but the eye of God penetrated beneath the surface. The inward thoughts, feelings, experiences, of Him who was led as a lamb to the slaughter, and who on Calvary prayed for the forgiveness of His murderers—all this, and infinitely more, far beyond what the intelligence of men or angels will ever know, in all its human preciousness, spiritual perfection, and divine excellence, furnished "the food of the offering made by fire unto Jehovah."

In Numbers xviii. 29-32 "the fat that covereth the inwards" is three times rendered "the best," and this is God's estimate of the internal preciousness of Him who hath reconciled us to God by the blood of His cross, and who is Himself in the presence of God our peace.

The fat tail of the eastern sheep has ever been regarded as a peculiar delicacy, and it was this which was taken off entirely and burnt as incense upon the altar, as a portion for God.

Verses 12-16.   As the LAMB represents the Lord Jesus in His personal character as the meek, lowly, and gentle One; so the GOAT sets Him forth, according to Rom. viii. 3, as made "in the likeness of sinful flesh," although Himself sinless.   And in His atoning sacrifice on Calvary's cross, He not only bore and put away the guilt of our actual and outward transgressions as the spotless LAMB, but also as the GOAT; our sin in the flesh in its internal springs, was judged and condemned by God, and full atonement made by the sinner's Substitute and full and perfect Saviour.   Whilst as to Himself, His inward thoughts and feelings were divinely pure and perfect, and infinitely acceptable to God.   Thus, in drawing nigh to God in the full consciousness of what we are in character and conduct, outward and inward, through Him we have boldness and confidence, for HE IS OUR PEACE.

Verse 17.   "It shall be a perpetual statute for your generations throughout all your dwellings, that ye eat neither fat nor blood."

As the prohibition of BLOOD (Gen. ix. 4) teaches man that as a sinner he has forfeited his claim to life, so the prohibition of "the fat of the beast, of which men offer an offering made by fire unto Jehovah" (Lev. vii. 25), teaches him that he cannot present his internal thoughts and feelings apart from atonement, as being acceptable to God, for in the estimate of God every thought and imagination of man's heart is only evil, and that continually (Gen. vi. 5).

The Sin Offering for Sins of Ignorance

(Leviticus iv.).

Verses 1, 2. "And Jehovah spake unto Moses, saying,
Speak unto the children of Israel, saying, If a soul
shall sin through ignorance against any of the commandments of Jehovah concerning things which ought
not to be done, and shall do against any of them."

"SIN is the transgression of *the* law" (1 John iii.
4), or, more literally, "sin is lawlessness"; it is,
as the original term implies, a missing of the
mark, or a coming short of the divine requirements,
either as to the whole or in any one of its particulars,
for he that offendeth in one point is guilty of all
(James ii 10). According to this, "All have sinned,
and come short of the glory of God" (Rom. iii. 23).

The sentence of the law is, "The soul that sinneth,
it shall die" (Ezekiel xviii. 20); but God, in the riches
of His grace, has provided a remedy. He has given
the blood of His own spotless Lamb upon the altar

to make an atonement for the soul, and that blood "cleanseth from all sin" (1 John i. 7).

But it is for sins of ignorance that the provision here is made. So said the Apostle Paul, " I obtained mercy, because I did it ignorantly in unbelief" (1 Tim. i. 13); and it is for such that Jesus made intercession on the cross, "Father, forgive them; for they know not what they do" (Luke xxiii. 34). For wilful continuance in sin after the truth is known there is no remedy, for "there remaineth no more sacrifice for sin" (Heb. x. 26). It is the sin-stricken, penitent soul that pleads the sacrifice and obtains a full salvation.

Verse 3. "If the priest that is anointed do sin according to the sin of the people; then let him bring for his sin, which he hath sinned, a young bullock without blemish unto Jehovah for a sin offering."

Here provision was made for the whole PRIESTLY FAMILY, including the high priest, for Aaron and his house; for the law made men high priests which had infirmity, who needed to offer sacrifice, first for their own sin, and then for the people (Heb. vii. 27, 28), in contrast to the "High Priest of our profession" (Heb. iii. 1), who was sinless, but who, when made sin for us, once for all, offered up Himself. And thus the high priest, on the great day of Atonement, presented a young bullock for a sin offering, and brought its blood within the veil to make an atonement for himself and for his house (Lev. xvi.),

Verse 4. "And he shall bring the bullock unto the door
   of the tabernacle [tent] of the congregation before
   Jehovah; and shall lay his hand upon the bullock's
   head, and kill the bullock before Jehovah."

The door of the tent of the congregation was the
place of communion with God (Ex. xxix. 42, 43).
There stood the altar, and there stood the laver; and
the personal act of the priest in killing the victim was
typical of Christ when He offered up Himself; and the
laying on of hands on the head of the sacrifice was
expressive of the identification of the offerer with his
offering.

Verses 5, 6, 7. "And the priest that is anointed shall take
   of the bullock's blood, and bring IT to the tabernacle
   [tent] of the congregation: and the priest shall dip
   his finger in the blood, and sprinkle of the blood seven
   times before Jehovah, before the veil of the sanctuary.
   And the priest shall put some of the blood upon the
   horns of the altar of sweet incense before Jehovah,
   which is in the tabernacle [tent] of the congregation;
   and shall pour all the blood of the bullock at the
   bottom [foundation] of the altar of the burnt offering
   [ascending offering], which is at the door of the tabernacle [tent] of the congregation."

As it was only on the great day of Atonement the
blood could be carried within the veil, and sprinked
before and on the ark of the covenant, on other occasions that which came nearest to it was to be done :
the blood was to be sprinkled seven times before Jehovah before the veil of the sanctuary. As it was against
Jehovah that the sin was committed, satisfaction
was made first, and above all, to Him. The blood was

also to be put upon the horns of the altar of sweet incense, as on the day of Atonement. The remainder of the blood was to be poured out at the bottom [foundation] of the brazen altar, teaching us that atonement by blood lies at the foundation of all our approach to God, our worship of God, and our communion with Him.

Verses 8, 9, 10. "And he shall take off from it all the fat of the bullock for the sin offering; the fat that covereth the inwards, and all the fat that is upon the inwards, and the two kidneys, and the fat that is upon them, which is by the flanks, and the caul above the liver, with the kidneys, it shall he take away, as it was taken off from the bullock of the sacrifice of peace offerings: and the priest shall burn [burn as incense] them upon the altar of the burnt offering [ascending offering]."

Reminding us, as in the peace offering, that when Jesus presented Himself on the cross "an offering and a sacrifice to God as a sweet-smelling savour" (Eph. v. 2), the inward experiences of His soul were infinitely precious in the sight of God, who alone could fully know and adequately appreciate them.

Verses 11, 12. "And the skin of the bullock, and all his flesh, with his head, and with his legs, and his inwards, and his dung, even the whole bullock shall he carry forth without the camp unto a clean place, where the ashes are poured out, and burn HIM on the wood with fire: where the ashes are poured out shall he be burnt."

With the exception of the blood, which was sprinkled and poured out, and the fat of the inwards, which was burnt as incense on the altar, the whole bullock was carried forth without the camp, and there consumed or burnt up on the wood with fire; so Jesus, who suffered for us without the gate, by that one offering has for ever and entirely put away sin, and to them that look for Him shall He appear the second time without sin unto salvation (Heb. xiii. 11-13; ix. 27, 28). The ashes which were left after the consuming of the burnt offering were to be taken and put beside the altar, and then carried forth to a clean place (Lev. vi. 10, 11).

This was typical of the taking down from the cross the sacred remains of the Lord Jesus, and the burial of the body in Joseph's tomb, where never man before had laid, and hence undefiled by death. The connection between the place of Sacrifice and of burial is beautifully expressed in the words of John xix. 41, 42: "Now in the place where He was crucified there was a garden; and in the garden a new sepulchre, wherein was never man yet lain. There laid they Jesus therefore because of the Jews' preparation day; for the sepulchre was nigh at hand."

Thus we see the wonderful coincidence between the type and the antitype.

FOR THE WHOLE CONGREGATION, OR FOR
THE ASSEMBLY.

Verses 13, 14. "And if the whole congregation of Israel sin through ignorance, and the thing be hid from the eyes of the assembly, and they have done somewhat against any of the commandments of Jehovah concerning things which should not be done, and are guilty; when the sin, which they have sinned against it, is known, then the congregation [assembly] shall offer [bring near] a young bullock for the sin [sin offering], and bring him before the tabernacle [tent] of the congregation."

" The WHOLE CONGREGATION of Israel" is typical of the entire Church of God, composed of ALL God's people, everywhere on earth.

"THE ASSEMBLY" is typical of a portion of the Church in any locality. In verse 13 both terms, CONGREGATION and ASSEMBLY, are correctly employed as in the Hebrew, though in the Authorized Version they are often misplaced. "Sin through ignorance." Something in Church order or practice which may be contrary to the Word of God and the commandments of the Lord Jesus. The universality of a practice is no excuse if it be contrary to the Word of God; it "should not be done." When the sin is known, then the local assembly have to deal with it as the sin of the whole, yet recognizing their own part in it. For the putting away of the sin, the obedience of Christ the perfect Servant, who never transgressed God's Word, and His atoning sacrifice, must be realized by faith, and pleaded in prayer, in the presence of God, and where He meets with His people.

"THE ELDERS" (verse 15) confess the sin and plead the sacrifice; the HIGH PRIEST of our profession (verse 16) presents before God His own blood, which makes perfect reconciliation and full atonement. As the BLOOD was to be POURED OUT at the bottom, or FOUNDATION, of the altar (verse 18), so the blood of atonement lies at the very foundation of all our worship and communion with God, whether individual or collective.

Verses 19-21. The internal preciousness of Christ gives its value to His atoning sacrifice, and the offering of Him who suffered without the camp has entirely and for ever put away the sin He bore.

THE SIN OFFERING FOR THE RULER.

Verses 22-26. There are those whom the Lord has made RULERS over His household, to give them their portion of meat in due season; for such to do anything contrary to the commandments of the Lord and Saviour, even though done through ignorance, it is sin which can only be forgiven on the ground of atonement. But for this sin provision is made through faith in Him who, though made in the likeness of sinful flesh, was Himself sinless, and offered Himself a sacrifice for sin, combining in Himself that which was typified by the sin offering (verse 24), the burnt or ascending offering (verse 25), and the peace offering (verse 26).

As the communion of the assembly in this case was not affected as in the two former instances, the blood of the sin offering is not brought into the sanctuary, nor put on the altar of incense, nor sprinkled before the veil; but upon the HORNS of the BRAZEN altar and poured out at the FOUNDATION (verse 25), the place of INDIVIDUAL communion with God.

THE SIN OFFERING FOR ONE OF THE COMMON PEOPLE, OR ONE OF THE PEOPLE OF THE LAND.

Verses 27-35. This is similar to the sin offering for the ruler, with this exception—that the GOAT was to be a FEMALE, whilst that for the RULER was to be a MALE. In the case of the ruler, though his sin was in ignorance, he was culpable, for he ought to have known the will of the Lord, and what was commanded or prohibited in His Word; but in regard to one of the people of the land he might have acted more under the influence of others, or have been led astray by erroneous teaching. The MALE offering contemplates the ACTIVE character, the FEMALE more the PASSIVE aspect of the offence.

The OFFICIATING PRIEST is CHRIST, who was in life the OFFERER, in death the SACRIFICE, in resurrection the PRIEST, in ascension the HIGH PRIEST entered within the veil. When faith pleads His person and work, and He Himself makes intercession for us, the assurance comes concerning any sin confessed before

God with the stamp of immutable truth upon it "it shall be forgiven him."

The GOAT for a sin offering, whether male or female, was typical of Christ, who was made in the likeness of sinful flesh, and who made atonement for sin in the flesh, whether active or passive, Himself sinless.

The LAMB (verse 32) represents Christ in the meekness and lowliness of His character, who was holy, harmless, undefiled, and separate from sinners, the Lamb of God, without a blemish and without a spot.

The Trespass Offering

(Leviticus v.).

"TRESPASS" is the transgression of law. There may be sin, but "where no law is, there is no transgression" (Rom. iv. 15). The transgression of known law is wilful or presumptuous sin, and this would require for its remission a male offering. But law may be transgressed inconsiderately or inadvertently, and it is for such that provision is made according to this chapter; hence the female sacrifice (verse 6).

Concealment of evil is sin. If a person sees or knows of evil, and is called upon to bear witness, if he does not declare it "he shall bear his iniquity." If one were called upon in a court of justice to give evidence on oath, so far from its being wrong for him to do so, it appears from this scripture it would be sinful for him to refuse. When Christ was adjured by the high priest, He at once responded (Matt. xxvi. 63, 64).

Verses 2, 3. "If a soul touch any unclean thing, . . . he also shall be unclean, and guilty."

Association with evil is defiling. It is not enough for a person to say, "I did not know evil was there"; he ought to have inquired. Contact with spiritual death is deadening and defiling to the soul.

Verse 4. Inconsiderate speech may involve the soul in sin, especially when we speak to God (Eccles. v. 1-9; James iii. 2-6).

Verse 5. When sin is known in any particular case, the confession of it is not sufficient; the offence might be against man, but the sin is against God; and nothing but the blood of atonement can put away its defilement.

Verse 6. The atoning sacrifice of Christ, the Lamb of God, pleaded by faith before God, avails to put away the defilement of transgression, as well as the sense of sin from the conscience.

Verses 7-10. There may be instances, as from infancy, feebleness of mind or faith, or want of instruction, when faith may fail in its full apprehension of the person of Christ. In such cases divine grace condescends to human infirmity. Jesus may be simply known in the kindness and tenderness of His feelings, as represented by the two turtle doves, or two young pigeons—the "gentle Jesus, meek and mild." He requires to be recognized not only as the perfect Example in life, but also in His sin-atoning sacrifice and death. The birds were not only to be brought, but killed, and the blood sprinkled and poured out—the one for a sin offering, and the other for an ascending

offering. For Christ was not only delivered for our
offences, but raised again for our justification—the
One who in life and death was in thought, purpose,
affection, and desire undivided towards God.

Verses 11-13. The apprehension of some as to the
person, character, and work of Christ may be exceedingly limited and imperfect; yet, if the faith of such
be real, divine grace condescends to their infirmity.
The tenth deal of fine flour without oil or frankincense
represents the Son of Man in His sinless humanity,
but made sin, and through His atoning death putting
sin away. The omer of manna, the daily portion of
Israel in the wilderness, was of the same quantity.
"The omer is the tenth part of the ephah" (Ex. xvi.
36); and it was an omer full of manna that was laid
up in the golden pot (verses 32-34), typical of Christ
in His humiliation and in His glory. Faith applies to
Christ the officiating priest, and Christ presents before
God the memorial of His sinless life and atoning
death; and on this ground the sin confessed, being
atoned for, is forgiven.

Verses 14-16. If a trespass against a neighbour
requires confession, atonement, and forgiveness, much
more does transgression in things pertaining to the
worship, service, or testimony for God. The RAM is
the type which represents Christ in His public, living
TESTIMONY, and also in His atoning death.

The TRANSGRESSOR brings the offering.

The PRIEST makes atonement.

And GOD assures the forgiveness.

" If any man sin, we have an Advocate with the Father, Jesus Christ the righteous : and He is the propitiation for our sins" (1 John ii. 1, 2). Spiritual offences need to be estimated and weighed in the balances of the sanctuary, and it must be a priestly estimate—that is, the estimate of one who has an unction from the Holy One—not simply according to human valuation. The discovery of error, failure, or shortcoming in service or testimony should lead to increasing diligence and more devoted service, so that not only amends may be made, but that the cause of God may be even furthered therby.

But the amendment made with the. fifth part added does not make the atonement; the ram for the trespass offering was requisite.

Verses 17-19. Ignorance regarding any of those things which God has forbidden or required in His service does not leave a person guiltless; and when the sin is known God requires amendment should be made, and the blood of atonement pleaded for forgiveness and acceptance.

The Consecration of the Priests

(Leviticus viii.).

Verses 1, 2. "And the Lord spake unto Moses, saying, Take Aaron and his sons with him, and the garments, and the anointing oil, and a bullock for the sin offering, and two rams, and a basket of unleavened bread.

THE priesthood of believers with the Risen Christ, and the qualifications for their office are typified in this chapter.

From Hebrews iii. 1, we learn that Moses was a type of Christ as the APOSTLE, communicating the mind and will of God, and Aaron a type of Christ as the HIGH PRIEST of our profession; while the sons of Aaron represent the priestly family, the children of God, as a royal priesthood (1 Peter ii.), the words "with him" expressing close association. "And the garments, and the anointing oil, and a bullock for the sin offering, and two rams, and a basket of unleavened bread"—a provision for the consecration.

Verse 3. God would have all His ransomed people to know that which, according to His mind, is essential to true priestly service and worship. The door, or open space in front of the TENT of the congregation, was the appointed place of communion between God and His people (see Ex. xxix. 42-44).

The expression "tabernacle of the congregation," never occurs in the original Scriptures; it conveys a different thought.

Verses 4, 5. All were thus present before God, to hear all things commanded of God (Acts x. 33).

Verse 6. The signification of this washing or BATH-ING is, I believe, taught us in Romans vi.—the death, burial, and resurrection of Christ, and of His people in association with Him, through the Pentecostal Spirit; for it is only in resurrection that the Lord Jesus truly entered on His High-priestly office, and it is only as dead and risen with Him that we can enter the holiest as a spiritual priesthood to offer up spiritual sacrifices acceptable to God.

All descended from Aaron were priests by BIRTH, but it was only after their CONSECRATION, as here set forth, that they could enter on the performance of their priestly office. So all the children of God by faith in Jesus are priests by birth; but do all, as a royal priesthood, recognize and enjoy the privilege? Are we all a consecrated priesthood?

There are two Hebrew words rendered "consecrated" in the Authorized Version which are never to be confounded. The one word signifies "set apart," or "SEPARATED AS HOLY TO GOD." The other word signifies "having the HAND FILLED," and it is this latter word which is employed in this chapter. All believers are saints, but all have not their hands filled for priestly service.

Verses 7-9. These garments, which are described at large in Exodus xxviii., set forth the various particulars in which the Lord Jesus is fully qualified for the High Priesthood, with which He is invested. "Coat," typifying the pure, sinless humanity of Christ. "Girdle," of righteousness and faithfulness. The "Robe" of the ephod was blue, the emblem of heavenly perfection—heavenly from its colour, and perfection from the Hebrew word. "Breastplate" of judgment (Ex. xxviii. 29), the Lord's estimate of His people. "Urim and Thummin," the LIGHTS and PER- FECTIONS of the Divine mind. "Mitre": this was a token of subjection; "The head of Christ is God." The priests wore "Bonnets" in token of subjection to Aaron. "Golden plate,"—"Holiness to Jehovah"; Christ in His Divine separation from evil, is our righteousness to God.

Verses 10, 11. The anointing oil is the type of the Pentecostal Spirit, and everything connected with the service and worship of God should be in the unction and power of the Spirit of the ascended Christ.

Verse 12. Typical of the Lord Jesus receiving the fulness of the Spirit in resurrection as the head of the priestly family, and also as the head of His body, the

Church (see Psalm cxxxiii. 2). Aaron's sons were virtually anointed in the anointing of Aaron, and each member of the mystic body of Christ receives from the fulness of the Head, as one Spirit with the Lord in glory.

Verse 13. The priestly family also invested with their priestly office.

Verse 14. Priesthood is founded on atonement, and for acceptable priestly service there must be the putting away of sin.

Verse 15. Aaron slays the victim, so Christ laid down His life, and no man took it from Him.

Without shedding of blood is no remission of sin; the blood of atonement lies at the very foundation of all acceptable worship or priestly service to God.

Verse 16. Even when made sin and suffering for sinners, there was that in the internal experience of Christ which went up as a sweet-smelling savour to God.

Verse 17. "Burnt with fire without the camp."

"Wherefore Jesus also, that He might sanctify the people with His own blood, suffered without the gate" (Heb. xiii. 12).

Verses 18-21. The burnt or ascending offering. Christ was not only delivered for our offences, but was raised again for our justification. And as a royal and holy priesthood, we are not only pardoned through the blood of Christ, but stand accepted and complete in Him who was raised from the dead.

Verse 22. "Aaron and his sons laid their hands upon the head of the ram."

The ram of CONSECRATION or FILLINGS. Not only is priesthood founded upon sacrifice, but with the preciousness of that sacrifice the hands of the priests are filled. This is true, not only of the High Priest, but of the priests. The Lord Jesus within the veil presents before God the remembrance of the same precious offering which His people plead on earth.

SANCTIFIED BY BLOOD.

Verse 23 "He slew it; and Moses took of the blood of it, and put it on the tip of Aaron's right ear, and upon the thumb of his right hand, and upon the great toe of his right foot."

Thus Aaron was set apart, or sanctified, by blood. So Christ through His atoning death sanctified Himself, or set Himself apart, becoming a Nazarite, as He said to His disciples, "I will not drink henceforth of this fruit of the vine, until that day when I drink it new with you in My Father's kingdom." So also in His prayer to the Father, He said, "For their sakes I sanctify Myself, that they also might be sanctified through the truth," linking them in association with Himself.

Verse 24. So also the blood was put upon Aaron's sons; it is the blood of atonement which separates the believer in his priestly character from sin; for Christ died to redeem him from all iniquity, setting apart the entire man for God, from head to foot.

Well for us if the blood of atonement stands sentinel at the ear, challenging every word that would pervert the truth, or defile the mind.

Well if a sense of redeeming love keeps us from engaging in any evil work, or walking in any evil way; as well as being that blood which we plead in our approaches to a throne of grace.

Verses 25-27. Moses took the fat, the kidneys, the right shoulder, one unleavened cake, a cake of oiled bread, and one wafer, "and he put all upon Aaron's hands, and upon his sons' hands, and waved them for a wave offering before Jehovah"—thus causing, as it were, all that Jesus was on earth, in the internal preciousness of His atoning sacrifice, His devoted service, His pure, undefiled, and excellent humanity, with which the hands of Christ and His people are filled, to pass and re-pass before the eyes of God.

Verse 28. "Moses took them from off their hands and burnt them [as incense] on the altar, upon the burnt offering [ascending offering]: they were consecrations [fillings] for a sweet savour [savour of rest] : it is an offering made by fire unto Jehovah."

Those spiritual sacrifices which the believer in his priestly character presents, whose hands are filled with the preciousness of Christ, being tested by the searching holiness of God, are found to be a savour of rest unto Jehovah. In the altar of burnt offering the fire was ever burning, and from that altar the sweet savour of the morning or evening lamb was ever ascending. Upon that altar all the sacrifices of the day were burnt

Verse 29. "Moses took the breast, and waved it for a
wave offering before Jehovah; for of the ram of consecrations [fillings] it was Moses' part."

In Hebrews iii. 1 we are exhorted to consider the
APOSTLE as well as the High Priest of our profession,
Christ Jesus. Of Christ as the APOSTLE, or communi-
cator to us of the mind and will of God, Moses was a
striking foreshadowing type. And the AFFECTIONS of
Christ's heart, as typified by the BREAST, while engaged
in this work were ever before the eye of God.

Verse 30. BLOOD SEPARATES; OIL UNITES. The oil
here used was not simple olive oil, as in the cleansing
of the leper, but the ANOINTING oil, in which the sweet
spices were incorporated. "Olive oil" is the emblem of
the Spirit of God, but the anointing oil shows not only
the Holy Spirit's testimony to Christ, but Christ
anointed at the right hand of God in resurrection, as
the risen Son of Man. It is the Spirit of the ascended
Christ, and the blood of His atoning sacrifice, which
have sanctified, or set apart, the Lord Jesus in His
priestly office—and the believer as associated with him
alike in their persons and in their offices—as a holy
priesthood unto God.

Verse 31. Those portions of the sacrifice and of the
gift-offering with which the hands of the priestly
family were filled, were burnt as incense upon the
altar, as "the food of the offering made by fire unto
Jehovah." The rest was for food for the priestly
family, to be partaken of in the place of communion
with God (Ex. xxix. 42-44). God's holy priesthood

are not only provided with that on the ground of which they could draw nigh to God, but also on which their souls may feed in unbroken communion with Him.

Verse 32. Whatever remained was to be consumed with fire, lest it should be put to any profane use.

Verse 33. These seven days, the complete or perfect number, stand for the whole period of the present dispensation, during which time God's royal and holy priesthood, fully furnished, are to abide in fellowship with God.

Verses 34-36. "That ye die not."

Spiritual life in its vigour can only be maintained by unbroken communion with God (See Rom. viii. 6-13).

The Eighth Day Consecration

(Leviticus ix.).

Verses 1-4. " On the eighth day."

THIS is additional to Exodus xxix., where no eighth day is mentioned. The eighth day is typical of resurrection, and of heavenly rest. When Israel is keeping her earthly and millennial seventh-day Sabbath on earth, the redeemed in heavenly and resurrection glory will enter on their eternal and eighth day Sabbath above.

Not only is it on the ground of sacrifice and redemption that the throne of grace is founded, where grace triumphant reigns; but the MANIFESTATION OF GLORY rests on the same basis. The same atoning work which secures mercy and grace now, secures millennial and eternal glory hereafter. It is on the ground of accomplished redemption that the Lord Jesus will appear in glory with His ransomed ones; and it is on the ground of redemption accomplished and peace made, that Israel will behold that manifested glory.

Verses 5, 6.   All this is preparatory to the manifestation of Jehovah in glory to His people Israel.

Verses 8-21.   Without entering on the details of these verses, we may simply say that atonement having been accomplished, acceptance being secured, and peace made; the curse was cancelled, and complete provision made for fulness of blessing to be pronounced.

Verses 22, 23.   The same gracious Lord who was taken away from His disciples in the act of blessing them, and carried up into heaven, having been hidden there for a season, will again appear in the glory of Jehovah, with unbounded blessings for Israel and the world.

Verse 24.   The righteousness of Jehovah having been fully vindicated, satisfied, and glorified by the sacrifice of Christ, provision has been made for Israel, and the earth's unlimited joy, and acceptable adoring worship.

The Cleansing of the Leper

(Leviticus xiv.).

Verses 1, 2. "This shall be the law of the leper in the day of his cleansing."

LEPROSY is the emblem of sin. There are no instructions in this chapter for the healing of the leper, but for his cleansing. The healing of leprosy was entirely in the hand of God. The officiating priest here primarily represents Christ, but in a secondary sense one employed by Christ.

When the leper had been seen by the priest, and pronounced unclean, his place was without the camp —his clothes rent, a covering on his upper lip, and with the cry, "Unclean, unclean!" (Chap. xiii. 45). A striking picture of a convicted sinner when by the Holy Spirit convinced of his real condition in the sight of God. What he then needs is such a presentation to the eye of faith of the person and atoning work of the Lord Jesus, that he might realize the putting away of sin, his standing in grace, and hope of glory (Romans v. 1-3). At first it was a work done for him.

Verse 3. "He shall be brought unto the priest: and the priest shall go forth out of the camp."

The priest is a priest by virtue of the anointing. The spiritual mind alone can discern in the convicted sinner the evidence of salvation by the grace of God.

Verse 4. The leper to be cleansed was not required at first to bring the offerings, but

"'Then shall the priest command to take for him that is to be cleansed two birds alive and clean, and cedar wood, and scarlet [worm scarlet] and hyssop.'"

So on the return of the prodigal the father commands the servants to bring hither the fatted calf, and to put the best robe upon the returning son. Two birds are to be taken, in order to show forth both death and resurrection. The typical import of the cedar wood, the worm scarlet, and the hyssop is best explained by Phil. ii. 6-8. The CEDAR WOOD is significant of HIGHEST DIGNITY, the HYSSOP that grows on the wall of DEEPEST HUMILIATION, and the WORM SCARLET of the EARTHLY DIGNITY of the Son of Man who was born of the seed of David, who in the form of God and of the Royal line of David humbled Himself even to the death of the cross. The birds here mentioned are in the Hebrew "sparrows," and strikingly remind us of Him who could say, "Foxes have holes, and birds of the air have nests; but the Son of Man hath not where to lay His head" (Luke ix. 58). Of little esteem among men, but ever the objects of His Father's care. "Are not two sparrows sold for a farthing? and one of them shall not fall on the ground without your Father" (Matt. x. 29).

Verse 5. "The priest shall command that one of the birds be killed."

In general the offerer kills the victim, but here the priest commands that one of the birds should be killed

in or over an EARTHEN vessel, emblem of the pure
HUMANITY of the Lord Jesus; over "running—literally
LIVING—WATER," type of Him who "through the eternal SPIRIT offered Himself without spot to God" (Heb.
ix. 14). It is important to see the part the Holy Ghost
takes in the crucifixion, this is too much overlooked.
The bird being killed over the living water contained
in the earthen vessel, the water would have become
saturated with the blood.

Verses 6, 7. "As for the living bird," etc.

The living bird, connected with the cedar wood,
scarlet, and hyssop, and dipped in the blood of the
slain bird, and let free in the open field, is a type of
the risen and ascended Saviour, who, like the high
priest of the day of Atonement, entered the holiest in
the value of the sprinkled blood, so our High Priest
ascended into the presence of His God and Father,
His divine glory, human excellency, and lowly obedience unto death giving their united value to His atoning work. On the ground of these perfectly applied
(sprinkled seven times), and fully apprehended, the
pardoned sinner is pronounced "CLEAN," the blood of
Jesus Christ, God's Son, cleansing him from all sin.

Verse 8. "He that is to be cleansed shall wash his clothes."

The *washing* of the clothes signifies the laying aside
all in outward character and conduct which is not con-
sistent with his profession. The *shaving* off of the
hair expresses the renunciation of nature's comeliness

and strength, having "no confidence in the flesh" (**Phil.** iii. 3). The washing or *bathing* in water is shown **by** Rom. vi. 4 to set forth fellowship through the **Holy** Ghost in the death, burial, and resurrection of the **Lord** Jesus. Are there not many who while they take **their** place among the people of God, and are recognized by them, yet for a season fail to enter into full **rest** and peace in their own souls, not at rest nor at home as to their inward experience. In the camp, but **not in** their own tent (Job iii. 26).

Verse 9. "It shall be on the seventh day."

We now come to the SEVENTH day cleansing, **that is,** to a more thorough renunciation of the comeliness **and** strength of the flesh. The shaving of the HEAD is **the** renunciation of his natural reason, of the BEARD **his** experience, of the EYEBROWS his powers of observation; and in the washing or bathing is set forth **the** realization of the fact that he is *dead* indeed unto **sin,** and *alive* unto God in Christ Jesus, through the indwelling Spirit.

Verses 10-13. "And on the EIGHTH day."

The EIGHTH day is the day on which Jesus AROSE from the dead, and the day on which, seven weeks after, the Comforter came. The eighth day cleansing sets forth the believer's apprehension, through faith in the death and RESURRECTION of Christ, that he is RAISED up together and made to sit together in heavenly places in Christ Jesus, being through the Holy Ghost one in Spirit with the RISEN, ascended, and glorified Lord.

Verses 14-20. In the cleansing of the leper much the same line is gone over as in the consecration of the priest, but with some exceptions. First, some of the blood of the trespass offering is put upon the ear, the hand, and the foot of the leper to be cleansed, and then the oil is put UPON the blood of the trespass offering. But secondly, it will be noticed that in the case of the leper it is not called AN ANOINTING. Thirdly, it is the pure olive oil which is applied, and not, as in the consecration of the priests, the anointing oil, which associates the priest with Christ in His priestly office, for he is "a priest by virtue of the anointing."

This is accompanied with the fresh realization of the atoning sacrifice and resurrection of the Lord Jesus. Thus he is pronounced clean. "Who shall lay anything to the charge of God's elect? It is God that justifieth. Who is he that condemneth? It is Christ that died, yea rather, that is risen again, who is even at the right hand of God, who also maketh intercession for us" (Rom. viii. 33-35).

THE PROVISION FOR THE POOR.

Verses 21-32. These verses show the goodness of God in thus meeting the poverty of the offerer when he is not able to bring all that was at first required, and expresses the condescension of divine grace towards those who are not able fully to comprehend the completeness and blessedness of their standing in Christ before God according to the Scriptures. Yet for the putting away of sin, the complete atonement of Christ in all its details, and the work of the Holy Spirit, were necessary IN THE SIGHT OF GOD; though the pardoned sinner may not be able fully to enter into the entire subject, yet the apprehension of the sacrifice of Christ is necessary for the soul's peace.

The Day of Atonement.

(Leviticus xvi.).

VERSES 1, 2. Although Jehovah appeared in glory upon the mercy-seat or propitiatory, His throne of grace, yet He was not to be approached without reverence, and it was to be in a way of His own prescribing; He would be sanctified in them that came nigh unto Him, and before all people He would be glorified, as He had reminded the children of Israel in the case of Nadab and Abihu (Lev. x. 1-3).

Verse 3. The YOUNG BULLOCK for a sin-offering was a type of Christ the perfect SERVANT in every detail of His life, who became obedient unto death, even the death of the cross, as the sin-atoning sacrifice.

The RAM for a burnt or ascending offering reminds us of Jesus Christ the faithful and true witness, on whose testimony God set His seal by raising Him again from the dead.

Verse 4. The HOLY LINEN GARMENTS typical of the pure and sinless humanity of the Lord Jesus, who was in all respects holy, harmless, undefiled, and separate from sinners. The LINEN GIRDLE as faithful in all things as Son of Man; and attired with the LINEN MITRE as subject throughout His life to the will of His heavenly Father.

Aaron BATHING his flesh in water before he put on the linen clothing rendered him a fit representative of the eternal Son of God, who was essentially pure and holy before He assumed humanity.

Verse 5.   The TWO KIDS of the GOATS for a sin-offering, and ONE RAM for a burnt or ascending offering, were to be taken of the congregation of the children of Israel, and were presented on behalf of that people as testifying Israel's participation in the atonement.

Verse 6.   But Jesus not only died for that nation, but that He might gather together in one the children of God which are scattered abroad (John xi. 51, 52). Jesus was the propitiation for the whole world, for "God so loved the world that He gave His only begotten Son" as the sinner's Substitute provided in the infinite mercy of God, on whom God laid the iniquity of us all.   It was in this sense He made atonement for Himself, though in His OWN PERSON perfectly SINLESS and pure, without a blemish and without a spot (Heb. vii. 26, 27).

"Christ also loved the CHURCH, and gave Himself for it" (Eph. v. 25), "as a Son over His own house; whose house are we" (Heb. iii. 6), including all who, as members of His body, are in living union with Him who is the Head of the body the Church, through the one Spirit uniting all in one.

Hence, in chapter xxiii. 27, 28, this day is twice spoken of in the Hebrew as the day of ATONEMENTS in the *plural*, because there is a threefold provision made—for the world, for the Church, and for the children of Israel.

Verses 7-10. In the TWO GOATS for a sin-offering we have a twofold representation of the Lord Jesus; first as putting away sin, and especially the sin OF Israel, by the sacrifice of Himself. Secondly, as removing sin FROM Israel in the latter day, in fulfilment of the word of the prophet Jeremiah (chap. l. 20), "The INIQUITY OF ISRAEL shall be sought for, and there shall be none; and the SINS OF JUDAH, and they shall not be found : for I will pardon them whom I reserve." "And so ALL ISRAEL shall be saved : as it is written, there shall come out of Zion the DELIVERER, and shall turn away ungodliness from Jacob : for this is My covenant unto them, when I shall take away their sins" (Rom. xi. 26, 27).

Verse 11. Aaron was to kill the bullock for the sin-offering which was for HIMSELF, and for his HOUSE, as a type of the Lord Jesus who, through the eternal Spirit, offered HIMSELF without spot to God, as He said, " I lay down My life, . . . No man taketh it from Me, but I lay it down of Myself. I have power to lay

it down, and I have power to take it again" (John x.
17, 18).

Verses 12, 13.   It is to be noticed that in Hebrews
ix. 4, where the vessels of the sanctuary are particu-
larized, no mention is made of the golden altar which
stood opposite the ark in the holy place, but without
the vail, though the golden censer in the Holiest is
spoken of.   It was this CENSER Aaron was to fill with
the fire which was taken from off the altar of burnt
offering.   The FIRE of the altar is a type of the HOLI-
NESS and JUSTICE of God, whereas the sin of Nadab
and Abihu was that they took strange or ordinary fire
typical of fleshly excitement, instead of fire from the
altar, and hence they died before Jehovah.

The SWEET INCENSE beaten small is described in
Exodus xxx. 34-38, composed of STACTE or freely-
flowing myrrh, emblem of grace; ONYCHA, the root of
the word signifying LION, the emblem of STEADFAST-
NESS; GALBANUM or FAT, the type of the inward PURITY
of Christ; and the FRANKINCENSE, the root of which
means WHITE, the type of PURITY, together the emblem
of the excellency of the Son of Man in His character
and life on earth, which subjected to the holiness of
God was found of sweet savour, the beloved Son in
whom the Father delighted, for Jesus when He ascended to His Father and our Father appeared before
Him in all the preciousness of His human life, before
He pleaded the blood of the atonement.   As the CLOUD
OF THE INCENSE covered the MERCY-SEAT or propitiatory, which was upon the ark of the testimony, so the

preciousness of Christ. in every minute particular, tested by the holiness of God, met all the requirements of divine glory. So that the Lord Jesus entered on His heavenly priesthood in all the power of an endless life.

Verse 14. Aaron sprinkled of the BLOOD of the BULLOCK with his finger upon the face of the MERCY-SEAT EASTWARD, thus putting the blood of atonement upon the propitiatory in a line with the eye of Him who dwelt between the cherubim and the worshipper in his approach, for the forefront of the Tabernacle was toward the east; the crimson blood thus covering the scarlet sins of him who approached, according to Isaiah i. 18, "Though your sins be as scarlet, they shall be as white as snow; though they be red like crimson, they shall be as wool." The scarlet geranium looked at through the crimson glass of a conservatory door in strong sunlight, appearing white, gives a forcible illustration of this. One drop of the precious blood of Jesus beneath the eye of a gracious and holy God is sufficient to cover all sin; but the worshipper in drawing nigh to God, conscious of the enormity of his sin, needs the blood to be presented SEVEN TIMES in order to give him boldness of access.

Verse 15. Aaron entered the Holiest in the sweet savour of the incense, and sprinkled the blood of the bullock for himself and for his house; so Christ entered once for all into the Holiest, having obtained eternal redemption both for Himself as Sin-bearer, and for the Church, and He is now appearing in the presence of God for us who now believe in His name. Hence, in His prayer in John xvii. He distinctly says, "I pray not for the world, but for them which Thou hast given Me . . . and those who shall believe in Me through their word" (*vv.* 9-20). In this prayer He makes no mention of Israel whatever, but Jesus died for the nation of Israel also, and the time will come when He will plead the same precious blood for the people of Israel. This is symbolized by the blood of the GOAT which was *for the people,* which was sprinkled on and before the mercy-seat in the same manner as was the blood of the bullock. This looks forward to ISRAEL in the latter day, and then all Israel will be saved, in fulfilment of God's covenant with them. There is no mention again of the incense because the sweet savour in which he first entered still remained. The atoning work is one, but there are two aspects of that atonement, for the Church now, and for Israel in due time.

Verses 16, 17. The blood of the New Covenant not only made atonement for the sin of the people of Israel, but also for their TRANSGRESSIONS in connection with the service and WORSHIP OF GOD, in the tabernacle, in the wilderness, and the temple in the land ; so that when the MOUNTAIN of JEHOVAH'S HOUSE shall be established in the top of the mountains, and all nations shall flow unto it (Isa. ii. 2, 3), the temple rebuilt, and the altar and sacrifices reinstituted according to Ezekiel's prophecy, the glory of Jehovah will fill the temple, which will be the house of prayer for all nations, and the sacrifices as a memorial of the once-

offered sacrifice of Christ will be accepted on behalf
of Israel, and on behalf of all who come up to worship
with them (see Isa. lvi. 6, 7). And as there was NO
ONE in the TENT of the congregation whilst Aaron went
in until he had completed the work, so in the work of
atonement the Lord Jesus stands perfectly alone, and
to Him be all the glory.

Verses 18, 19. It is a fact little apprehended but
amply attested in the Word of God, that when Israel
are restored again to their land in the LATTER DAY,
their holy CITY and the TEMPLE rebuilt, then the ALTAR
of Jehovah and its memorial sacrifices, with certain
important alterations, will be reinstituted according to
Ezekiel xliii. 13-27, and after its dedication with the
BLOOD of the GOAT and of the BULLOCK, strikingly coin-
ciding with the portion in Leviticus under consideration; then God says, "Upon the eighth day and forward, the priests shall make your ascending offerings
upon the altar, and your peace offerings; and I will
accept you, saith Adonahy Jehovah."

Verses 20-22. The word translated SCAPEGOAT is in
the Hebrew composed of two words, the one signifying
"goat," the other "departure," that is the goat that is
sent away. On the HEAD of this goat Aaron was to
LAY BOTH his HANDS "and confess over him all the
iniquities of the children of Israel, and all their transgressions in all their sins," and "send him away by
the hand of a fit man into the wilderness," or land of
separation. The best interpretation of this type, so

far superior to man's perversion of it, will, I believe,
be found in Jer. 1 20, "In those days, and in that
time, saith Jehovah, The iniquity of Israel shall be
sought for, and there shall be none; and the sins of
Judah, and they shall not be found : for I will pardon
them whom I reserve." And as the Psalmist says
(Ps. ciii. 12), "As far as the east is from the west,
so far hath He removed our transgressions from us."
And according to the New Covenant Jehovah says, "I
will forgive their iniquity, and I will remember their
sin no more" (see Jer. xxxi. 31-34; Heb. x. 15-17).

Verses 23-25.   In the expression "holy place," where
the word "place" is printed in italics, it signifies the
SANCTUARY; but when the word "place" is printed in
Roman characters the COURT of the Tabernacle is intended.   Aaron went into the SANCTUARY and there left
the HOLY LINEN GARMENTS which he had put on at the
commencement.   And after he had bathed his flesh
in water he put on other garments, in which he appeared, and then prepared his ASCENDING OFFERING,
and the ascending offering for the people.   And the
FAT of the SIN OFFERING he burnt as incense upon
the altar.   In this we have a foreshadowing of the
Lord Jesus on the day of His resurrection, when He
appeared in another form to two of His disciples on
the way to Emmaus (Mark xvi. 12), and afterwards in
the upper room where the disciples were assembled.
It was the same body, but in another condition to
that in which He had formerly appeared.   Previously
it was a natural or soullish body, but now it was a

spiritual body (see 1 Cor. xv. 42-46); for Him to eat of the portion of the broiled fish and honeycomb previously would have been a natural act, but now it was supernatural, an action performed by spiritual power. The BATHING of the flesh in water was typical of His death, burial, and resurrection; but the ASCENDING OFFERING represents Him as going back to the Father, entering the holiest of all, and there making atonement both for Himself and for Israel, in all the SWEET SAVOUR of His internal PERFECTNESS whilst suffering for sin, as signified by the FAT of the SIN OFFERING burnt as incense.

Verses 26-28. He that SENT AWAY the SCAPEGOAT, and he that BURNT the bodies of the SIN OFFERING were to WASH THEIR CLOTHES and BATHE their FLESH; not till then could they come into the camp, showing that contact with that which bears sin rendered them ceremonially defiled, and this defilement needed to be put away. "For the bodies of THOSE beasts, whose blood is brought into the sanctuary by the high priest for sin, are burned without the camp. Wherefore Jesus also, that He might sanctify the people with His own blood, suffered without the gate. Let us go forth therefore unto Him without the camp, bearing His reproach" (Heb. xiii. 11-13).

Verses 29-31. The apprehension of the full atonement, which is in Christ Jesus, leads to the deepest humiliation, repentance, and sorrow for sin, together with the entire renunciation of all human effort for salvation. This looks forward prophetically to that

day when God "will pour upon the house of David, and
upon the inhabitants of Jerusalem, the spirit of grace
and of supplication : and they shall look upon Me
whom they pierced, and they shall mourn for Him,
as one mourneth for his only son, and shall be in
bitterness for Him, as one that is in bitterness for his
firstborn. In that day there shall be a fountain opened
to the house of David and to the inhabitants of Jerusalem for sin and for uncleanness" (Zech. xii. 10; xiii. 1).

Verses 32-34.   The return of every fresh year
brought to Israel a fresh remembrance of their sins,
for it was not possible that the blood of bulls and goats
should take away sins (Heb. x. 3, 4).   The high priesthood could not be continuous by reason of death, but
the High Priest of our profession when He had offered
one sacrifice for sins for ever, sat down on the right
hand of God, having obtained eternal redemption for
all who believe in Him, whether Jew or Gentile ; and
because He continueth ever hath an unchangeable
priesthood, a high priest for ever after the order of
Melchisedec.   "Christ was once offered to bear the
sins of many; and unto them that look for Him shall
He appear the second time without sin unto salvation"
(Heb. ix. 28).

The Ashes of the Red Heifer

(Numbers xix.).

WE have the divine comment on this chapter in those words of the inspired Apostle (Heb. ix. 13, 14), "For if the blood of bulls and of goats, and the ashes of an heifer sprinkling the unclean, sanctifieth to the purifying of the flesh : how much more shall the blood of Christ, who through the eternal Spirit offered Himself without spot to God, purge your conscience from dead works to serve the living God?"

The subject of this chapter is the DEFILEMENT of DEATH, and how it is to be put away. The application of the ASHES of the HEIFER had only a value as rendering a defiled person CEREMONIALLY CLEAN, but it could not "make the comers thereunto perfect" (Heb. x. 1, 2) as pertaining to the conscience.

"God is a Spirit : and they that worship Him must worship Him in Spirit and in truth" (John iv. 24). Dead works bring defilement to the conscience, and render one unfit for LIVING service to a LIVING God.

89

What is man's condition till he is born of the Spirit? Spiritual death. Death reigned from Adam to Moses (Rom. v. 12-14), and to the present time, and men are "dead in trespasses and sins"; hence the words of Christ, "Ye must be born again" (John iii. 7).

When the Triune God created man in His own image and after His likeness (Gen. i. 26, 27) He made him spirit, soul, and body, three natures in one person, "Jehovah Elohim formed man of the dust of the ground, and breathed into his nostrils the breath of life; and man became a LIVING soul" (Gen. ii. 7). The inferior creatures became living souls by an act of CREATIVE POWER, MAN by the BREATH of the LIVING GOD. LIFE is in the blood, mortal life is sustained by breathing the atmospheric air; DEATH is ceasing to breathe. A prayerless soul is a dead soul; as the soul of man became living by the inbreathing of life FROM the Father, THROUGH the Son and BY the Holy Ghost, so when Adam and Eve ate the fruit of the forbidden tree they ceased to breathe spiritually, communion with God ceased; and the word was fulfilled, "in the day that thou eatest thereof thou shalt surely die" (Gen. ii. 17). "Their eyes were opened," but their mouths were closed to communion with God, their SOULS DIED and their BODIES became MORTAL. Communion lost is PARADISE LOST; communion restored is PARADISE RE-GAINED. A picture of Paradise is graphically drawn by the Spirit of God in the first chapters of Genesis. How much is enfolded in those words (ch. iii. 8, 9), "They heard the voice of Jehovah Elohim [the Triune God] walking in the garden in the cool [breeze] of the day."

How did they know the voice of God? When God put our first parents in the Garden of Eden, He gave them occupation for the body in dressing and keeping it, food for the mind in the study of natural history, but reserved the evening hour for Himself. The evening BREEZE which refreshed the body was a type of the SPIRIT who maintained their communion with God. In the evening of that day when Adam and Eve had sinned, the footfall of God was heard as usual. Where was the response? Communion was gone. "Adam, where art thou?" Out of communion with God, hid behind the trees of the garden. This condition of spiritual death could only be met by atonement, as suggested by those words, "the seed of the woman shall bruise the serpent's head"; and by the action of God, Who clothed our first parents in the skin of the slaughtered victim.

In the type of the RED HEIFER we have God's provision for putting away the defilement of spiritual death. "Jehovah spake UNTO MOSES AND UNTO AARON," not to them separately as before; and ELEAZAR was to carry out the ordinance. The "red heifer" was a type of the Lord Jesus Christ INCARNATE, "God manifest in flesh." The name "Adam" signified RED EARTH, ·out of which man was formed, and the word "red" here employed conveys in the original that thought. Typically there is a distinction between the male and female offerings : the male was offered for actual sin, the female for passive defilement, such as by contact or the contamination of nature. It was to be a red heifer on "which never came yoke," emblem of the sinless obedience of the Lord Jesus, Who was never subject to the will of man, but to His heavenly Father.

Verses 1-3.   The children of Israel were to GIVE the RED HEIFER to ELEAZAR the priest.   AARON was a type of the Lord Jesus in His humiliation on earth who offered Himself without spot to God.   ELEAZAR is a type of the Lord Jesus NOW in His RESURRECTION PRIESTHOOD, bringing to remembrance the sacrifice. already offered.   In MELCHISEDEC the kingly and priestly offices were united, and in the MILLENNIUM CHRIST will be a priest after the order of Melchisedec. As Eleazar brought the heifer without the camp, and one slew her before his face ; even so Jesus, that He might sanctify the people with His own blood, once for all suffered without the gate (Heb. xiii. 12).   This action of Eleazar is like the Lord's Supper, the memorial of an action once accomplished, whereas the mass is a fictitious repetition of it.

Verse 4.   On the day of atonement the blood was carried within the vail, but in this case Eleazar with his finger sprinkled the blood towards the face of the tent of the congregation seven times, to show that the blood had efficacy to restore communion in its sevenfold perfection.

Verse 5.   The entire victim was carried without the camp and consumed.   The Lord Jesus was treated by God as made sin, though Himself sinless.

Verse 6.   As the cedar wood, hyssop, and scarlet were cast into the midst of the burning, so the divine glory, human humiliation, and earthly dignity of the Lord Jesus gave their value to His atoning work.

Verses 7, 8, 10. The priest, he who burnt the heifer, and also he that gathered the ashes, were all three to wash their clothes, and be unclean until the evening; showing that, as these things represented realities, there was need for ceremonial purification.

Verse 9. The ashes of the heifer, which included the blood, were to be laid up in a clean place, and by a clean man without the camp to be KEPT. They were to be treated as holy, and not to be counted an unclean thing (see Heb. x. 28, 29). The place of keeping was to be without the camp, so as to be available for those who could not enter into the camp. It was to be for a water of separation or cleansing; for its antitype, the blood of Jesus Christ, God's Son, cleanseth us from all sin. But the BLOOD of CHRIST not only cleanses the heart from all unrighteousness, and from the contamination of sin, but it also, THROUGH THE ETERNAL SPIRIT, purges the conscience from the guilt of sin, and "from DEAD WORKS TO SERVE THE LIVING GOD." In Hebrew the words "it is a purification for sin," are, literally, "it is a sin offering." because it is that which has made atonement for it.

Verse 10. "A statute for ever."

An everlasting statute; there is no cleansing in any other way, for any, either saint or sinner (Acts iv. 12).

Verses 11-13. God has graciously shown us the danger of defilement in such a world of sin and spiritual death as this. Also, the secret cause of hindered communion through its defilement, and the remedy in Christ Jesus.

The BURNING of the HEIFER and GATHERING the ASHES showed the crucifixion and burial of Jesus; the THIRD DAY typified His resurrection, it was therefore on the third day it was to be applied, that is, the. soul should realize not only His death but His resurrection for His cleansing. "He was delivered for our offences, and was raised again for our justification" (Rom. iv. 25).

The SEVENTH DAY, or day of rest, when the cleansing was complete, typified the perfect atonement of Jesus, and the consequent REST into which the soul enters by faith in Him.

"He shall purify himself with it." There is no true purification by any other means.

"Purifieth not himself." It is remarkable that this in Hebrew really is, make one's self sin, because the only way to purify is by taking the guilt, confessing it, and then applying to the sacrifice of Christ by faith we are cleansed.

" Defileth the tabernacle of Jehovah." If through the influence of surrounding evil, or evil things, our souls have got into a dead and carnal state, without applying the remedy as here set forth, we bring in the withering power of spiritual death when we meet the assembled saints, and lose the blessing of living communion; and until by the Holy Spirit the truth of the death and resurrection of Jesus is applied, the soul continues in this sad condition.

Verses 14-16. This the defiling influence of spiritual deadness in one professing the name of Christ in his HOUSE and around him, and those who are not GUARDED, but open to the influence, as many are; yet the soul in the lively exercise of faith and watchfulness may escape. The heart should be kept carefully CLOSED to the influence of dead, carnal profession.

"Seven days." It is not temporary, which will pass off in a time, but SEVEN DAYS is put for continuance, and it can only be removed in God's appointed way.

Verses 16-22. In the twelfth verse the command was "He shall purify himself with it"; a personal application by faith in Christ.

In these verses it is an action to be done by another who is CLEAN; as said the apostle, "Brethren, if a man be overtaken in a fault, ye which are spiritual, restore such an one in the spirit of meekness" (Gal. vi. 1); it is by way of discipline, one dealing with the sin of another, that it may be put away; and the spiritual man may have need to cleanse himself from the defiling influences with which he has to deal.

The ASHES of the burnt heifer were the memorial of the sacrifice of Christ; the running or LIVING WATER, a type of the Holy Spirit giving divine and spiritual efficacy to that atoning blood when applied to the heart and conscience. The HYSSOP may remind us of that deep contrition and humiliation in which the blood of atonement should be applied and apprehended, so that we may well say with the psalmist, "Purge me with hyssop, and I shall be clean : wash me, and I shall be whiter than snow" (Psalm li. 7).

Shadows of the Cross

THE cross of Calvary throws its shadow back through the long ages. We may trace it in the Garden of Eden. See that innocent victim whose skin formed a covering for the nakedness of our first parents. It was *one* skin—for the word is in the singular—with which our first parents were arrayed by the hand of God in substitution for the fig-leaf covering which they had themselves devised. We see in that victim the first shadow of the cross. The firstling of the flock, which was Abel's offering, forms another part of the shadow of Calvary's cross.

In the altars erected by the patriarchs that shadow is lengthened out. The altar erected by Abraham on Mount Moriah, on one of the mountains which God told him of, is a marvellous shadow of the cross of Calvary. If we wanted a proof of the inspiration of Scripture, that twenty-second chapter of Genesis would furnish it. We see there an unmistakable shadow of the cross, clear in all its outlines, sharply cut, accurate, and true in every detail. Let us connect the altar in

97

the centre of Solomon's court with that Abraham erected on the spot pointed out by the finger of God on Mount Moriah. It may be that Solomon's altar stood on the very self-same spot. At the present day, on the crest of that mountain, there is a remarkable projection of limestone, a few feet above the surface of the surrounding platform of marble, on which the Dome of the Rock now stands. That irregular limestone projection is regarded by the Mohammedans to the present day as the sacred site where their father Abraham built an altar on which to offer up his son Isaac. The Dome of the Rock, or Mosque of Omar, is, so to speak, a monument erected over that sacred spot.

What a wondrous shadow of the cross of Calvary is given in this twenty-second chapter of Genesis, which describes the sacrifice that Abraham offered. We are told that God did tempt Abraham—that is, put him to the test. Satan's temptations act upon the evil of our nature to bring out evil. God's testings are rather the actings of His own grace to bring out that grace to the full. God tried Abraham in the most severe manner. He put the gold into a crucible at white heat. He tried him at the tenderest point. How it reminds us of that wondrous fact : "God so loved the world, that He gave His only begotten Son, that whosoever believeth in Him should not perish, but have everlasting life" (John iii. 16).

Abraham takes the wood and lays it on his son Isaac. This brings Isaiah liii. to our remembrance—another deep shadow of the cross — where we learn that

"Jehovah laid on Him the iniquity of us all." Abraham and Isaac, we read, "went both of them together." How instructive and full of deep meaning is this expression. It was the grace of God that caused Him to give His only begotten Son; it was the grace of the Son that led Him to give Himself up to the fulfilment of the Father's will—"they went both of them together." Isaac said,"Behold the fire and the wood : but where is the lamb for a burnt offering?" How suggestive was Abraham's reply : "My son, God will provide Himself a lamb for a burnt offering." Did Isaac understand it? Perhaps he did. If there was in Abraham the spirit of the Father's surrender of the Son, there was also in Isaac the spirit of the Son's surrender to the Father's will. "So they went both of them together."

Let us transfer the question of Isaac to the altar of burnt offering. In the centre of Israel's camp in the wilderness was the altar of burnt offering—five cubits square, and three cubits high. At the dedication of the tabernacle the fire of God descended and consumed upon the altar the sacrifice. Henceforth, the command of God was that the fire should ever be burning upon the altar; it should never go out. So also, when Solomon's temple was dedicated, the fire again descended and consumed the sacrifice upon the altar, that the same ordinance might be observed—"The fire shall ever be burning on My altar"; "It shall never go out"; "It shall never be put out."

What is the fire that came from God, which consumed the victim on the altar, and caused it to ascend as a sweet savour, or savour of rest— that fire which, when the rebels presented strange fire, came forth and consumed them.   What is that fire the emblem of? "Behold the fire." It was in the very centre of Israel's encampment; there was the smoke ever ascending, the fire ever burning.   "Our God is a consuming fire."

The fire is the emblem of God's righteousness and holiness.   God never ceases to be the righteous and holy God, of purer eyes than to behold iniquity, and who cannot look upon sin.   Never for one single moment or twinkling of an eye, in time, or for one single moment throughout eternity, will that fire cease to burn.   It shall never go out.   In the glory above God will be ever righteous and holy; and in the bottomless pit, the lake that burns with fire and brimstone, His righteousness shall for ever be manifested.   That fire shall never cease to burn.   There the fire is not quenched, and there the worm dieth not.   "For Tophet is ordained of old; yea, for the King it is prepared; He hath made it deep and large : the pile thereof is fire and much wood; the breath of Jehovah, like a stream of brimstone, doth kindle it" (Isa. xxx. 33).   When the lake of fire is open to receive the lost, all the sin of a guilty world will be cast into it, as fuel for the everlasting burnings.   It shall never go out.   "Behold the fire."

"Behold the wood."   It was the occupation of the Gibeonites to be hewers of wood for God's altar.   Daily the priests were to lay the wood in order upon the fire. What is the wood?   The wood is the emblem of sin.

"Thou hast set our iniquities before Thee; our secret sins in the light of Thy countenance." The wood was each day set in order upon the fire. God is righteous; behold the fire. Man is a sinner: behold the wood. Look round upon the world. Look at London: behold the wood. Oh! what heavy faggots will be carried down to the everlasting burnings. Men's sins will follow them; every sin that man hath committed, and that goes unconfessed and unpardoned, unwashed in Emmanuel's blood, will be a faggot for the burning.

"Behold the fire and the wood: but where is the lamb for a burnt offering?"

Behold the holiness and righteousness of God, for "our God is a consuming fire." Behold the wood. From all parts of the world the echo comes back: Behold the wood! From heathendom, Popedom, Christendom, comes the echo: Behold the wood! "But where is the lamb for a burnt offering?" Let us send up the challenge to the heavens above: "Where is the Lamb?" Angels, where is the Lamb? Gabriel, will you step forward? The echo comes back: "Where is the Lamb?" Where? Where? Ah beloved friends, that was the cry for ages and ages, till one day John the Baptist pointed with his finger to a man walking along, and said, "Behold the Lamb of God, which taketh away the sin of the world." "My son, God will provide Himself a lamb for the burnt offering." That is He.

See "the carpenter's son," despised and rejected of men, led as a lamb to the slaughter, and dumb before

its shearers—behold the Lamb that God has provided.
"None other can by any means redeem his brother, nor
give to God a ransom for him" (Psalm xlix. 7). God
could see none amongst the ranks of the angels mighty
enough, and worthy enough, to be laid on His altar.
But God has Himself provided a Lamb. He looked
round upon a sinful world; God is holy : "behold the
fire." "The wrath of God is revealed from heaven
against all ungodliness and unrighteousness of men" :
"behold the wood." Oh, blessed thought : "Behold the
Lamb of God, which taketh away the sin of the
world !" The fire ever burning, the wood ever consuming, the sweet savour of the Lamb ever ascending.
God always holy, man ever a transgressor, but the
sweet savour of the Lamb of God ever ascending from
God's altar.

Look down now to the cave below, and see in Tophet
the fire and the wood. People want to know what the
brimstone is (Isa. xxx. 33); it is the wrath of God.
The breath of Jehovah, like a stream of brimstone,
doth kindle it, and adds intensity to the flames. Look
down and say : Behold the fire, and behold the wood,
but where is the Lamb? And these caves of darkness
utter back the sorrowful echo : Where? *Where?*
WHERE? Behold the fire; it shall never go out. Behold the wood; but no lamb for a burnt offering there.

Look up to the regions of light above, and say,
Behold the fire. Yes, He Who sits upon the throne of
the universe—God the Judge of all—is a God of infinite justice, infinite holiness, infinite purity : behold

the fire. Where is the Lamb? Behold, in the midst of the throne, "a Lamb as it had been slain." But where is the wood? From those regions of light, and from the midst of the throne, there comes the echo back : Where? *Where?* WHERE? There is no evil there, no wood there, no sin there.

The lamb on the altar was God's centre for Israel's camp; the lamb on the altar was God's centre of Israel's kingdom under Solomon; the lamb on the altar —not the evening lamb, but the morning lamb—will be God's centre for Israel and for the earth in the millennial period. But God's centre for heaven, for the universe, and for eternity, will be "the Lamb as it had been slain," in the midst of the throne of God—no longer led as a lamb to the slaughter, but reigning for ever and ever.

QUESTIONS AND ANSWERS

QUESTIONS AND ANSWERS.

The following questions, which were primarily answered by Mr Newberry for the benefit of a Bible-class consisting of several hundreds of young believers, being of general importance, and intimately connected with the subject of Christ's sacrifice and Priesthood as set forth in the "Types" of the foregoing pages, have, with their answers, been here given a permanent place, in the hope that they may yield help on the points which are acknowledged difficulties with many students of the sacred Word.

QUESTION 1. *With what object were the Sacrifices of Antediluvian and Patriarchal times instituted?*

The purpose of God from the beginning, in the institution of sacrifices, appears to have been to convey to the eye of man, by object-lessons, His plan for the putting away of sin through the atoning sacrifice of His beloved Son, during the entire period from the fall of man, until, in the fulness of times, the Son of Man appeared, and the atonement was made. Hence,

on the entrance of sin into the world, He announced
His purpose in that wondrous prophecy concerning the
woman's seed (see Gen. iii. 15), and this He illustrated
by the introduction of the first sacrifice, which is implied by those words, "Jehovah-God made coats of
skin, and clothed them" (Gen. iii. 21). If we apply
the law of the offerings as laid down in the book of
Leviticus to these words, a beautiful and striking light is thrown upon them. We there
learn that the offerer himself killed the victim;
the offerer in this case must have been Adam
acting as the patriarchal priest, the victim appears to have been a lamb, suggested in Abel's offering "of the firstlings of his flock." From Leviticus
vii. 8 we learn. "The priest that offereth any man's
burnt offering, even the priest shall have to himself
the skin of the burnt offering which he hath offered."
Therefore "Jehovah-God made coats of skin, and
clothed them." In the Hebrew the word SKIN here is
in the singular number. It will be observed that the
first death after man's sin was the death of atonement,
and the first blood that stained the ground was the
blood of the innocent victim that was shed for the
guilty.

" It was not possible that the blood of bulls and of
goats should take away sin." hence the law had only a
"shadow of good things to come." of which the body
and substance is Christ. But when the Spirit of God
explained and applied to the mind and heart of the
children of faith the spiritual import of these things,
they were enabled to lay hold of and embrace them, to

rejoice in present grace, and in prospect of future glory, confessing they were strangers and pilgrims on the earth (see Heb. xi.).

QUESTION 2. *Will Sacrifices be resumed in Millennial times? If so, where, by whom, and for what purpose?*

The pattern of the TABERNACLE and its ALTAR was given to MOSES on the MOUNT. The pattern of SOLOMON'S TEMPLE and its courts was given to DAVID by God. So in like manner the pattern of the MILLENNIAL TEMPLE and its altar was given to EZEKIEL in the visions of God. We have the records of this in Ezek. xl.-xlviii. The TEMPLE will be erected on the MOUNTAIN of JEHOVAH'S house (Isa. ii. 2, 3), and not on Mount Moriah as the former temples were, whilst the city of Jerusalem will occupy its former site.

The directions for the Millennial temple and altar are given with instructions for the SACRIFICES in Ezek. xliii. 10-27. This altar will be intermediate in size between the one of the tabernacle and the one of Solomon's temple. The Millennial temple will be the house of prayer for all nations, all flesh will worship there, and their SACRIFICES shall be accepted (Isa. lx. 7, lxvi. 23; Psalm li. 18, 19; Zech. xiv. 16, 17).

In the ordinances connected with the altar, etc., it will be observed there are significant and striking alterations. There will be the DAILY MORNING lamb (Ezek.

lxvi. 13-15); but no evening sacrifice is mentioned. This type was fulfilled at the crucifixion of Jesus. The FEAST OF THE PASSOVER will be observed (Ezek. xlv. 21-24); but not the feast of Pentecost, that is being fulfilled in the present dispensation.

The FEAST OF TABERNACLES will be kept (Ezek. xlv. 25; Zech. xiv. 16), but not the Day of Atonement. The type of the bullock for the household is being fulfilled now, and the type of the goat for Israel will be fulfilled then. There is no mention of the Lord's day; but the NEW MOONS and SABBATHS will be observed (Isa. lxvi. 23; Ezek. xlvi. 1-7). There is no mention of the high priest; but the PRINCE who will be the earthly representative of the KINGLY and PRIESTLY MELCHISEDEC offices of the Lord Jesus, occupies a prominent place.

The former SACRIFICES looked FORWARD to Calvary; the LORD'S SUPPER, as a MEMORIAL of the sufferings of Christ, looks UPWARD to Him, risen and glorified. The MILLENNIAL SACRIFICES will look BACK and be a MEMORIAL of the atoning work of Jesus on the cross.

QUESTION 3. *Are the Levitical Offerings as types restricted in their application to believers, or may they be used as gospel types for the unconverted?*

They were intended for the profit of *all*, and are written "for our admonition, upon whom the ends of the ages are come" (1 Cor. x. 1-12). They pointed to Christ, the Lamb of God, THE TAKER AWAY of the sin of the world (John i. 29). And it is written, "He is the propitiation for our sins : and not for ours only, but also for the whole world" (1 John ii. 2). And again, "As Moses lifted up the serpent in the wilderness, even so must the Son of Man be lifted up : that WHOSOEVER believeth in Him should not perish, but have eternal life" (John iii. 14, 15).

QUESTION 4. *What is the meaning of the words in Hebrews x. 12 : "After He had offered one sacrifice for sins for ever, sat down"? and ought the comma to be after "sins" or "for ever"?*

In Hebrews x. 10-12 the CONTRAST is between the former priests, who stood DAILY offering OFTENTIMES the SAME SACRIFICES, and Jesus Christ, who, when He had offered ONE sacrifice of INFINITE value for sins, which was effective ONCE FOR ALL, then sat down, which shows that the work was finished. I prefer placing the pause after the word "ever," because the Greek phrase expresses COMPLETENESS. Standing and sitting are figurative expressions, and must *not* always be taken as expressing CONTINUATION of posture. Stephen saw "Jesus *standing* on the right hand of God" (Acts vii. 55); and in Rev. v. 6 we read, "In the midst of the throne . . . *stood* a Lamb as it had been slain."

QUESTION 5. *What do the words, " We have an"*
altar" (Heb. xiii. 10) mean?

To the true believer JESUS is both SACRIFICE and
ALTAR, and also PRIEST, and it is only those who, by
receiving Him, are "born not of blood, nor of the will
of the flesh, nor of the will of man, but of God"
(John i. 13), who have a right or title to feed on Him
"whose flesh is meat indeed." It was only those who
were born of the tribe of Levi and of the family of
Aaron who were permitted to feed on the victims
offered on the altar of burnt-offering. But their being
born into the family of Aaron gave them no title to
feed at the altar which is Christ Himself; so now
neither a pious ancestry, nor outward ceremonies, can
give a title to feed on the true and living Bread.
Hence the exhortation, "Let us go forth therefore unto
Him without the camp, bearing His reproach. . . By
Him therefore let us offer the sacrifice of praise to God
continually, that is, the fruit of our lips giving thanks
to His name" (Heb. xiii. 13, 15).

QUESTION 6. *Was the Lord Jesus a Sin-bearer all*
His life, or only on the cross? The words of 1 Peter
ii. 24 are given in the margin of the Revised Version,
"carried up . . . to the tree." Is this correct?

The Lord Jesus in His life was holy, harmless, undefiled, and separate from sinners; He Himself knew
no sin. He could say to the last, "My Father hath not

left Me alone, for I do always those things that please Him"; and His Father's repeated testimony was, "This is My beloved Son, in whom I am well pleased." As stated in 1 Peter ii. 24, "Who His own self bare our sins in His own body ON the tree." The reading given by the revisers in the margin of the R.V. (like many other of their alterations) is *absolutely false*. It was ONLY ON THE CROSS that He, the sinless One, was made sin for us, it was there and then ONLY that He, the blessed One, was made a curse, but not accursed. It was *our* death He died; He Himself (though as incarnate He was capable of dying) was not *liable* to death. It was OUR transgressions, which were laid on Him, that hid God's face from Him. This is beautifully expressed in Psalm xxii. 24, when rightly translated : "For He (Jehovah) did not despise nor abhor the affliction of the afflicted; neither did He hide His face from Him; but when He cried unto Him, He heard."

QUESTION 7. *What is the difference between Priesthood and Advocacy as exercised by the Lord Jesus?*

ADVOCACY is a part of the PRIESTLY office of the Lord Jesus. The word ADVOCATE is only so translated in 1 John ii. 1. In other places it is translated " COMFORTER," and applied to the Holy Ghost (John xiv. 16, 26; xv. 26; xvi. 7).

The Greek word PARAKLETOS signifies "one acting on behalf of those who are called." The Holy Ghost acts on their behalf on earth, instructing, counselling, and comforting them, while the Lord Jesus acts on their behalf before His Father in heaven.

QUESTION 8. *Does the Lord Jesus exercise His Melchisedec Priesthood at present, or does it belong to the future?*

Both *now* and for ever. In Heb. v. 5-10 it is applied to the Lord Jesus, when having become "Author of eternal salvation unto all them that obey Him," He *is* addressed by God "High Priest after the order of Melchisedec."

Then in chapter vi. 20, when He is spoken of as "Forerunner" within the veil, "Jesus, having become [margin, Newberry Bible] High Priest for ever after the order of Melchisedec." Chapter vii. continues the subject; chapter viii. 1 begins, "Now of the things which we have spoken this in the sum : WE have SUCH AN HIGH PRIEST, Who is set on the right hand of the throne of the Majesty in the heavens."

QUESTION 9. *To what cleansing do the words "The Blood of Jesus Christ His Son cleanseth us from all sin"* (1 John i. 7) *apply?*

If we walk in the light as God is in the light, we shall be conscious of many evils which otherwise may not be realized; so Job experienced when he said, "I have heard of Thee by the hearing of the ear : but now mine eye seeth Thee. Wherefore I abhor myself, and repent in dust and ashes" (Job xlii. 5, 6). That which keeps the soul in conscious peace and confidence, is the apprehension of the infinite value and efficacy of the blood of Jesus Christ, God's Son.

The word "cleanseth" is not in the aorist or past tense, "cleansed"; nor as some explain it as the present participle, "is cleansing"; but it is in the PRESENT tense. It "CLEANSETH" moment by moment. And when the Word is applied by the Holy Ghost, it purges the conscience and purifies the heart, leading to a holy walk and conversation.

QUESTION 10. *What is the "fountain opened" for* " *sin and for uncleanness* " *in Zech. xiii. 1?*

We read in John xix. 34, "One of the soldiers with a spear pierced His side, and forthwith came there out blood and water." And when applied by the Spirit of grace (Zech. xii. 10), " I will pour upon the house of David, and upon the inhabitants of Jerusalem, the spirit of grace and of supplication : and they shall look upon Me whom they pierced." In Zech. xiii. 1, we read, "In *that day* there shall be a fountain opened to the house of David and the inhabitants of Jerusalem for sin and for uncleanness."

I believe the lines by Toplady—

> Let the water and the blood,
> From Thy wounded side which flowed
> Be of sin the double cure;
> Cleanse me from its guilt and power.

express the true meaning.

QUESTION 11. *What are the " things in heaven"* (Col. i. 20) *said to be reconciled by Christ? and for what cause was their reconciliation necessary?*

In Ephesians i. 9 we read that God has "made known unto us the mystery of His will, that in the dispensation of the fulness of times He might head up in one all things in Christ, both which are in THE HEAVENS, and which are on earth, even in Him."

When God created man in His own image as His earthly representative, He put all things in subjection under his feet, and with Adam He associated Eve. In their fall creation was made subject to vanity. The purpose of God now is in the fulness of times to head up together in the second Adam, together with the second Eve, the Church, not only things on earth, but THINGS IN THE HEAVENS, making Him the Head of the creation of God, the keystone of the arch of universal security, "and put all things under His feet, and gave Him to be the Head over all things to the Church, which is His body, the fulness of Him that filleth all in all" (Ephesians i. 22, 23).

The fall of Satan and his angels had brought sin into the heavens, before, through his temptation, sin had entered into the world. But God, through the cross of Christ, has reconciled THINGS IN HEAVEN as well as things on earth; so then, when God's present dealing with the earth is finished, in the new heavens and the new earth everlasting security and peace will be established, for by Christ were not only ALL THINGS CREATED that are IN THE HEAVENS, and that are on earth, visible and invisible, whether thrones, or dominions, or principalities, or powers, but also by the blood of His cross ALL THINGS ARE RECONCILED and set on an established basis (Col. i. 16, 20), whether they be things on earth, or things IN THE HEAVENS.

QUESTION 12. *What is the force of the words " The times of the restitution of all things" (Acts iii. 21)? It is asserted by some that all men and things shall be finally redeemed and restored to God, as a result of the cross of Christ.*

The times of the restitution of all things will probably be the period of millennial blessedness under the new covenant, when Israel will be restored to their own land, and the creation delivered from the bondage of corruption (Rom. viii. 19-21), under the rule of the Prince of peace, which shall be finally established in the new heavens and the new earth (Rev. xxi.).

The eternal condition, both of the saved and unsaved, is asserted in a variety of scriptures, which must not be set aside, for the Scripture cannot be broken. The Judge of all the earth will do right, a God of truth, and without iniquity, just and right is He. And the equity of His dealings, God Himself in due time will make manifest to all the universe (Rom. iii. 4).

Blind unbelief is sure to err,
And scan God's work in vain,
God is His own Interpreter,
And He will make it plain.

APPENDIX

APPENDIX.

The following words, with their significations and use, are all intimately connected with the sacrifice of Christ.

Atonement.

THE English word ATONEMENT signifies "at-one-ment," setting AT ONE, or reconciliation, as in Acts vii. 26.

It occurs once in the New Testament (Rom. v. 11).

In Hebrew the root of the word means to COVER OVER; we get the same signification in Genesis vi. 14, "PITCH it within and without with PITCH."

It also means RECONCILIATION, as in Daniel ix. 24.

The word rendered MERCY-SEAT or PROPITIATORY is from the same root. It was the COVERING lid of the Ark of the Covenant, containing the two unbroken tables of the law.

Propitiation.

This signifies RECONCILIATION. In Romans iii. 25, and Hebrews ix. 5, it means the mercy-seat or propitiatory. In 1 John ii. 2, and 1 John iv. 10, it is "a propitiatory offering," or sacrifice for sin.

In Luke xviii. 13, "God be merciful" should be "God be propitious," on the ground of reconciliation made, as in Hebrews ii. 17, "To make reconciliation [propitiation] for the sins of the people."

121

Substitution.

We have a beautiful example of SUBSTITUTION in Genesis xxii. 13, where we read, "And Abraham lifted up his eyes, and looked, and behold behind him a ram caught in a thicket by his horns: and Abraham went and took the ram, and offered him up for an ascending offering IN THE STEAD OF his son."

In Leviticus i. 4, in the case of the burnt or ascending offering, we have the promise, "And it shall be accepted for him, to make atonement for him."

Sin-bearing.

In the Scriptures SIN is looked at in three aspects.

First, as INIQUITY; sin the nature, or bud.

Second, as SIN which in both Hebrew and Greek signifies "missing the mark," or "coming short" of God's requirements—the omission of righteousness.

Third, TRANSGRESSION, the breach of a positive commandment, for "where no law is, there is no transgression" (Rom. iv. 15). First the bud, then the ear, then the full corn in the ear.

Thus we read in Psalm xxxii. 1, 2, 5, "Blessed is he whose whose transgression is forgiven, whose sin is covered. Blessed is the man unto whom Jehovah imputeth not iniquity, and in whose spirit there is no guile. I acknowledged my sin unto Thee, and mine iniquity have I not hid. I said, I will confess my transgressions unto Jehovah; and Thou forgavest the iniquity of my sin." See also Exodus xxxiv. 7. In Isaiah liii. 5, 6, the Lord Jesus is presented as bearing and putting away sin. "He was wounded for our transgression. He was bruised for our iniquity; .. and Jehovah laid on Him the iniquity of us all"

Righteousness.

This means rectitude of character or conduct; what i right, just, and proper.

"Abraham believed God, and it was counted unto him for righteousness" (Rom. iv. 3); that is, God reckoned him righteous—"through the redemption which is in Christ Jesus"; for on the ground of His atoning sacrifice God is just, while He "justifieth the ungodly" (Rom. iii. 21-26; iv. 5).

Holiness.

In the Hebrew holiness signifies SEPARATION, especially separation from evil to God, as was expressed on the golden plate of the mitre of the high priest, "Holiness to Jehovah."

In the Greek it means "NOT OF THE WORLD." This is beautifully shown in what is said of Christ. He was "holy, harmless, undefiled, separate from sinners, and made higher than the heavens" (Heb. vii. 26).

Sanctification.

Sanctification means "a setting apart" from that which is evil and worldly for the service and glory of the God of heaven. This may be best accomplished practically—

First, by living, thinking, acting in the presence of God. The holiest human life on record is that of Enoch, whose name signified DEDICATED and INITIATED, of whom it is said, "Enoch walked with God: and he was not; for God took him" (Gen. v. 24).

Second, by abiding in Christ, for he that "abideth in Him sinneth not" (1 John iii. 6), and he who abideth in Christ, and Christ in him, the same "bringeth forth much fruit" (John xv. 5).

Third, by living and walking in the Spirit, for the righteousness of the law is fulfilled in us, who walk not after the flesh, but after the Spirit (Rom. viii. 4).

Covenant and Testament.

The Hebrew word "Berith" is COVENANT.

The Greek word "Diatheke is TESTAMENT, or WILL.

Hence in Hebrews ix. 15-20, the words may have a double sense.

Words or titles must always be considered in the connection where they are found. Many more synonymous words and titles, with their meanings, will be found in "The Companion to the Englishman's Bible," by Thomas Newberry.

TYPES OF
THE TABERNACLE

Types of
The Tabernacle

THOMAS NEWBERRY

THE TABERNACLE IN THE WILDERNESS

Contents

List of Illustrations.

Types of

The Tabernacle.

INTRODUCTION.

(Exodus, Chapter xxv. 1-9).

IT is not here Israel seeking to provide a dwelling-place for God, as in David's case (Psa. cxxxii. 1-5), but God desiring a dwelling-place for Himself amongst them. Man naturally desires not the presence of God with him here on earth, but God in the riches of His grace seeks to dwell with men. We must remember when this request from God was made. In the twentieth chapter, we have the giving of the law, in the three following chapters further precepts, then in chapter xxiv., Moses, Aaron, Nadab, Abihu, and seventy of the elders were called up unto mount Sinia. "And the glory of Jehovah abode upon mount Sinai, and the cloud covered it six days : and on the seventh day He called unto Moses out of the cloud. And the sight of the glory of Jehovah was like devouring fire. And Moses was in the mount forty days and forty nights." There, shut in with God, he receives directions concerning the Tabernacle. Thus the law includes within itself "a shadow of good things to come," and patterns of things in the heavens were given on mount Sinai.

It is in the heart of man God desires His dwelling-place, hence it was from those who offered " willingly with the heart " His offering was to be taken. Where there is first a willing mind, it is accepted according to that a man hath. The widow's two mites given out of her penury, were more acceptable to God than the offerings of the rich out of their abundance.

THE MATERIALS.

Verse 3. "And this is the offering (heave-offering) ye shall take of them."

There are two kinds of offerings frequently mentioned. The wave-offering which was made to pass and re-pass before the eye of Jehovah, and the heave-offering which was lifted up to God and presented to Him. In this case it is the "heave-offering" (see margin of *The Englishman's Bible*).

In the original there are two distinct terms employed for tent and tabernacle; in our Authorized Translation these terms are frequently confused, but the Spirit of God always uses them with precision. The tent (*ohel*) is the ordinary term for transitory habitations in the desert; hence "to dwell in tents" is characteristic of pilgrimage. The Tabernacle *mishcahn*, from *shahcan*, "to dwell," is more immediately connected with the presence of God. As God says in verse 8, " Let them make Me a sanctuary that I may dwell among them." God's dwelling-place among men must be holy, for holiness becometh God's house for ever.

In the original Scriptures the term employed is "The Tent of the congregation." It is never written " Tabernacle of the congregation," although frequently so translated. The term " Tent of the congregation " is connected with the assemblage of God's people, at the door or entrance, where God promised to meet with them. The children of Israel were to encamp far off, round about the Tabernacle, thus leaving ample space in front and around, for the congregation to assemble. Those who brought a sacrifice entered the court, and killed and cut it into its pieces on the north side of the altar; the priests only were allowed to enter into the Sanctuary.

THE METALS.

GOLD is the emblem of that which is divine, divinely excellent and precious, and reminds us of GOD THE FATHER. SILVER is typical of atonement and atonement price. "Ye were not redeemed with corruptible things such as silver or gold . . . . but with the precous blood of Christ " (1 Peter i. 18, 19). The children of Israel when numbered, were required to give a half shekel of silver as a ransom for the soul, unto Jehovah (Exodus xxx. 11-16). This brings the SON OF GOD to our remembrance. BRASS is the emblem of stability and enduring strength, as iron is the emblem of overcoming strength. "Thy shoes shall be iron and brass, and as thy day thy strength shall be" (Deut. xxxiii. 25), reminding us of the divine, eternal SPIRIT. "Not by might nor by power, but by My Spirit, saith Jehovah of hosts" (Zech. iv. 6). And "strengthened with might by His Spirit in the inner man" (Eph. iii. 16). The boards of the Tabernacle were overlaid with GOLD. The sockets of the Tabernacle were of SILVER. And the sockets for the Court were of BRASS. In Nebuchadnezzar's image there was the same order—gold, silver, brass. In light there are three primary colours—yellow, red, and blue. The *gold* corresponds with the yellow, as emblematic of God the Father; the *silver* with the red, as typical of the Son of God, His incarnation and atoning blood; the *brass* corresponds with the blue, as emblematic of the Holy Spirit, and His regenerating and resurrection power. First, divine sovereignty; second, redemption by Christ Jesus; third, sanctification by the Spirit.

THE COLOURS.

Verse 4. "And blue, and purple, and scarlet."

BLUE, according to the root of its Hebrew name, signifies "perfection"; it is also the colour of the heavens above, typical of that which is spiritual, heavenly, and perfect.

SCARLET, Hebrew *tôlahath shanee,* or the splendour of a worm, typical of earthly dignity and glory, as

Jesus Christ was born King of the Jews, and heir of David's royal throne.

PURPLE is a combination of scarlet and blue, reminding us of the union of the earthly dignity and the heavenly perfectness in the Melchisedec priesthood of the Lord Jesus, who will sit as a priest upon His throne.

What is symbolized by the Tabernacle in the wilderness? The first explanation is given in John i. 14, "The Word was made flesh and tabernacled among us." We have seen that in the Hebrew, the terms "tent" and "tabernacle" are distinct, but in the Greek one word is used for both, so the Lord Jesus was at once the Tabernacle in which God dwelt, and the Tent in which He sojourned among men, during the thirty-seven years of His life on earth. (For we must not leave out of account the four years of His infancy, before A.D. commenced).

In a secondary sense, the Tabernacle in the wilderness is a type of the Church of the present dispensation from Pentecost to the return of the Lord Jesus. In Christ Jesus, Jew and Gentile are now builded together for a habitation of God through the Spirit (Eph. ii. 22). The Temple of Solomon is the type not only of the Church, but of the whole of the redeemed in resurrection and heavenly glory.

THE COVERINGS.

"And fine linen, and goat's hair, and rams' skins dyed red, and badgers' skins and shittim wood." Exod. xxv. 4, 5.

In these materials we have symbolically presented God's estimate of the human nature of the Lord Jesus Christ as Son of Man.

First, fine linen, Hebrew, *sheesh,* signifying white, corresponding with the fine flour of the meat or gift-offering, nothing coarse or uneven. The pure, sinless humanity of the Lord Jesus, the Woman's seed, the Virgin's son, "that holy thing" begotten of the Holy Ghost, and called the Son of God. Though made in all points like unto His brethren, yet without sin; holy, harmless, undefiled. The finest texture woven in God's loom.

Second, the goat's hair. In the parable of the sheep and goats in Matthew xxv. 32, the sheep represent the righteous, and the goats the wicked. In the sin-offering, it was generally the kid of the goats that was to be offered. Romans viii. 3, beautifully explains this. "God sending His own Son in the likeness of sinful flesh, and for sin, condemned sin in the flesh." It was not in sinful flesh but "in the likeness of sinful flesh" that Jesus came. "He knew no sin." He was "found in fashion as a man;" hence he experienced hunger and thirst, sat weary at the well, fell asleep in the storm after the labours of the day. God never suffered His Holy One to see corruption, neither by disease in life nor decay after death. God not only numbered Him with transgressors on the tree, and made His soul an offering for sin, but in the person of Him who was

made in the likeness of sinful flesh though Himself
sinless, God condemned and executed judgment on sin
in the flesh. Hence there is "no condemnation to them
which are in Christ Jesus," neither because of actual
transgression, nor of duty omitted, nor for that inward
depravity which they are conscious of. For the judgment of "sin in the flesh" has been borne in the sinless
person of Immanuel on the Cross. On the great day
of atonement, the sacrifice of the bullock, whose blood
was brought into the Holiest, was for Aaron and his
house, typical of Christ and the Church. (See Heb.
iii. 6). The goat was on behalf of Israel, and the
scape-goat prefigured the putting away of Israel's sins
nationally, on the ground of the new covenant. (See
Jer. l. 20).

Third, "Rams' skins dyed red." The bullock represents Christ in service, the lamb in His meekness and
gentleness, and the ram in His public testimony. As
the lamb He increased in wisdom and stature and in
favour with God and man; but as the ram, the world
hated Him, because He testified of it that the works
thereof were evil. It was to be "rams' skins dyed red,"
because He was not only the Faithful Witness in life,
but sealed the testimony with His blood. The " coats
of skin" with which God clothed our first parents in
Eden, fore-shadowed this. And Joseph's coat of many
colours, which his brethren took and dipped in the
blood of a kid of the goats and presented to their
father, was likewise typical. The rider on the white
horse in Revelation xix., is clothed with "a vesture
dipped in blood," which probably has a twofold mean-

ing; symbolical at once of His own atoning death, and of judgment which He executes on His foes.

Fourth, "And badgers' skins." The term badgers' skins occurs elsewhere only in Ezekiel xvi. 10, "And shod thee with badgers' skins," hence used where strength and durability were required. It was the external covering of the Tabernacle. This suggests the outward appearance of Jesus of Nazareth, the Son of Joseph, who, whilst the foxes had holes, and the birds of the air had nests, had not where to lay His head; having no form nor comeliness, but despised and rejected of men. His outer garments were divided among the soldiers who nailed Him to the tree. He was a stranger and a pilgrim here.

Fifth, "And shittim wood." Wood from the wilderness of Shittim, typical of human nature; in the case of Christ, of sinless humanity. The children being partakers of flesh and blood, "He Himself likewise took part in the same" (Hebrews ii. 14). "He was made in all points like unto His brethren, yet without sin" (Hebrews iv. 15).

The Tabernacle and Tent may also be regarded as typical of the Church in its present wilderness condition. "For whatsoever things were written aforetime were written for our learning" (Rom. xv. 4).

First, the "fine linen," typical of the Church, looked at in the Spirit, regenerated and sanctified by the Holy Ghost, and conformed to the example of Christ.

Second, the "goats' hair," emblematic of what we truly are in the flesh, whilst Christ was only made in the likeness of it. It is also similar to the two wave loaves baken with leaven (Lev. xxiii. 17), representing the Church of the present dispensation, composed of Jew and Gentile, not sinless according to the flesh, but conscious of and confessing the law of sin which is in their members. (Romans vii.)

Third, "Rams' skins dyed red." As in Leviticus xxiii., the two wave loaves were accompanied by various sacrifices, so here the goats' hair curtains were covered over with the rams' skins dyed red. Thus while we confess our sinfulness, we realize that the blood of Jesus Christ, God's Son, cleanseth us from all sin; that our iniquity is forgiven, our sin covered.

Fourth, the "badgers' skins." Whilst seeking a city yet to come, we confess that we are strangers and pilgrims here.

Fifth, "Shittim wood." Though now by divine grace children of God, yet having been born in sin, shapen in iniquity, and by nature children of wrath even as others, there was need of the regenerating power of the Holy Ghost, and of redemption through the blood of the Lamb. The Church is composed of sinners saved by grace.

Oil for the Light.

"Oil for the light." (Exodus xxv. 6).

THE word "light" here, signifies "light-giver"; that is, the lampstand with its seven lamps which stood in the Tabernacle. In the Sanctuary natural light was in a measure shut out. Light during the night was supplied by the golden lampstand. The lamps were ordered by Aaron and his sons from evening to morning before Jehovah (Exodus xxvii. 20, 21). The children of Israel were commanded to bring the pure oil olive beaten for the light, to cause the lamp to burn continually (Lev. xxiv. 1-4).

Primarily, the lampstand represents Christ, who, whilst He was in the world was the light of the world; on Him the Spirit of God rested in all its fulness. He was anointed to teach and preach (Isaiah xi. 2, 3; lxi. 1). And even after His resurrection, it was through the Holy Ghost that He gave commandment to His apostles whom He had chosen (Acts i. 2). Now believers are exhorted to shine as lights in the world, holding forth the word of life (Philippians ii. 15, 16), bearing their testimony, not in the words which man's wisdom teacheth, but in the words the Holy Ghost teacheth (1 Cor. ii. 13). It was for this purpose the apostle Paul besought the saints to pray on his behalf, for the supply of the Spirit of Jesus Christ (Philippians i. 19). The Greek word here used implies

16

"additional supply." Testimony for God in the Church and in the world, can only be kept up in its spirituality and efficiency, by the continual communication of grace from God through the Holy Ghost, out of the sufficiency which is in Christ Jesus.

In Acts ii. we read, the Spirit was given at Pentecost; and in Acts iv., in answer to prayer, the disciples were again filled with the Holy Ghost, and with great power gave their testimony. The lamp is provided for the night season. It is during the present night-time of the world that the Church is called upon to hold forth the Word of life in the power of the Spirit of God. Whilst Christ was in the world He was the light of it, but that sun set behind the hill of Calvary when the Son of Man bowed His head upon the Cross. From that time till the appearing of "The Morning Star" the word of Christ to His disciples is, "Ye are the light of the world." "Let your light so shine" (Matt. v. 14-16) that God may be glorified. And Pentecost supplied the oil for the light, that the lamp might burn continually. What is now needed is the continual additional supply.

In Exodus xxvii. 20, the word to Moses is, "Thou shalt command the children of Israel, that they bring thee pure oil olive beaten for the light, to cause the lamp to burn always." The supply of the Spirit of God is to be kept up in answer to prayer; and if the people of God were diligent in seeking that supply, would there not be additional power in the ministry of the Word?

Ministry should not be haphazard talk, but the result of careful study of the Word in dependence on the Holy Ghost. When Stephen, full of the Holy Ghost, spake in the council, they were not able to resist the wisdom and the spirit by which he spake (Acts vi. 10). The secret of effective speaking is said to be "prepared unpreparedness," being thoroughly up in the subject, but leaving to the Spirit of God to direct the utterance. Then after the feast there may be twelve baskets left, and there is always a fresh supply, for God's truth is never exhausted.

The lamp in the Tent of the Congregation was to be ordered by Aaron and his sons continually " BEFORE JEHOVAH." It is a matter of great importance, that ministry should be exercised consciously in the presence of God. The divine presence not only realized by the assembly according to Acts x. 33, "Now therefore are WE all here present before God, to hear all things commanded thee of God," but also by the speaker as delivering God's message, and with the ability which God giveth, that God in all things may be glorified (1 Peter iv. 10, 11). Remembering that God hears every word, and that He is his most discriminating listener. If preaching before an earthly potentate would call for such care and circumspection, how much greater should it be, when speaking in the presence of the Majesty of heaven and earth.

Spices for Anointing Oil.

(Exodus xxv. 6: xxx. 22-23).

"Moreover Jehovah spake unto Moses, saying 'Take THOU also unto thee principal spices, of pure myrrh five hundred shekels, and of sweet cinnamon half so much, even two hundred and fifty shekels, and of sweet calamus two hundred and fifty shekels, and of cassia five hundred shekels, after the shekel of the Sanctuary, and of oil olive a hin: and thou shalt make IT an oil of holy ointment, an ointment compound after the art of the apothecary: it shall be a holy anointing oil.'"

"PRINCIPAL SPICES." The anointing oil was to be composed of the chief or most excellent spices.

"PURE MYRRH;" literally, freely-flowing myrrh—a fragrant spice, bitter to the taste, but sweet to the scent. The ordinary kind was obtained from the tree by lacerating the bark, but that which flowed freely and spontaneously without laceration was considered the most excellent and valuable. This is the kind here indicated by the Hebrew word.

What do these four spices represent? They are all the produce of trees, the result of vegetation and life. They represent the excellencies and perfections of Christ as Son of Man, the chiefest among ten thousand and the altogether lovely. His humanity was so excellent and perfect, that infidels can but admire His por-

19

trait as drawn in the Gospels. The Bride in Canticles
(v. 13) says, "His lips are like lilies, dropping sweet-
smelling myrrh." His townsmen at Nazareth marvelled at "the gracious words which proceeded out of His
mouth," and the officers which were sent to take Him
returned with the report, "Never man spake like this
Man." And even His laceration on the Cross only
brought out the words, "Father, forgive them; for they
know not what they do." Myrrh is also a soother of
pain, and the sympathy of Jesus how comforting!

"SWEET CINNAMON" is the inner bark, sweet and
also fragrant. Expressive of the sweetness and excellency of the character of Jesus, as witnessed by those
who were familiar with His private walk.

"SWEET CALAMUS" is the pith. Emblematic of the
sweetness of the Spirit of Christ in all His internal
thoughts, feelings, and affections; similar to the fat of
the inwards, burnt as incense on the altar, which was
for God alone, and only fully estimated by Him.

"CASSIA" is the outer bark. Expressive of the
sweetness and excellency of the external character and
conduct of the Lord Jesus in His daily walk.

Pure Myrrh -	- 500 shekels -	- Bitter.
Cinnamon -	- 250 „ -	- Sweet.
Calamus -	- 250 „ -	- „
Cassia -	- 500 „ -	- „

500 shekels bitter, 1000 sweet; such is the composition.

"After the shekel of the Sanctuary." Not man's estimate, but God's holy estimate of the graces of the Spirit of His Christ, which is here set forth.

"AND OF OIL OLIVE A HIN." This pure olive oil symbolizes the Holy Ghost, the eternal Spirit of the Triune God. It was to be a full hin, for the Father gave not the Spirit by measure unto Him.

"IT SHALL BE A HOLY ANOINTING OIL." "A COMPOUND COMPOUNDED." Two things strike us here. First, its holiness. This is twice mentioned, for the Spirit of Christ was a Holy Spirit. Secondly, the tempering of the precious spices together. Expressive of the incomparable excellency of the Spirit of Christ, produced by the exquisite blending of the various graces of His character, in perfect and harmonious oneness. It should be observed that the pure OIL OLIVE represents the Spirit of God apart from the Incarnation. The ANOINTING OIL with the spices added, is typical of the Spirit of Christ and the various graces of His Spirit, which are communicated to believers, and shared by them through the anointing of the Holy Ghost sent down from Christ exalted. "Like the precious ointment upon the head, that ran down upon the beard, even Aaron's beard : that went down to the skirts of his garments" (Ps. cxxxiii. 2). Thus they become Christ-like. Thus the character and graces of Christ as the anointed Son of Man are reproduced in those who drink into His Spirit.

Not only under the law were almost all things sprinkled with blood (Heb. ix. 18-22), but we may say that almost all things also were anointed with oil.

THE TABERNACLE TO BE ANOINTED.

"And thou shalt take the anointing oil, and anoint the Tabernacle, and all that is therein." (Ex. xl. 9).

For believers " are builded together for a habitation of God THROUGH THE SPIRIT" (Eph. ii. 22). So on the day of Pentecost, the Spirit from Christ risen and glorified, constituted the assembled believers the dwelling-place of God, and by that one Spirit are we all baptized into one Body.

THE TENT OF THE CONGREGATION.

"And thou shalt anoint the tent of the congregation therewith." (Ex. xxx. 26).

When believers are gathered together in the presence of God, and in the Name of the Lord Jesus, that which is of all importance is the power of the Spirit unquenched. This makes the assembly of believers the place of power, and joy, and blessing.

THE ARK ANOINTED.

"And the ark of the testimony." (Verse 26).

Christ risen, exalted, anointed, having received of the Father the promise of the Holy Ghost, is the centre of gathering to the Church of God. He is the subject of testimony, and in Him all the promises of God are, Yea and Amen.

THE TABLE ANOINTED.

"And the table and all his vessels" (verse 27).

The communion of saints, in the sacred remembrance of the sufferings and death of their divine

Saviour, must be in the present power of the Spirit of Christ, and all things connected therewith should be done by the unction of the Holy Ghost.

THE LAMPSTAND ANOINTED.

"And the lampstand and his vessels " (verse 27).

Testimony to Jesus and the ministration of God's Word is to be in the exercise of the gifts of the Spirit given by Christ exalted, and by His present guidance and grace, and everything connected with this ministry is to be in the power of the Spirit of Christ.

THE GOLDEN ALTAR ANOINTED.

"And the altar of incense " (verse 27).

The worship of the Father in truth, can only be by the Spirit of Adoption—the Spirit of an ascended Christ. He helps our infirmities, He makes intercession, He causes our prayers and praises to ascend accompanied with all the fragrance of the Name of Jesus.

THE BRAZEN ALTAR ANOINTED.

"And the altar of burnt offering, with all his vessels " (verse 28).

It was through the Eternal Spirit, that Jesus offered Himself without spot to God; and it is by the Holy Ghost sent down from heaven, that testimony is to be borne to the value of His blood, and to the fact of His resurrection, as the ground of communion between God and the soul.

THE LAVER.

"And the laver and his foot" (verse 28).

The Spirit of God reveals Jesus in the holiness of His Person and walk down here, and makes Him practical sanctification to us.   He also reveals to us a glorified Christ, and conforms us to Him, changing us into the same image from glory to glory (2 Cor. iii. 18).

THE ANOINTING OF AARON AND HIS SONS.

"And thou shalt anoint Aaron and his sons" (verse 30).

The risen Jesus was anointed to His heavenly priesthood, and it is the Spirit of the ascended Christ, received by the believer, which constitutes him one of God's holy and royal priesthood (1 Peter ii. 5, 9).

A HOLY ANOINTING OIL.

Verses 31-33.

This unction of the Holy One is not to be imitated. In Acts v. we have a solemn illustration of this, when the graces of the Spirit of Christ manifested in the church as received in Acts iv., were imitated by Ananias and Sapphira, they were cut off from the people of God.   The substitution of the energy of the flesh for the power of the Spirit, cuts off from real spiritual communion with the people of God.   God and Christ are most jealous for the honour of the Holy Ghost. All manner of sin and blasphemy may be forgiven unto men, but the blasphemy against the Holy Ghost hath no forgiveness (Matt. xii. 31, 32).

The Sweet Incense.

(Exodus xxv. 6; xxx. 34-38).

"And for sweet incense." "And Jehovah said unto Moses, Take unto thee sweet spices."

THESE sweet spices express the divine estimate of the excellencies of the character of the Lord Jesus as Son of Man, "whose Name is as ointment poured forth" (Cant. 1, 3).

The name of the first spice, "stacte," comes from a Hebrew word signifying to drop, to fall in drops, to distil, similar to the freely flowing myrrh used in the composition of the holy anointing oil.

"Onycha" in Hebrew means also a lion, and suggests the thought of the uncompromising faithfulness, firmness, and decision of the character of Christ, setting His "face like a flint," boldly acting for God and reproving all manner of evil. He was not only the Lamb of God, but also the Lion of the tribe of Judah (Rev. v. 5, 6).

"Galbanum." The root of the word signifies "milk," or "fat," and connects the thought with the "fat which covered the inwards"—God's portion of the sacrifices, and emblematical of the internal preciousness of Jesus.

"With pure frankincense." The Hebrew word signifies white. The richness and abundance of its perfume suggested the English word, meaning frank or liberal incense. It reminds us of the purity, piety, and acceptability of Him who was holy, harmless, undefiled, and separate from sinners.

"Of each shall there be a like weight."

How expressive of the character of Christ! What an even balance do we there discover! His grace, His firmness, His internal excellency and outward piety how exactly proportioned!

"And thou shalt make IT a perfume, a confection after the art of the apothecary, tempered together (salted together), pure and holy" (verse 35).

Perfume and incense are the same. There is but one word in the original. The graces and virtues which compose and make up the character of Jesus, how exquisitely tempered together! Not only equal, but harmonized, blended, and combined. "Tempered;" Hebrew, "salted," or seasoned. The art of the apothecary so combining as to bring out the perfume in its exquisite perfection. "Pure and holy." What purity and holiness also are seen in the character and ways of Jesus!

"And thou shalt beat some of it very small, and put it before the testimony in the tabernacle (tent) of the congregation, where I will meet with thee: it shall be unto you most holy " (verse 36).

These sweet spices, beaten very small, may suggest the thought that the various excellencies and perfections of the Lord Jesus are to be searched out and discovered in His minutest recorded action and word, as well as in the more important occasions of His life.

Some of it was to be put before the testimony in the tent of the congregation, where God promised to meet with His people. And when the people of God are gathered together in His presence, then the preciousness of the name of Jesus gives a perfume to their prayers and praises. And this is there for the encouragement of faith, and for the comfort and joy of our souls before God, "for ointment and perfume rejoice the heart."

"And as for the perfume which thou shalt make, ye shall not make to yourselves according to the composition thereof: it shall be unto thee holy for Jehovah. Whosoever shall make like unto that, to smell thereto, shall even be cut off from his people" (verses 37, 38).

This preciousness of Jesus is inimitable, and must not be counterfeited. Self-conceit through supposed resemblance will put the soul out of communion. Strange fire is natural, or fleshly excitement. Strange incense is Nature's imitation of the peerless preciousness of Christ. Both are alike forbidden of God. But fire from God's altar, and the sweet perfume of the excellency of Jesus, are provided for the true worshippers of the Father through the Son, and in the power of the Holy Ghost.

God's Holy Dwelling Place.

"And let them make Me a sanctuary, that I may dwell
among them. According to all that I show THEE,
after the pattern of the tabernacle, and the pattern of
all the instruments thereof, even so shall ye make it."
(Exodus xxv. 8, 9).

GOD having redeemed the people of Israel out
of Egypt, desired to have a dwelling-place
among them in the wilderness. So God now
desires that sinners redeemed by the blood of the
Lamb should be builded together for a habitation of
God through the Spirit (Eph. ii. 22), and be built up
a spiritual house composed of living stones (1 Peter
ii. 5).

When Jesus was here upon the earth, He Himself
was the sanctuary and dwelling-place of God. In Him
the glory of the Godhead dwelt. "The Word was made
flesh and dwelt (tabernacled) among us, and we beheld His glory" (John i. 14). Before His death, in
this respect, He abode alone (John xii. 24). But
having finished His work, and ascended up on high,
He built the church of the living God, as a habitation
for God (Matt. xvi. 15-18). Upon this foundation,
upon Himself, and on the confession of His name as
the Christ, the Son of the living God, made known to
the soul by the revelation of the Father, He built His
Church, as the house of God, to be the pillar and
ground of the truth (1 Tim. iii. 15).

How perfect, how suggestive are the words of God! He does not say, "Let them make themselves a tabernacle, or meeting-place, that I may come and visit them." It is natural to man to think of himself first, and to begin from himself. But God's thoughts and ways are the opposite of man's. God begins from Himself—"Let them make ME a sanctuary! that I may dwell among them."

O for grace to learn this lesson perfectly! so that in meeting together in church fellowship our first thought may be, not of our own comfort and convenience, nor even our edification—God will take care of that—but that God may have a dwelling place among us, and that God, through Christ, may be glorified. "That I may dwell among them," not as a wayfaring man that turneth aside to tarry for a night, but to be at home there. And Jesus has told us the secret of this (John xiv. 23). And the secret is love and obedience—love to Christ and obedience to Him, "If a man love Me, he will keep My words; and My Father will love him, and We will come unto him, and make Our abode with him." The VISIT of Divine grace, in a Father's love and a Saviour's pity, to the abodes of the saints in the midst of their unworthiness and self-will, is one thing; the HOME-DWELLING of Divine love, where holiness is cultivated, truth maintained, and obedience sought, is another, and far more blessed. Again the Lord adds, "He that loveth Me not, keepeth not My sayings : and the word which ye hear is not Mine, but My Father's which sent Me." One proof of love to the Lord Jesus, and of regard to the authority of God, is keeping, retaining, and guarding the words of the Lord Jesus which He spake on earth, even those words which were given Him by His Father to make known to us. Surely it becomes us to be careful, lest on the authority of some two or three Arian manuscripts of the fourth and fifth centuries, we blot out large numbers of these inspired utterances from the sacred page. The Lord's message of commendation to the messenger to the church in Philadelphia was, "Thou hast a little strength, and hast kept My word, and hast not denied My name" (Rev. iii. 8).

A SANCTUARY.

God does not say, "Let them make Me a tabernacle, or a tent," as though anything would do for God; but "Let them make Me a SANCTUARY," a holy habitation, "that I may dwell." Yes, "holiness becomes God's house for ever." In the Gospel, God comes down to sinners; it is grace abounding amidst the aboundings of sin. But the truth for the saint is the doctrine which is according to godliness. To the sinner, by the gospel, God says : "Though your sins be as scarlet, they shall be white as snow : though they be red like crimson, they shall be as wool." But to the believer He says, "What fellowship hath righteousness with unrighteousness? And what communion hath light with darkness? And what concord hath Christ with Belial? And what part hath he that believeth with an unbeliever? And what agreement hath the temple of God with idols? Wherefore come out from among

them, and be ye separate, saith the Lord, and touch
not the unclean thing, and I will receive you : I will
dwell in them, and walk in them; and I will be their
God, and they shall be My people" (2 Cor. vi. 14-18).

"Having, therefore, these promises, dearly beloved,
let us cleanse ourselves from all filthiness of the flesh
and spirit, perfecting holiness in the fear of God"
(2 Cor. vii. 1).

THE PLAN.

In the things of God no place is left for human
reason, and no margin for self-will. God has arranged
everything according to infinite wisdom, and the word
of God contains full instructions.

These earthly types were the "example and shadow
of heavenly things, as Moses was admonished of God
when he was about to make the tabernacle : for, see,
saith He, that thou make all things according to the
pattern showed to thee in the mount" (Heb. viii. 5).
Weighty and important words? May they be brought
to bear upon our consciences, and tell upon our hearts !

The assembly of believers on earth should be the
reflection down here, of what the Church of the firstborn is in Christ above. Is the Church above redeemed
to God from an evil world?

The Church on earth is to be separate to God, as not
of the world, even as Christ is not of it.

Is the Church above one in Christ its glorious Head?
The Church on earth should exhibit this oneness. Is

the Church above a holy and true church? The Church
on earth should be conspicuous for holiness and truth,
"the epistle of Christ known and read of all men," the
pillar and ground of the truth." And just as Christ
on earth was "God manifest in flesh;" so the Church
should exhibit Christ manifest in His people.

In that marvellous prayer of the Lord Jesus recorded in John xvii., this separateness, holiness, and
oneness of the Church are the main subjects of His
petitions. The Lord distinctly said, "I pray not for
the world," neither is Israel mentioned, but His prayer
is for those whom the Father had given Him out of
the world. Of these He said, "They are not of the
world, even as I am not of the world. I pray not that
Thou shouldest take them out of the world, but that
Thou shouldest keep them from the evil. Sanctify
them through Thy truth; Thy word is truth."

Three times He prays for their oneness. First, that
they may be one after a Divine model (*v.* 11), "That
they may be one as We are." Second, that they may
be all one in the Spirit from Pentecost till His return,
"That they all may be one; as Thou Father, art in Me,
and I in Thee, that they also may be one in Us" (*v.*
21). And this oneness in the Spirit, notwithstanding
their outward divisions, might be a proof to the world
that He was the sent One of God, "That the world
might believe that thou didst send Me." Third, that
they might be one in the glory, "And the glory which
Thou hast given Me I have given them : that they may
be one, even as We are one" (*v.* 22). That when thus

THE HIGH PRIEST IN GARMENTS OF GLORY

To face page 32

manifested with Him in glory, it may be a proof to the world that He was not only the sent One, but that they also were loved with the same love. The answer to this prayer commenced at Pentecost, when the Holy Ghost came to sanctify them, and to baptise them into one body, and He has continued in the world ever since to carry on the work, and will not cease until the whole body is complete, and until He has established them, "unblamable in holiness before God, even our Father, at the coming of our Lord Jesus Christ with all His saints" (1 Thess. iii. 13).

The Ark of the Covenant.

(Exodus xxv. 10-22).

Verse 10. "And they shall make an ark of shittim wood: two cubits and a half shall be the length thereof, and a cubit and a half the breadth thereof, and a cubit and a half the height thereof."

NOAH was commanded to make "an ark" for the saving of his house; the Hebrew word there used is "tebah," as also in the "ark" of bulrushes in which Moses was laid. But the Hebrew word here employed is "ahrohn," which signifies a chest. This ark of the covenant is one of the most complete and comprehensive types of the Lord Jesus, a full length portrait. In the instructions given for the vessels of the tabernacle, the first mentioned is the ARK. As to worship, service, and testimony, God's centre is Christ. The SHITTIM WOOD is a type of the sinless humanity of the Lord Jesus. And its dimensions being fixed by God, reminds us of the words of the Lord Jesus, "A body hast Thou prepared Me" (Hebrews x. 5).

Verse 11. "And thou shalt overlay IT with pure gold, within and without shalt thou overlay it."

Pure gold is the emblem of that which is divine, divinely excellent and holy. It typifies the Word which was in the beginning with God, and was God, made

34

flesh and tabernacling among us, the great mystery of
godliness, God manifest in flesh.   To the carnal mind
the human was conspicuous, He was Jesus the Naza-
rene.   The badger's skin hid the glory of the tabernacle; but to the spiritually minded the gold hid the
shittim wood, such could say, "And we beheld His
glory, the glory as of the only begotten of the Father."
And "The God shone glorious through the man."   At
the foot of the Mount of Transfiguration, Jesus was
seen in contact with sinners, and in conflict with
Satan; but to the disciples on the mount He appeared
in glory, and the Father Himself bare witness to Him.

The ark was to be overlaid within as well as without
with gold.   Every internal thought, feeling, and affection of the Lord Jesus was not only perfect as human,
but spiritually and divinely excellent; like the fat of
the inwards burnt upon the altar which was for God
alone.   In Him dwelt all the fulness of the Godhead
bodily, and in Him the Church of God is blessed with
every Spiritual blessing.   This ark of the covenant is
the treasure chest of the family of God, in which all
the title deeds and promises of God in Him, Yea and
Amen, are contained.

**"And thou shalt make upon it a crown of gold round
about."**

This crown of gold surrounding the ark and sur-
mounting it, kept the propitiatory or mercy-seat in its
place; even so was it with Jesus, He for the joy that
was set before Him endured the cross, despising the

shame; and, though for a season, made a little lower than the angels, He is now crowned with glory and honour. The obedient and humbled Son of man is now seated on the right hand of majesty and power, and glorified with the glory He had with the Father before the world was.

Verses 12-15. "And thou shalt cast four rings of gold for it, and put them in the four corners thereof; and two rings shall be in the one side of it, and two rings in the other side of it."

"And thou shalt make staves of shittim wood, and overlay THEM with gold. And thou shalt put the staves into the rings by the sides of the ark, that the ark may be borne with them. The staves shall be in the rings of the ark: they shall not be taken from it."

These rings and staves adapted the ark to the wilderness condition of God's people, ready at all times, not only to accompany them in their journeyings, but also in their wanderings. The rings were to be of gold, but the staves of shittim wood, overlaid with gold. The divine grace and human sympathy of the Lord Jesus renders Him sufficient to meet our every need. The staves were never to be taken from the rings; even so Jesus assures us, "Lo, I am with you alway"; "I will never leave you nor forsake you." The three families of Levites, Gershonites, Merarites, and Kohathites, may represent the evangelists, pastors and teachers of the Christian ministry. The Gershonites and Merarites, when the camp set forward, went before and set up the tabernacle, for these six wagons and twelve oxen were provided; but none were given to the sons of Kohath, because the service of the sanctuary belonging unto them was that they should bear upon their shoulders (Numbers vii. 9).

To the charge of the Kohathites was committed the ark and other sacred vessels of the sanctuary. The teacher is specially thrown upon his individual responsibility before God in treating on those subjects which pertain to the person, offices, and perfections of the Son of God; he needs, in an especial manner, the unction from the Holy One. God is especially jealous of human interference in regard to the glory of His Son. When David put the ark upon a new cart, and Uzzah put forth his hand to steady it, God made a breach upon Uzzah. What is needed is not human intellect, invention, nor imagination, but the teaching and revealing of the Holy Ghost.

Verse 16. "And thou shalt put into the ark the testimony which I shall give thee."

Whilst Moses was on the Mount, receiving these instructions from God, respecting the tabernacle and its vessels, the children of Israel were impatient at his delay, had made the golden calf, and worshipped it. The law which they had undertaken to keep they had broken in its most essential parts. Thereupon Moses, on his coming down from the Mount, with the two tables of the testimony in his hand, which he had received from God, written with the finger of God, moved with holy indignation, brake the tables at the foot of the Mount.

And Jehovah said unto Moses, "Hew thee two tables of stone like unto the first : and I will write upon these tables the words that were in the first tables, which thou brakest." These two tables of the testimony Moses was commanded to put into the ark. This type was fulfilled in Christ, who is the Mediator of the New Covenant, whose language was, according to Psalms xl. 8, "I delight to do Thy will, O My God : yea, Thy law is within My heart." Made of a woman, born under the law, He magnified that law, and made it honourable. And it is by abiding in Him that the righteousness of the law is fulfilled in us, who walk, not after the flesh, but after the Spirit.

The Propitiatory and the Cherubim.

(Exodus xxv. 17-22).

Verse 17. "And thou shalt make a mercy-seat [propitiatory] of pure gold: two cubits and a half shall be the length thereof, and a cubit and a half the breadth thereof."

THE spiritual import of this is clear from Rom. iii. 24, 25, where there is a manifest allusion to it by the Holy Ghost. "Christ Jesus, whom God hath set forth to be a propitiation [a propitiatory, or mercy-seat] through faith in His blood"—the word rendered "propitiation," in Rom. iii. 25, being the same word that is used in Heb. ix. 5, and there translated "mercy-seat." This is the import of the publican's prayer in Luke xviii. 13—"God be merciful [propitious on the ground of reconciliation made] to me a sinner." The Hebrew word rendered "mercy-seat" signifies "to cover over;" to make atonement; to appease, or pacify.

The material is of "pure gold," the emblem of that which is divine, or divinely pure and excellent. No shittim wood is in the propitiatory, therefore nothing human or angelic is symbolized, neither Church nor angels. This is a consideration too often overlooked. The propitiatory formed the lid if the ark in which were deposited the unbroken tables of the testimony; for the exercise of divine mercy towards guilty sinners, can only be on the ground of atonement made, and righteousness established. On this propitiatory the blood was sprinkled on the great day of atonement (Lev. xvi.)

The propitiatory was of the same dimensions and extent as the ark of the covenant. The exercise of divine mercy and grace is founded on the Person and work of the Lord Jesus Christ Himself, and is co-extensive therewith. It has for its basis and foundation the incarnation, obedience, life, and death of Him who was eternally God, and is now the risen and glorified Christ, at God's right-hand above.

Verses 18-20. "And thou shalt make two cherubim of gold, of beaten work shalt thou make THEM, in [from] the two ends of the mercy seat. And make one cherub on [from] the one end, and the other cherub on [from] the other end: even of [from] the mercy-seat [propitiatory] shall ye make the cherubim on the two ends thereof. And the cherubim shall stretch forth their wings on high, covering the mercy-seat with their wings, and their faces shall look one to another; toward the mercy-seat shall the faces of the cherubim be."

Cherubim is the plural of cherub, as we say ox, oxen; the "s" at the end is incorrect. The forms of these cherubim appear to be simpler than those described in Ezekiel i. x., which have four faces fronting four different directions; whereas here, the expression "toward the mercy-seat shall the faces of the cherubim be," implies but one face to each. These cherubim of glory represent the fulness of the Spirit, received by the ascended Christ, on the completion of His atoning work. As we read in Psalm lxviii. 18, "Thou hast

ascended on high, Thou hast led captivity captive :
Thou hast received gifts for men [Heb. in the man] ;
yea, for the rebellious also." Acts ii. 33, "Therefore
being by the right hand of God exalted, and having
received of the Father the promise of the Holy Ghost,
He hath shed forth this, which ye now see and hear."
And in Eph. iv. 10, 11, "He that descended, is the same
also that ascended up far above all heavens, that He
might fill all things.   And He gave some, apostles ; and
some, prophets ; and some, evangelists ; and some,
pastors and teachers."   The ascended Son of Man has
received the Holy Ghost in His own person, He has
given gifts to the Church, and He has also received the
Spirit for the rebellious children of Israel, to be communicated in due time, when Jehovah will again dwell
among them.

The propitiatory and cherubim were of one solid
piece, of wrought or beaten gold.   The cherubim
formed the extension of the propitiatory from either
end, and represent the provision made by God, through
the Spirit, for the extension of divine mercy and grace,
founded on the finished work of Christ.

The wings of the cherubim, from the propitiatory on
either side, meeting in the centre form a complete
circle, and overshadow the mercy-seat.   According to
Ps. ciii. 17, "The mercy [loving kindness] of Jehovah
is from everlasting to everlasting."   The three Persons
in the Godhead, in the counsels of eternity, laid the
plan of redeeming love ; the eternal Spirit from the
beginning, in promise, type, and prophecy, foretold and

foreshadowed it; the incarnate Son of God, by His
atoning death, accomplished the work; and the Holy
Spirit is now making it known, and will continue to
manifest it, long as eternal ages roll.

> Verses 21-22. "And thou shalt put the mercy-seat above
> upon the ark; and in the ark thou shalt put the testi-
> mony that I shall give thee. And there I will meet
> with thee, and I will commune with thee from above
> the mercy-seat, from between the two cherubim which
> are upon the ark of the testimony, of all things which
> I will give THEE in commandment unto the children
> of Israel."

The throne of divine grace is founded on the Person
and work of the Lord Jesus; and all God's purposes,
promises, and covenant blessings centre in Him. He is
the true ark of the covenant, and the ark of the testimony also. All the lines of divine truth centre in
Him, and radiate from Him. This is the meeting-place
and place of communion between God and those who,
like Moses, receive the word from God's mouth, and
give testimony from Him (Ezek. iii. 17); those who
stand in the secret counsel of Jehovah, who perceive
and hear His word, who mark His Word and hear it
(Jer. xxiii. 18).

The secret of ministry in the power of the Holy
Ghost is communion with God, over His own Word,
in spirit in the holiest, God occupying the mercy-seat,
Jesus Himself our meeting-place; while from Him
who has received the fulness of the Spirit for testimony, gift is not only received at first, but is replen-
ished for constant exercise.

The Table of Shewbread.

(Exodus xxv. 23).

"Thou shalt also make a table of shittim wood."

THE table presents Christ as the centre and ground of communion to the Church of God. "A table," not tables; for there is but one. Where believers are gathered together unto the Name of Jesus, it is God's will that His dying love should be commemorated among them.

"Of shittim wood." The incarnation and humanity of the Lord Jesus lies at the foundation, and an incarnate Saviour—God manifest in the flesh—is the centre of our communion in church fellowship.

THE DIMENSIONS OF THE TABLE.

"Two cubits shall be the length thereof, and a cubit the breadth thereof, and a cubit and a half the height thereof."

God has fixed the dimensions of His own table, and man is not at liberty to extend or limit it. In length and breadth it extends to all believers, while walking worthily, yet excluding the unconverted, and the defiled. Its height also is of divine appointment. It is on a level with the propitiatory, for it is for those who through atonement have their iniquities forgiven, their sins covered. The length and breadth of the

43

table is half a cubit less than the ark and propitiatory; for their are more saved by Christ, than actually and worthily sit at His table.

THE OVERLAYING.

Verse 24. "And thou shalt overlay IT with pure gold."

Gold is the emblem of divine excellency, and pure gold of the purity and holiness of the divine nature. That is not the Lord's table, according to the mind of God, where the divinity of Christ, and His divine excellency and glory, is not held and maintained. The Christ in whose Name we meet is Immanuel—God with us.

THE GOLDEN CROWN.

"And make thereto a crown of gold round about."

He who was once made a little lower than the angels for the suffering of death, that He by the grace of God should taste death for every man, is now crowned with glory and honour. While we commemorate therefore His dying and redeeming love, we do it also in the apprehension of His glory where He now is, at God's right-hand. And we do this "until He come," in the expectation of His return to receive us to Himself.

THE BORDER.

Verse 25. "And thou shalt make unto it a border of a hand-breadth round about."

The table which was extended and limited by divine grace and infinite wisdom, was also guarded. There was to be a border to the table of a handbreadth. There are four fingers to a handbreadth, and there are four things indispensable to real and right communion at the Lord's table, according to God and His Word, if there is to be real and full blessing. First, saving FAITH in Christ, which admits into the family of God, for, "Ye are all the children of God by faith in Christ Jesus" (Gal. iii. 26; John i. 12). Secondly, the HOLINESS and consistency of walk which becomes the confession of the Name of the Lord Jesus (1 Cor. v.) Thirdly, soundness in holding and maintaining the TRUTH of the Person of Christ (1 John i. 10). Fourthly SUBJECTION to the Lordship of Christ. For we meet at the Lord's table as believers, in brotherly love, and in the Name of Him that is holy, Him that is true, and of Him that hath the key of David, that openeth and no man shutteth (Rev. iii. 7). It should be observed that the Lord Jesus, at the Passover, previous to His instituting the Lord's Supper, having first washed His disciples feet (John xiii. 1-11), then led His disciples into the closest self-examination (Matt. xxvi. 20-25; John xiii. 12-30); the result of which was that Judas, having received the sop, went immediately out. Then, and not till then, could Jesus divide the bread among them, and also the cup, saying, "Drink ye all of it."

In Luke's account, who states things in their moral order and connection, and not always in their historical order, it would appear otherwise; but a careful examination of all the passages will confirm the fact.

THE BORDER CROWNED.

"And thou shalt make a golden crown to the border thereof round about."

This is very striking! There is not only a divine
glory connected with the Person of the Lord Jesus as
the ground of communion, as shewn by the golden
crown to the table, but also God has put divine honour
on the jealousy which guards the communion of saints
because it is connected with the glory of the Person
of His Son. And as the border extends all round, so
does the crown : for it is the jealousy that guards the
Person of Jesus in every point, in the matter of communion, that has this divine honour put upon it by
God Himself.

THE RINGS AND STAVES.

Verse 26. "And thou shalt make for it four rings of gold,
and put the rings in the four corners that are on the
four feet thereof."

Thus adapting the table to the wilderness condition
of God's people. And God also has provided for His
people now, so that wherever two or three are gathered
to the Name of the Lord Jesus, there they might break
the bread, and drink of the cup in remembrance of
Him.

Verse 27. "Over against the border shall the rings be for
places of the staves to bear the table."

Thus especially connecting the rings and staves with
the border. And are we not thus reminded that our
exposed condition in such a wilderness as this, renders
the border of great importance and necessary in every

place? The border was to extend all round the table, not in the middle, dividing loaf from loaf.

"And thou shalt make the staves of shittim wood, and overlay THEM with gold."

Both the human tenderness and sympathy of the Lord Jesus, as shewn by the shittim wood; and His divine grace and all sufficiency, as shewn by the gold, adapt Him to the wilderness need of His people in their church communion here.

"That the table may be borne with them."

Neither the ark nor the table were to be carried, after the example of the Philistines, on a new cart. That is, both testimony to the Person of Christ, and communion together in His Name, are to be matters of individual responsibility to God.

THE VESSELS OF THE TABLE.

Verse 29. "And thou shalt make the dishes thereof, and spoons thereof, and covers thereof, and bowls thereof, to cover [pour out] withal: of pure gold shalt thou make THEM."

All that is connected with the communion of saints, on the ground of the Person of the Lord Jesus, is to be of God, and done in the power of divine grace. Human will, human authority, human wisdom, have no place here. " If any man speak, let him speak as the oracles of God ; if any man minister, let him do it as of the ability which God giveth : that God in all things may be glorified through Jesus Christ " (1 Pet. iv. 11). Let all things be done, not only decently and in order, but also by the grace of God, and to God's glory. And however important these directions are in all manner of service, they are never more so than in things connected with the table of the Lord.

THE SHEWBREAD.

Verse 30. "And thou shalt set upon the table shewbread [Heb. bread of faces] before Me alway."

Lev. xxiv. 5-9. "And thou shalt take fine flour, and bake twelve cakes [pierced cakes] thereof: two-tenth deals shall be in one cake."

The fine flour is typical of the pure and sinless humanity of Jesus, for it was without leaven. The twelve pierced cakes, for so the Hebrew expresses, foreshadowed Christ as the Man of Sorrows and acquainted with grief, for " His visage was so marred more than any man, and His form more than the sons of men" (Isaiah lii. 14); and likewise His sufferings on the Cross. The Hebrew expression for shewbread is literally "bread of faces," for these twelve cakes were the representation and remembrance of the twelve tribes of Israel before God continually; and they also typify Christ as God's provision for all His people, the whole Israel of God (John vi.).

Two-tenth deals, or two omers to each cake. A double portion; a portion for time, and for eternity. As the provision of manna made on the sixth day, which was for that day, and also for the Sabbath. (See Ex. xvi. 22-26).

THE HOLY PLACE AND ITS FURNITURE

To face page 48

Verse 6. "And thou shalt set them in two rows, six on
a row, upon the pure table before Jehovah."

Christ, the bread of life, set forth a full provision
for all believers. But it must be on a PURE table. A
pure and holy Christ the basis of communion; and the
table guarded from defilement. And "before Jehovah,"
for the eye of a jealous and holy God is ever resting
on the communion of saints.

Verse 7. "And thou shalt put frankincense upon each
row, that it may be on the bread for a memorial, even
an offering made by fire unto Jehovah."

The frankincense, which is white and fragrant, is
emblamatic of the purity and excellency of the Lord
Jesus, both in His life and in His death, especially in
the estimate of God His Father, so that His language
in the contemplation of Him was, " This is My beloved Son, in Whom I am well pleased." It was to be
" an offering made by fire." From this we learn that
the shewbread was to be unleavened, for in Lev ii. 11,
we read, " Ye shall burn no leaven, nor any honey, in
any offering of Jehovah made by fire."

Verse 8. " Every Sabbath he shall set it in order before
Jehovah continually, being taken from the children
of Israel by an everlasting covenant."

Renewed weekly. So on the first day of the week
the disciples came together to break bread (Acts xx.
7). And on the day of Christ's resurrection, and the
following Lord's Day, Jesus Himself allowed His
disciples to handle, in His own precious body, the sacred memorials of His sufferings and death (John xx).

To the Church, the weekly period is not the seventh day, the token of creation rest; but the eighth day, the emblem of resurrection rest, and the rest of completed redemption, being the first day of the week, on which day also the Comforter was given.

"BEFORE JEHOVAH CONTINUALLY." This is repeated for it is important. The feast is not provided for the guests only, but in honour of the Father and of the Son. The table is not spread for the children alone; the Father takes His seat at the head. His language is, "Bring hither the fatted calf, and kill it; and let us eat and be merry." For the full joy of communion is in the Father's presence. We are but partakers at the altar : the first and best portion belongs to God.

Verse 9.   "'And it shall be Aaron's and his sons'; and they shall eat it in the holy place."

"Aaron's and his sons'." The High Priest and His house. That is, to us, "Christ as a Son over His own house, Whose house are we" (Heb. iii. 6). By virtue of the anointing as a holy priesthood, our fellowship is not only with the Father, but also with His Son Jesus Christ. "If any man hear My voice," says Jesus, "and open the door, I will come in to him, and will sup with him, and he with Me" (Rev. iii. 20). At the Lord's table we have fellowship with Jesus, our High Priest above, in the remembrance of His sufferings and death.

" For IT is most holy [holy of holies] unto Him of the offerings of Jehovah made by fire."

How God guards the holiness of this feast of love! The very atmosphere of the place where it is eaten must be holy, for that which is here set forth, and on which the believer feeds, is "most holy."

" A perpetual statute."

"As often as ye eat this bread, and drink this cup," says the Apostle,"ye do shew the Lord's death till He come." It is of perpetual obligation till then. It is an ordinance peculiar to the present dispensation. After this, Jesus will drink the new wine with us in His Father's kingdom.

In the millennial period, the divinely appointed and restored sacrifices, which till then will never have fully accomplished their original intention, will take the place of the present simpler but grand memorials of a Saviour's sufferings; and then "the mountain of Jehovah's house" will be the centre of communion to the whole earth.

While in heaven the Lamb in the midst of the Throne—"a Lamb as it had been slain, having seven horns and seven eyes"—will be God's memorial for the universe, and for eternity.

The Lampstand.

"And thou shalt make a lampstand of pure gold."
(Ex. xxv. 31).

THE golden lampstand, with its seven lamps and centre shaft, is the type of ministry according to God in the power of the Holy Ghost, in its various branches of testimony, having Christ for its centre, source, and subject. In the CHERUBIM, on the mercy-seat, we have ministry in its heavenly and divine source; in the LAMPSTAND, ministry in its exercise on earth.

THE MATERIAL.

That which is here signified by the "pure gold" is ministry according to God, and not according to the principles and practices of men—ministry after a divine model, maintained in the power of divine grace.

"If any man speak," says Peter, "let him speak as the oracles of God; if any man minister, let him do it as of the ability which God giveth; that God in all things may be glorified through Jesus Christ" (1 Peter iv. 11). Not cultivated intellect, putting forth its strongest efforts to the credit of the preacher, and to the honour of the ministry, but divine grace, manifested to the glory of God.

This ministry looks to no earthly source for its authority, but has its sanction and its strength in God. It is GIFT received from the Lord Jesus Christ, risen and glorified; distributed by the Holy Ghost according to His own will, and exercised in subjection to the supreme authority of Christ (1 Cor. xii. 11). There are diversities of gifts, but the same Spirit; differences of administration (or services), but the same Lord; diversities of operations, but it is the same GOD which worketh all in all (1 Cor. xii. 4-6).

THE WORKMANSHIP.

"Of beaten work shall the lampstand be made."

"Beaten work" for the lampstand, and "beaten oil" for the light (Exod. xxvii. 20). The lampstand was not cast by one simple operation, but wrought. This shews the labour, care, and skill which is required in ministry according to God. It is not simple gift, but gift stirred up, laboriously fulfilled, and strengthened by its exercise. (See 1 Tim. iv. 13-16; and 2 Tim. i. 6).

THE CENTRE SHAFT AND BRANCH.

" His shaft, and his branch (not branches, see chap. xxxvii. 17), his bowls, his knobs, and his flowers, shall be of of the same."

This is the centre shaft and branch, which is called, by way of pre-eminence, "the lampstand," in v. 34, and is typical of the Lord Jesus Christ Himself, the centre and source of testimony in the power of the Spirit, and the great example and pattern of it in His personal ministry on earth.

As to fruit-bearing, He is the true vine, and His disciples are the branches. And as to testimony-bearing, He is the true lampstand, and His servants are branches of the same. In either case, without Him we can do nothing.

THE SIX BRANCHES.

Verse 32. "And six branches shall come out of the sides of it; three branches of the lampstand out of one side, and three branches of the lampstand out of the other side."

The apostles and prophets of the present dispensation, having laid the foundation, and all the fundamental points, whether of truth or practice, being settled, and contained in the inspired Scriptures, the three standing branches of ministry in the Church, and for its adding to, and building up, until it is complete, are those of the EVANGELIST, the PASTOR, and the TEACHER (Eph. iv.). The six branches proceed from the main shaft in PAIRS, expressing fellowship and concurrence in testimony. They proceed from the sides, and not the front; for the object of ministry is not to make it or the minister prominent, but for the exhibition of Christ. "We preach not ourselves, but Christ Jesus the Lord, and ourselves your servants for Jesus' sake." Standing aside that He may be visible to all, and thus giving Him in testimony His own proper place, "Jesus in the midst."

These branches, as the original implies, are hollow. In Zech. iv. we have a lampstand of gold; the representation of ministry in the power of the Spirit, in the latter day in connection with Israel. This lampstand had a bowl on the top, and seven pipes leading to the seven lamps. While two olive trees supply the oil to the bowl, and thence to the seven branches and lamps. The two olive trees are representations of Zerubbabel and Joshua; but these again are typical of the Lord Jesus in His Melchizedec character as priest and king. The great lesson is—"Not by might, nor by power, but by My Spirit, saith Jehovah of hosts." " Branches," hollow, thus adapted to receive and convey the oil. The import is expressed by the apostle, "Not that we are sufficient of ourselves to think anything of ourselves; but our sufficiency is of God." "We have this treasure in earthen vessels, that the excellency of the power may be of God, and not of us."

The SOURCE of supply for ministry is in Christ, the POWER for all testimony is the Spirit of God. Three branches on either side. The EVANGELIST begins the work, and lays the foundation, which is Christ Jesus; his sphere is the widest, his parish is the world. The PASTOR carries on the work in caring for the blood-bought flock of God. The TEACHER leads the soul yet higher into the truth of God, and the apprehension of the divine glories of the person of Christ.

THE BOWLS.

Verse 33. " Three bowls made like unto almonds, with a knop and a flower in one branch; and three bowls made like almonds in the other branch, with a knop and a flower; so in the six branches that come out of the lampstand."

The oval form, "made like unto almonds," is significant. The root of the Hebrew word for " almond "

signifies to WATCH, also TO BE EARLY, READY or PRE-
PARED. The almond tree was noted for its early blos-
soming. See Jer. i. 11, 12, "Moreover, the word of
Jehovah came unto me, saying, Jeremiah, what seest
thou? And I said, I see a rod of an almond tree.
Then said Jehovah unto me, Thou hast well seen : for
I will hasten [am watching over] My word to perform
it."

So also 2 Tim. ii. 21, "If a man, therefore, purge
himself for these, he shall be a vessel unto honour,
sanctified, and meet for the Master's use, prepared
unto every good work." And 2 Tim. iv. 5, " But
watch thou in all things, . . . do the work of an evangelist, make full proof of thy ministry." These bowls,
therefore, made like almonds, express watchfulness,
readiness, and preparedness for the Christian ministry.
But this preparedness consists in an acquaintance with
divine truth; the Word of Christ dwelling richly in the
heart, in all wisdom.

Like the scribe instructed unto the kingdom of
heaven, bringing forth out of His treasure things new
and old (Matt. xiii. 52).

So Paul wrote to Timothy, "Meditate upon these
things; give thyself wholly to them; that thy profiting
may appear to all" (1 Tim. iv. 15). "Study to shew
thyself approved unto God, a workman that needeth
not to be ashamed, rightly dividing the word of truth"
(2 Tim. ii. 15).

THE KNOPS AND FLOWERS.

" KNOP." Round, the original word signifies, and smaller in size than the bowls. These knops I understand to be typical of GIFT, such as that of the evangelist, pastor, or teacher.

"AND A FLOWER." The Septuagint says, a lily. As the bowls express PREPAREDNESS for ministry, through a deep acquaintance with the Word of God ; and the knops, distinct GIFT for its ministration ; so by the flower is expressed the FULL UNFOLDING of divine truth in actual testimony.

This suggests an instructive lesson, that God would have His truth presented in attractive form. "The preacher sought to find out acceptable words," or words of delight (Eccles. xii. 10). "The sweetness of the lips increaseth learning" (Prov. xvi. 21). On the lips of the great Teacher, the people hung, and marvelled at the gracious words that proceeded from Him ; and no wonder, for "never man spake like this Man."

Three bowls, one knop, and one flower in each branch. Significant of a threefold capacity or preparedness, a general acquaintance with each branch of divine truth—"three bowls." One distinct gift, as that of evangelist, pastor, or teacher—"a knop." And one manifestation of gift—"a flower." Every EVANGELIST should not only be acquainted with the truth of the gospel, but with other truths of God's Word, so as to be prepared to give the word of exhortation and instruction as needed, though his distinct work be that of preaching the gospel.

So the PASTOR's especial call may be, to deal with souls experimentally, "To reprove, rebuke, exhort with all long-suffering and doctrine," but he should be ready also to present the gospel of the grace of God to perishing sinners, and to instruct the souls he deals with.

And while the TEACHER makes full proof of his own ministry, he will find it profitable to "do the work of an evangelist" as God gives him opportunity (2 Tim. iv. 5). Experimental dealings with souls in secret, will tend to increase the richness and value of his ministry in teaching.

THE CENTRE SHAFT.

Verse 34. "And in the candlestick [lampstand] shall be four bowls made like unto almonds, with their knops and their flowers."

"The Lampstand." This is the centre shaft and branch, the type of the Lord Jesus, the great Pattern, Centre, and Source of ministry in the Spirit.

"Four bowls." All treasures of wisdom and knowledge are in Him.

"Four knops." He was the great Evangelist, the Good Shepherd, and the perfect Teacher, and the great Apostle and Prophet of our profession.

"And their four flowers." The very perfection of beauty and excellency shone out in His ministry. When He PREACHED THE GOSPEL, all the publicans and the sinners drew near unto Him for to hear Him. And what can equal the rich unfoldings of grace contained in the fifteenth of Luke? When He FEEDS HIS SHEEP, what green pastures and still waters do His cheering words provide! When He INSTRUCTS HIS DISCIPLES, what rich unfoldings of divine truth! what revelations of a Father's love! And when He UNFOLDS THE FUTURE, how distinct the prophetic visions stand before the eye! How vivid the brightness of His coming! How gorgeous the mansions of His Father's House appear! and that ONE place which He is gone to prepare for us!

In verse 31 we have noticed "HIS BRANCH," for He too was the empty and dependent One in ministry on earth. His language was, "I can of Mine own self do nothing. As I hear I judge," and "My doctrine is not Mine, but His that sent Me." And when, from the height of His glory, He gives the revelation to His servant John, He writes upon it the title, "The Revelation of Jesus Christ, which God gave unto Him." What an example for us!

THE KNOPS UNDER THE BRANCHES.

Verse 35. " And there shall be a knop under two branches of the same, and a knop under two branches of the same, same, and a knop under two branches of the same, according to the six branches that proceed out of the lampstand."

The word "AND" shews that this is additional. There are four knops in the centre BRANCH above, and three in the SHAFT below the six branches, making seven in all, the perfect number; for the PERFECTION OF GIFT IS IN CHRIST; He has received gifts, all gifts for men And it is beautiful to see how each several branch of ministry is sustained, as it were, by the corresponding office and grace of the Lord Jesus, as we read, "A knop under two branches of the same," &c. The evangelist, the pastor, and the teacher all fall back on **Him**, that, out of His fulness, they may receive grace for grace in the exercise of their several gifts.

THE ONENESS OF THE LAMPSTAND.

Verse 36. "Their knops and their branches shall be of the same: all of it shall be one beaten work of pure gold."

How beautifully expressive of the oneness of His ministry, and labour, and patience! "He that planteth, and he that watereth are one," and one in Christ. Howsoever diversified the gift, the labour, the characters, and service of each; and though each one will receive his own reward according to his own labour; yet, in the end, he that soweth and he that reapeth will rejoice together. By the grace of God they are one in the service, and, when the whole shall result in the glory of God, they shall share in the joy. "There are diversities of gifts, but the same Spirit; differences of administrations, but the same Lord; diversities of operations, but it is the same God which worketh all in all" (1 Cor. xii. 4-6).

THE LAMPS.

Verse 37. "And thou shalt make the seven lamps thereof: and they shall light the lamps thereof, that they may give light over against [Heb. the face of] it."

"Seven lamps"—the perfection of testimony to divine truth. Six in the side branches, and one in the centre shaft, making the seven. For all testimony is incomplete apart from Christ. He gives it its perfection.

That ministry alone is complete, according to God, which has Christ for its central subject. "And they shall light the lamps thereof." Where God has given the gifts, it is that they may be exercised. "No man lighteth a lamp and putteth it under a bushel, but on a lampstand."

"That they may give light over against it." The design of testimony in the power of the Spirit, is the manifestation of the glory of God in the Person of the Lord Jesus. The whole circle of truth is to be connected with Him, that it may not merely be truth, but "as the truth is in Jesus."

How beautifully the Lord Jesus has taught this in speaking of the Comforter, through whom it is that this ministry is exercised! He shall glorify Me : for He shall receive of Mine, and shall shew it unto you. All things that the Father hath are Mine : therefore said I, that He shall take of Mine, and shall shew it unto you" (John xvi. 14, 15).

THE OIL.

In Ex. xxvii. 20, we read, " And thou shalt command the children of Israel, that they bring thee pure oil olive beaten for the light [light-giver] to cause the lamp to burn always."

How this oil—that is, the supply of the Spirit—is to be obtained, we learn from the example of the early disciples, recorded in Acts iv. 23-31 : "They lifted up their voice to God with one accord, and said, . . . And now, Lord, . . . grant unto Thy servants, that with all boldness they may speak Thy word. . . . And when they had prayed, the place was shaken where they were assembled together; and they were all filled with the Holy Ghost." Paul says: "Brethren, pray for us," "and for me, that utterance may be given unto me, that I may open my mouth boldly, to make known the mystery of the gospel . . . that therein I may speak boldly, as I ought to speak" (Eph. vi. 19). "Through your prayer, and the supply of the Spirit of Jesus Christ" (Phil. i. 19).

If the lamp of testimony should burn dim in the sanctuary, the real cause may not be so much on the part of the testimony-bearers, as that those ministered to may have neglected to seek from above, the needful supply of spiritual unction and power, in order that the lamp of God may burn with continual and increasing brightness.

THE VESSELS BELONGING TO THE LAMPSTAND

Verse 38. "And the tongs thereof, and the snuff dishes thereof, shall be of pure gold."

In Rev. i., ii., iii. we have a beautiful example of the use of these golden instruments by the Lord Jesus, where He is seen in the midst of the seven golden lampstands, trimming the lamps. So also in the ministry of the apostle Paul, as seen in his Epistles to Timothy and Titus. And how, when needed, ministry is to be regulated, not by human authority, nor on human principles, but on those which are of God, and according to God, by godly counsel and admonition, exercised in spiritual wisdom and grace.

A TALENT OF GOLD.

Verse 39. "Of a talent of pure gold shall he make it, with all these vessels."

A talent of gold is computed to be about 114 lbs. in weight, and about £5,475 in value.

Ministry according to God, in the exercise of the gifts of His Spirit, and in connection with Christ, is a WEIGHTY and VALUABLE thing. That which gave the lampstand its weight and value was the pure gold of which it was composed. The highest order of natural ability, however cultivated, is but as inferior metal. It is the GRACE OF GOD, and the GIFTS OF CHRIST, exercised in the POWER OF THE HOLY GHOST, which gives to ministry its true dignity and real value.

THE EXHORTATION.

Verse 40. "And look that thou make them after their pattern, which was shewed thee in the mount."

God has given us a divine and heavenly pattern for the ministration of His own Word; and our true wisdom will be, to seek conformity to this pattern in all its details, and this will secure to us the richest and fullest blessing.

The Curtains of the Tabernacle.

(Exodus xxvi. 1-6).

Verse 1. "Moreover thou shalt make the tabernacle with ten curtains of fine twined linen, and blue, and purple, and scarlet: with cherubim of cunning work shalt thou make THEM."

HAVING considered the principal vessels of the sanctuary, we now come to the consideration of the Tabernacle itself. In this Tabernacle of Witness, there are two sets of CURTAINS and two COVERINGS. The ten curtains of fine twined linen, and blue, purple, and scarlet, with cherubim, form the TABERNACLE; and the eleven curtains of goats' hair, form what is called the TENT over the Tabernacle.

Then the COVERING of the TENT was of rams' skins dyed red, and the COVERING above that was of badgers' skins (Ex. xxxvi. 8, 13, 14, 18, 19).

It is of importance to keep the Tabernacle and Tent distinct in our minds, for although the translators often confound the terms "Tabernacle" and "Tent" ("*Mishcahn*" and "*Ohel*"), the Holy Ghost employs the most exact and beautiful precision; and it is by attention to it that we may hope, through Divine grace, to ascertain the mind of God.

64

THE CURTAINS OF THE TABERNACLE

To face page 64

The TABERNACLE, as the Hebrew word *"Mishcahn"* signifies (which is from *"shahcan"* to dwell) is God's DWELLING-PLACE, according to Ex. xxv. 8, "Let them make Me a sanctuary, that I may dwell among them," and is more immediately connected with God's abiding presence.

The TENT (*"Ohel"*) is connected with the congregation, because in the open space before the door or entrance of the tent the congregation of Israel assembled therefore the Holy Ghost never uses the expression "tabernacle of the congregation;" but in the Authorized Version the terms are frequently confounded. In the "Englishman's Bible" the distinction is invariably shown. "THOU SHALT MAKE THE TABERNACLE." A dwelling-place for God with men. Oh, marvellous, condescending grace! "Will God in very deed dwell with men on the earth? Behold, heaven and the heaven of heavens cannot contain Thee" (2 Chr. vi. 18).

Christ Himself, whilst He was on the earth, was God's tabernacle, and as such He abode alone (John i. 14, and xii. 24). "The Word was made flesh, and dwelt (or tabernacled) among us." He was God manifest in flesh : the Godhead and the glory dwelt in Him. But Christ having died, and being by the right hand of God exalted, and having received of the Father the promise of the Holy Ghost, and sent down the Comforter : by that One Spirit all believers are now baptized into one body, in union with their glorified Head. The Church on earth forms the tabernacle or dwelling-place of God, as we read in Eph. ii. 22, "In whom (Christ) ᴠᴇ also are builded together for an habitation of God through the Spirit."

In this sense the Tabernacle represents the whole Church of God, looked at in the Spirit, not in the flesh, composed of all true believers in Jesus throughout the world. I speak not of any manifest oneness, but of that which exists in the Spirit, notwithstanding all the outward failure and division. It was for this spiritual unity the Lord Jesus prayed in John xvii., and this unity we are exhorted "to keep," that is, to recognize and manifest (see Eph. iv. 3-6).

As to the ᴍᴀᴛᴇʀɪᴀʟs of which these curtains are composed. "Oꜰ ꜰɪɴᴇ ᴛᴡɪɴᴇᴅ ʟɪɴᴇɴ." Let it be borne in mind, that here the Church is not looked at only as the purchase of the blood of the Lamb—the ram's skins, dyed red, will give us that thought in due time—but as the workmanship of the Eternal Spirit. " The new man, which is renewed in knowledge after the image of Him that created him " (Col. iii. 10). "God's workmanship, created in Christ Jesus unto good works " (Eph. ii. 10). " The new man, which after God is created in righteousness and true holiness " (Eph. iv. 24).

"The fine linen is the righteousness of saints" (Rev. xix. 8), is expressive of conformity, through the Spirit, to the image of Christ as the Holy One. For he that is begotten of God sinneth not (1 John iii. 9). " The righteousness of the law is fulfilled in us, who walk not after the flesh, but after the Spirit " (Rom. viii. 4).

When the Tabernacle is regarded as a type of the Lord Jesus during His earthly sojourn, the fine linen represents His pure, sinless humanity.

" AND BLUE." Blue is the colour of the heavens, and the root of the Hebrew word rendered " blue " signifies PERFECTION. Therefore BLUE is the emblem of heavenly perfectness. And how beautifully these two thoughts of righteousness and heavenly perfectness are expressed by the Lord Jesus in His sublime prayer in John xvii.! " I pray not that Thou shouldest take them out of the world, but that Thou shouldest keep them from the evil." " Sanctify them through Thy truth : Thy Word is truth " (v. 17). Here is the FINE LINEN. And, again : " They are not of the world, even as I am not of the world " (v. 16). Here is the BLUE. " And for their sakes I sanctify Myself " (set Myself apart from the world to God), " that they also might be sanctified through the truth " (v. 19). Here is the fine linen and the blue combined. For by the Holy Ghost, sent down from heaven, uniting the believer with a glorified Christ at God's right hand, just so far as his soul enters by faith into the truth, is he in heart separated from the world, and brought into fellowship with God. And thus the *holiness* and the *heavenliness* of Jesus are wrought by the Holy Ghost into the saint's spiritual being.

When on earth, Christ was the heavenly Man, as He Himself said, " No man hath ascended up to heaven, but He that came down from heaven, even the Son of Man which is in heaven " (John iii. 13).

"AND PURPLE." The emblem of earthly and heavenly glory combined. For through the indwelling of the Holy Spirit the believer is identified with the Lord Jesus, in whom the *earthly* glories of the SON OF DAVID, and the divine and *heavenly* glories of the SON OF GOD, meet and centre.

"AND SCARLET." The emblem of earthly glory. Jesus as the offspring of David was born King of the Jews, and as King of the Jews He was crucified, witness the title written over Him on the cross. At present Jesus is rejected as King both by Jew and Gentile, and believers share with Him in that rejection. But "it is a faithful saying, that if we suffer with Him we shall be also glorified together." PURPLE is the combination of scarlet and blue, and Christ in His Melchizedek character unites the earthly glories of the kingdom with the heavenly glory of His eternal priesthood. And "till He comes" believers, like John, share in "the kingdom and patience of Jesus Christ" (Rev. i. 9).

"WITH CHERUBIM OF CUNNING WORK SHALT THOU MAKE THEM." The Cherubim inwrought with these various materials beautifully express the gifts of the Spirit for service to God, for the building up and knitting together of the Church as the body of Christ in the Spirit. While Jesus was on earth, these various gifts of the Spirit were manifested in His personal ministry.

"TEN CURTAINS." We have hitherto looked at the Church in the Spirit, in its unity; we now contemplate it as composed of various parts or assemblies. Thus, in the apostles' time, there were the churches of Galatia, the church in Corinth, Ephesus, etc. And so now believers, though one in the Spirit, are dispersed in various localities. True, in the times of the apostles, there was an outward expression of local oneness which no longer exists. Yet, nevertheless, in Spirit and in truth, all believers in a given place are one as God sees them.

THE TABERNACLE.

Verse 2. "The length of one curtain shall be eight and twenty cubits, and the breadth of one curtain four cubits; and every one of the curtains shall have one measure."

The length and breadth of every curtain was fixed by God. God's measure of the Church, in Spirit, in any one place, takes in every real believer in that place; but no more. It is inclusive of every quickened soul, but exclusive of every unconverted person. The Church of God, in Spirit, as here represented, in any given place, is composed of every real believer in that place—of every converted sinner, of every true-born child of God.

Wherever the Spirit of God has come as a quickening Spirit, there He remains as an indwelling Spirit. And every one in whom He dwells, is, by Him, baptized into the one body, of which Christ is the risen and glorified Head.

And God's principles are the same everywhere. He has not one measure for one place and another for another. "Every one of the curtains shall have one measure."

Verse 3. " The five curtains shall be coupled together one to another; and other five curtains shall be coupled one to another."

When the different local assemblies of believers were outwardly, as well as spiritually one, as in the Church at Ephesus, or at Philippi, composed of all believers in Christ in those cities, how real and sweet the fellowship of churches ! How close and intimate the fellowship between Colosse and Laodicea ! Hence, writes the Apostle Paul, "When this epistle is read among you, cause that it be read also in the Church of the Laodiceans ; and that ye likewise read the epistle from Laodicea" (Col. iv. 16). And so writes the Apostle Peter, to the elect strangers : "The church that is at Babylon, elected together with you, saluteth you" (1 Peter v. 13).

But even now, while the outward oneness is gone, the fellowship of God's churches, in the Spirit, remains,—hindered, hampered, and feeble though it be. And where two or three are gathered together unto the Name of Jesus in different localities, a little of the sweet fellowship of the early churches may still be enjoyed. Then, again, the vital interests of believers, though sundered by distance of place, are inseparably connected. One member cannot suffer without all the members with it, little as they may healthfully sympathize the one with another. The membership of the body, in Spirit, is the all-important point. Denominational membership, is a thought entirely unknown to Scripture.

Five of these curtains together covered the outer Sanctuary, the other five the Holiest of all.

> The saints above, and those below,
> But one communion make;
> All join in Christ, their living Head,
> And of His grace partake.

They are worshippers in one holy Temple, the rent veil alone being between them, whether they serve here in the shadow, or there in the light Divine.

Verse 4-6. "And thou shalt make loops of blue upon the edge of the one curtain from the selvedge in the coupling; and likewise shalt thou make in the uttermost edge of another curtain, in the coupling of the second. Fifty loops shalt thou make in the one curtain, and fifty loops shalt thou make in the edge of the curtain that is in the coupling of the second; that the loops may take hold one of another. And thou shalt make fifty taches [hooks] of gold, and couple the curtains together with the taches: and it shall be one tabernacle."

The marvellous prayer of the Lord Jesus, recorded in John xvii., gives us, I believe, in the Lord's own words, the precious truth set forth by the loops of blue and taches of gold, uniting the whole into one tabernacle, the dwelling-place of God.

This prayer of Jesus is occupied with the Church of God; it takes in neither Israel nor the world (*v.* 9), neither the Old Testament, nor the millennial saints; but those who were then the disciples of Christ, and those who should believe in Him through their word— the Church, as built upon the foundation of the apostles and prophets. Having first reminded His heavenly

Father of His earthly obedience, and asked to be glorified, as the obedient God-man, with the glory which, as the Eternal Son, He had with the Father before the world was, He then prays for His disciples. He had given to them eternal life, for they had known both Him and the Father, and now, taking His place in spirit, as no longer in the world, but as ascended to His Father—He at the right hand of God, above, and they still on the earth—He prays that they may be ONE, as the Father and the Son are one, through the one Eternal Spirit who unites the Father and the Son in a divine and eternal oneness. And this prayer was accomplished when, being by the right hand of God exalted, having received the promise of the Father, He sent down the Holy Ghost at Pentecost, who baptized into one body all believers in Jesus, in union with their glorified Head.

Then setting Himself apart to the Father from the world which crucified and rejected Him, thus sanctifying Himself for their sakes, He prays for them, that they, being one with Him risen, and thus no more of the world, than He is of the world, through the knowledge and apprehension of this truth in the power of the Holy Ghost, that they might be practically sanctified, and separated, through the Spirit, from the world to God.

He next proceeds to include all those who should believe on Him, during the present dispensation, through faith in the inspired Word, previous to His return to receive the Church : that they ALL, through the Holy Ghost, might be ONE in this divine, perfect, eternal oneness. And so they are. And this oneness is the proof to the world of the mission and Messiahship of Jesus.

He is not here contemplating their outward manifested oneness, but their inward oneness in the Spirit. (*v* 20, 21).

Then, making them the sharers of His given glory, He asks that they might be ONE, as the Father and Himself are one, in that glory.

Marvellous grace! Glorious and blissful prospect!

And when associated with Him in that resurrection glory, their bodies fashioned into the likeness of His own, they shall be MADE PERFECT IN ONE, and the perfection of the oneness will be manifest. (*v*. 22, 23).

And when Christ, who is their life, shall appear, and every eye shall see Him, and they also appear with Him in glory, then will the world KNOW that Jesus is the sent One of the Father, and that they also are loved with the same love as that with which the Father loves the Son. (*v*. 23).

Then, as not having yet exhausted the desires of His loving heart, He asks that they may not only be associated with Him in His manifested glory to the world, but that they also may be with Him and near Him in His own eternal dwelling-place with the Father, there to gaze on His divine glories, and share His everlasting love (*v*. 24).

This divine, heavenly, perfect oneness of the Church is beautifully typified by these "taches of gold" and "loops of blue." GOLD is the emblem of that which is

DIVINE; BLUE of that which is HEAVENLY, PERFECT. Their oneness is of God. It is even as the Father and the Son are one, effected by the indwelling of the divine Spirit, the Spirit of the Father and the Son.

This oneness is PERFECT, although the glorious perfection of it will only fully appear when the one Church, having no spot, wrinkle, nor any such thing, shall descend out of heaven from God, having the glory of God, and shining with a light clear as crystal (Rev. xxi. 10, 11).

And this DIVINE, HEAVENLY, and PERFECT ONENESS still exists, and nothing can touch it. The loops of blue and taches of gold, never let go their holdfast. The prayer of Christ secures it. A prayer heard and answered.

THE TENT.

Verse 7. "And thou shalt make curtains of goats' hair to be a covering [tent] upon the tabernacle: eleven curtains shalt thou make them.

The TEN curtains of fine twined linen formed the TABERNACLE; these ELEVEN curtains of goats' hair composed the TENT. Looking on the tent as typical of the Lord Jesus while on earth, it presents Him as taking upon Him the form of a servant, and made in the likeness of men (Phil. ii. 7). Yea, more; Oh marvellous stoop of condescending love, as made in the likeness of sinful flesh (Rom. viii. 3). For the goat in Scripture was especially selected for the sin-offering, as typical of Christ; though it was only on the Cross that He was "made sin for us." And the parable in Matt. xxv. 31, to the end, shews the marked distinction in the figure between the sheep and the goat. We know that He personally "knew no sin;" yet, in outward form and appearance, He was found in fashion as a man. At the same time, like the tent enclosing the tabernacle, He was the habitation of God, the glory of the Godhead dwelt within.

In the second place, looking at the tent as typical of the Church of God on earth, it presents the Church as composed of individuals living in the world; not as the Church inwardly in Spirit, but the Church outwardly in the flesh; not as to standing, for in that sense we are not in the flesh but in the Spirit (Rom. viii. 9), but being as yet in the body.

It is called "the Tent of the CONGREGATION," as representing those who are associated, or gathered together, to the confession of the Name of Jesus—the assembly, or assemblies, of the saints. And the "Tent of WITNESS," as representing them as the witnessing company for Christ in the earth.

"I am black, but comely," said the bride (Song of Sol. i. 5), "as the tents of Kedar," such is the Church's outward appearance in the flesh; "as the curtains of Solomon," such she is within, as the workmanship of the Divine and Eternal Spirit.

THE DIMENSIONS OF THE CURTAINS.

Verse 8. "The length of one curtain shall be thirty cubits and the breadth of one curtain four cubits: and the eleven curtains shall be all of one measure."

The length of the curtains of the TABERNACLE was twenty-eight cubits, the curtains of the tent were thirty cubits long, two cubits extra, and there was one curtain more to the tent, thus entirely covering the tabernacle.

"Whosoever shall call upon the Name of the Lord shall be saved." This is true of all who compose the Tabernacle, or Church of God in Spirit. And, "Let every one that nameth the name of Christ depart from iniquity." This is the precept which is imperative on all who form part of the Tent of the congregation— the witness to the Name and truth of Christ on the earth.

THE COUPLING TOGETHER OF THE CURTAINS.

Verse 9. "And thou shalt couple five curtains by themselves, and six curtains by themselves, and shalt double the sixth curtain in the forefront of the tabernacle [tent]."

How beautifully and expressively this sets forth the happy fellowship of assemblies, where holiness, and truth, and subjection to Jesus has been maintained! And God would have this fellowship experimentally and practically realised. And does not this also express the communion together which God would have enjoyed by assemblies of believers in any particular district, more or less extended?—such as between the Churches of Galatia, or the seven Churches of Asia; while provision is made, as we shall see presently, that ALL may be one.

THE LOOPS AND BRAZEN TACHES.

Verses 10, 11. "And thou shalt make fifty loops on the edge of the one curtain that is outmost in the coupling, and fifty loops in the edge of the curtain which coupleth the second. And thou shalt make fifty taches of brass, and put the taches [hooks] into the loops, and couple the tent together, that it may be one."

The Spirit of God baptizes into one body all believers in Jesus, as the tabernacle or dwelling-place of God; and the apostles and their fellow-labourers, under the direct guidance and control of the Spirit, carried out the Divine thought in the original formation of the outward Church; for it was one, in a manifest and unbroken outward unity,—one tent.

And God had made full provision for the continuance of this oneness, in the one doctrine of His Word, the one teaching of His Spirit, and the supreme Lordship of His Son. But human traditions having been permitted to mingle with, and to supersede the pure doctrines of the Word; and the teachings of the so-called Church to interfere with the teaching of the Spirit; and the authority of man to set aside the SOLE Lordship of Christ in His Church, the outward oneness which once existed, exists no longer. This was wonderfully foreshadowed in the outward garments of the crucified Redeemer, divided among the four Roman soldiers that crucified Him, while the inner coat, woven from the top throughout, remained intact.

But God's principles are unchangeably the same. The Word of God continues to be the depository and criterion of revealed truth; the Comforter remains, and the Lord Jesus retains His supremeacy. And the blessing, the privilege, and the profit, are to be realized and enjoyed still, whenever two or three are found to carry into practice God's original instructions, by meeting on God's principles. The testimony of the Lord

Jesus to the Church in Philadelphia is the witness of this (see Rev. iii. 7-13).

And the five disciples seen at the last, gathered around the Cross of the expiring Redeemer, furnish the standing type of this special and sacred fellowship.

THE TENT COVERING THE TABERNACLE.

Verses 12, 13. "And the remnant that remaineth, of the curtains of the tent, the half curtain that remaineth, shall hang over the backside of the tabernacle. And a cubit on the one side, and a cubit on the other side of that which remaineth in the length of the curtains of the tent, it shall hang over the sides of the tabernacle on this side and on that side, to cover it."

By this arrangement, the beautifully wrought curtains forming the tabernacle were entirely enclosed and hidden by the curtains of the tent; the tabernacle, as we have shewn, representing the Church inwardly in Spirit, and the tent the Church in outward manifestation.

THE RAMS' SKIN COVERING.

Verse 14. "And thou shalt make a covering for the tent of rams' skins died red. And a covering above of badgers' skins.

It is not called a covering for the TABERNACLE, though, in one sense, that is true, but a covering for the TENT; for it is not the Church in Spirit, but the Church in testimony, that especially needs this covering. The curtains of goats' hair formed a tent upon the Tabernacle. These rams' skins dyed red form a covering for the Tent.

The LAMB was the type of the Lord Jesus in the meekness, gentleness, and lowliness of His *character;* the RAM the type of Him in the strength, firmness, and decision of His *testimony.*

The rams' skins being dyed RED add another thought; that of the atoning death and precious blood of Him who was "The faithful and true Witness." The tent under the covering of the rams' skins dyed red shews the Church as accepted in the Person, and under the cover and shelter of the blood of the Lamb.

When the first intimation of gospel grace was given by God Himself to our first parents in the garden of Eden, in those words, "The seed of the woman shall bruise the serpent's head," Adam, on the part of himself and of his wife, made his confession of faith, by calling his wife's name Eve, the mother of all LIVING, though the sentence of death had just been pronounced on himself and his posterity on account of sin. Yet he calls her not the mother of all dying, but of all living, for faith laid hold on the promise, and associated in life and victory with the Virgin's Seed who was to come, all who should believe in Him. Thereupon God made, as a substitute for the aprons of fig leaves, which unbelief had sewn together, COATS OF SKIN, and clothed them. Thus Adam and Eve no longer appeared in their nakedness and shame, but clothed and covered by God Himself in the skin of that victim which probably was the first sacrifice, foreshadowing the bruising of the heel, and the atoning death of the woman's promised seed.

In like manner the tent, covered with this covering
of rams' skins dyed red, shews the Church in its testimony as seen in Christ, "in Whom we have redemption
through His blood, the forgiveness of sins, according
to the riches of His grace." And, as THUS SEEN, notwithstanding all the failure in testimony of those composing it, and their unworthiness in themselves, what
was said of Israel may be applied to them, "He hath
not beheld iniquity in Jacob, neither hath He seen
perverseness in Israel" (Num. xxiii. 21). While, at
the same time, we know that there was no iniquity nor
perverseness that God did not discover and deal with,
as walking in their midst.

It is important to remember this, that the Church's
completeness in Christ above, does not exempt her
from God's fatherly discipline, and the judgment of
the Lord Jesus down here. Totally the reverse. We
are called to "walk worthy of God unto all well
pleasing," and to "adorn the doctrine of God our
Saviour in all things." And we are dealt with on the
ground of this high responsibility. "You only have I
known," said God to Israel, "of all the families of the
earth; therefore I will punish you for all your iniquities" (Amos iii. 2). The more God's presence is manifested in the assembly, the more will be felt that He
is of purer eyes than to behold iniquity, and cannot
look on sin.

THE BADGERS' SKIN COVERING.

This covering typifies the Church in its outward
appearance, as seen by man. "As the tents of Kedar"

THE GOLDEN CANDLESTICK

To face page 80

(Song of Solomon, i. 5). "I clothed thee also with broidered work, and SHOD THEE WITH BADGERS' SKIN" (Ezekiel xvi. 10). It is the PILGRIM ASPECT of the Church, which is thus presented, in which it is conformed to the lowly appearance of Jesus of Nazareth when on earth. Therefore, whilst walking in conformity with the pattern thus set us by our Lord, "the world knoweth us not, because it knew Him not" (1 John iii.1).

SOLOMON'S TEMPLE was "exceeding magnifical," for it was the type of all the redeemed in glory.

The TABERNACLE, though all glorious within, was covered with a covering of badgers' skins : for it is the figure of the Christ in the wilderness.

SUMMARY OF THE CURTAINS.

Looking on the Lord Jesus while on earth as typified by the tabernacle (John i. 14), the inner wrought curtains of Fine Linen, answer to Him as the SON OF GOD in His spiritual excellency and beauty. "Declared to be the Son of God with power, according to the Spirit of holiness" (Rom. i. 4).

The Goats' Hair Curtains, as the SON OF MARY (Luke i. 35), made in the likeness of sinful flesh (Rom. viii. 3), yet personally "that holy thing" born of the Virgin.

The Rams' Skins dyed red present Him as the SON OF MAN in testimony, both in life and in death.

And the Badgers' Skin covering, as Jesus of Nazareth, the supposed Son of Joseph, the stranger here, to whom the world was a wilderness, and life a pilgrimage from the manger to the Cross.

But regarding the Tabernacle and Tent, with its coverings, as typical of the Church of God, the curtains of Fine Linen represent the Church in Spirit as the workmanship of the Holy Ghost.

The Goats' Hair curtains, the Church in outward responsibility.

The Rams' Skins dyed red, the Church in testimony, as seen of God in Christ, under the shelter of His atoning blood.

And the Badgers' Skin, the Church as seen by the world in her pilgrimage character, and her outward condition here.

In Resurrection glory, however, the internal workmanship of the Holy Spirit, as typified by the curtains of the tabernacle, will appear in all its Divine perfection and beauty.

The flesh, with all its imperfections, will be done away for ever, these vile bodies fashioned like Christ's glorious body, this mortal will have put on immortality, and this corruptible, incorruption. The goats' hair tent will be exchanged for the "building of God, a house not made with hands, eternal in the heavens" (2 Cor. v. 1).

But the Church will ever appear as accepted in God's Beloved Son, with robes washed and made white in the BLOOD OF THE LAMB.

While the PILGRIM garb will be exchanged for the becoming robes of royalty and triumph, the priestly garments of glory and beauty. No longer the badgers' skin covering externally visible, but "having the glory of God" (Rev. xxi. 11).

The Boards.

"And thou shalt make boards for the tabernacle of shittim wood standing up" (v. 15).

REGARDING the Tabernacle as typical of Christ, these boards of shittim wood overlaid with gold, the framework of the Tabernacle, represent Him in the combination of the human and divine natures in His blessed Person, the foundation truth of Christianity, "God manifest in flesh." But, taking the Tabernacle as typical of the Church, these boards represent the individual believers of whom the Church of God is composed.

THEIR POSITION.

Boards of shittim wood "standing up." This intimates that they had been previously cut down. Believers were once the children of wrath, even as others, growing wild in nature's forest; but they had been selected by divine grace, and had been brought low by the convictions of the Spirit, and they are here seen standing in grace (Rom. v. 2).

THE DESIGN.

This is stated in Exodus xxv. 8, "Let them make Me a sanctuary; that I may dwell among them." These boards represent believers in Christ, builded together for a habitation of God through the Spirit (Eph. ii. 22). This is God's ideal of the Church as a whole, according to the pattern shewn in the Mount (Heb. viii. 5). It is also designed to be a model for believers gathered together in Church fellowship on earth.

THE DIMENSIONS OF THE BOARDS.

" Ten cubits shall be the length of a board, and a cubit and a half shall be the breadth of one board " (v. 16).

Taking the cubit to be nearly one foot ten inches in length, the height of each board would be about eighteen feet three inches, and the breadth two feet nine inches. Thus, ten cubits was the height of the Tabernacle, one third of the height of the holy place in Solomon's Temple, which was thirty cubits, and half the height of the most holy place there, which was twenty cubits.

Though every regenerate soul is born into the family of God, and as such has his place in the Church of God, yet, in order to fill that place profitably in the assembly of believers, three things are requisite— faith, hope, charity. Faith in the atonement, hope of the glory, and love to all saints. Faith, hope, charity, these three—depth, height, and breadth. DEPTH— down to the sockets of silver, FAITH in redemption. HEIGHT—up to the rings of gold, HOPE of coming glory. BREADTH—extending to the other boards on either side. "LOVE in the truth" to all them that have known the truth, for the truth's sake which dwelleth in us (2 John i. 2).

THE   TENONS.

"Two tenons [hands] shall there be in one board, set in
order one against another [made parallel one to an-
other]; thus shalt thou make for all the boards of the
Tabernacle" (v. 17).

According to their Hebrew name, they appear to
represent the HANDS of faith, laying hold of the redemption which is in Christ Jesus; and according to
their position at the bottom of the boards, they suggest
the idea of the FEET of faith, standing firm on redemption, and the redemption price. "Set in order." So
as to fit exactly into the sockets. No slackness, no
wavering, but steadfast and unmovable, stablished,
strengthened, settled.

THE BOARDS ON THE SOUTH AND NORTH SIDES

"And thou shalt make the boards for the Tabernacle,
twenty boards on the south side southward. And for
the second side of the Tabernacle on the north side
there shall be twenty boards" (vv. 18, 20).

Twenty boards, of a cubit and a half, measure thirty
cubits, which would be about fifty-five feet long. The
length of the holy place and of the most holy together,
of the Temple, was sixty cubits, or double the length
of the Tabernacle.

THE SOCKETS OF SILVER.

"And thou shalt make forty sockets of silver under the
twenty boards; two sockets under one board for his
two tenons [hands], and two sockets under another
board for his two tenons" (v. 19).

The comparison of Exodus xxx. 11-16 and xxxviii.
25-28, with 1 Peter i. 18, 19, will give us most clearly

and beautifully the spiritual import of these sockets of silver. Every Israelite passing among them that were numbered, whether rich or poor, was required to give a ransom for his soul, of half a shekel, after the shekel of the sanctuary, in value about fifteen pence. Peter explains this, " Forasmuch as ye know that ye were not redeemed with such corruptible things, as silver and gold . . . but with the precious blood of Christ, as of a lamb without blemish and without spot."

All God's people are numbered as a RANSOMED people; to be reckoned among them on the ground of profession merely, is to come under judgment. This is illustrated by the numbering of Israel by David, as recorded in 2 Samuel xxiv., where no mention is made of the redemption price having been paid. In the instance recorded in Matt. xvii. 24, the tribute required was not the tribute to Cæsar, but the half shekel of the sanctuary; the Son of Man required no ransom for His soul. But from the abundance of the sea, the piece of money, " the stater," value two shillings and sixpence—was provided, double the ransom price, as Christ said to Peter, " For Me and thee." In Exodus xxxviii. 25-27, we read, " And the silver of them that were numbered of the congregation was a hundred talents, and a thousand seven hundred and threescore and fifteen shekels after the shekel of the sanctuary .. And of the hundred talents of silver were cast the sockets of the sanctuary, and the sockets of the vail; a hundred sockets of the hundred talents, a talent for a socket." A talent of silver is computed at £342 3s 9d; a talent being about 114 lbs. weight.

Each board had two tenons, and under each tenon there was socket of silver, each weighing a talent. What an idea this gives us of the security of every believer as founded on the atoning work of Christ; securing at once a firm foundation for the foot of faith, for it is redemption from the wrath to come; and a firm grasp to the hand of faith in laying hold of eternal life, and hope of everlasting glory.,

THE BOARDS FOR THE WEST SIDE.

"And for the sides of the Tabernacle westward, thou shalt make six boards. And two boards shalt thou make for the corners of the Tabernacle in the two sides. And they shall be coupled [twinned] together beneath, and they shall be coupled together [perfected together] above the head of it unto one ring: thus shall it be for them both; they shall be for the two corners. And they shall be eight boards, and their sockets of silver, sixteen sockets; two sockets under one board, and two sockets under another board " (vv. 22-25).

The corner boards were coupled or twinned beneath. So believers are one in the confidence of FAITH. Each board standing firm in the sockets of silver, and each believer established in the faith of the gospel. The corner boards were also coupled or perfected together to one ring above. Believers are one in the rejoicing of HOPE. We have " ONE FAITH " and " ONE HOPE OF OUR CALLING." Christ crucified is the foundation of our FAITH, and Christ glorified the substance and centre of our HOPE, Christ Himself being " the chief

CORNER STONE," uniting the Jew and the Gentile in one, on earth beneath. And He is also the HEAD STONE of the corner, uniting them together in one in heaven above. Thus we read in Hebrews iii. 6, " Christ as a Son over His own house; whose house are we, if we hold fast the confidence and the rejoicing of the hope firm unto the end." And again, *v.* 14, "For we have been made partakers of Christ, if we hold the beginning of our confidence steadfast unto the end."

The Bars of the Tabernacle.

"And thou shalt make bars of shittim wood; five for the boards of the one side of the Tabernacle, and five bars for the boards of the other side of the Tabernacle, and five bars for the boards of the side of the Tabernacle for the two sides westward. And the middle bar in the midst of the boards shall reach from end to end" (vv. 26-28).

WE have considered the BOARDS fitly framed together, firmly fixed in the sockets of silver, as typical of believers standing in redemption. We have now to consider the BARS of shittim wood overlaid with gold—God's provision for compacting together and securing the whole.

In the first six verses of Eph. iv. the sevenfold unity of the Church is mentioned : One body, one Spirit, one hope, one Lord, one faith, one baptism, one God and Father of all. From verses 7-11, the FIVE gifts given from an ascended and glorified Saviour are noticed; apostles, prophets, evangelists, pastors and teachers.

The object for which they are given is stated from verses 12 to 16 : "For the perfecting of the saints, for the work of the ministry, for the edifying of the body of Christ. Till we all come in the unity of the faith, and of the knowledge of the Son of God, unto a perfect man, unto the measure of the stature of the

90

fulness of Christ. That we henceforth be no more children, tossed to and fro, and carried about with every wind of doctrine, by the sleight of men, and cunning craftiness, whereby they lie in wait to deceive; but speaking the truth in love, may grow up into Him in all things, which is the head, even Christ. From whom the whole body fitly joined together and compacted by that which every joint supplieth, according to the effectual working in the measure of every part, maketh increase of the body unto the edifying of itself in love."

The FIVE BARS answer strikingly to these FIVE GIFTS from a risen Christ, and the object and the end is the same, both in the Tabernacle and the Church: the "perfecting," "edifying," and "compacting of the whole together."

THE MATERIAL.

They were to be of SHITTIM WOOD; reminding us that those who have received gifts for service to the Lord and to His saints, are men of like passions with others. They have this treasure in earthen vessels, that the excellency of the power may be of God, and not of them. Not sufficient of themselves to think anything as of themselves, their sufficiency is of God.

THE ARRANGEMENT OF THE BARS.

God's arrangements and provisions for ministry are simple, perfect, and uniform, adapted to the need of the Church of God throughout the whole world. All

believers everywhere have need of all the gifts of the
Spirit for their compacting and edifying; and according to God's arrangements, whatever gifts there may
be, are designed for all.

The leading of the Spirit, or the providence of God,
may place some in certain localities; all believers have
a title to their service, and they are debtors, according
to their ability and opportunity, to all. Two of the
bars were placed near the bottom of the boards; one
in the centre extending from end to end, and two near
the top, thus :

Pastors and Teachers.
Evangelists.
Apostles and Prophets.

The two UNDER bars may be taken to represent the
gifts of the APOSTLES and PROPHETS.   These, as to
doctrine and practice, according to the ability given
them of God, have laid the foundation.   The Church
is said to be "built upon the foundation of the apostles
and prophets, Jesus Christ Himself being the chief
corner stone."   They laid the foundation by their
labours, example, and teaching in their lifetime; and
in the inspired Scriptures in the New Testament which
they have left, the Church has still the benefit of their
gifts.

The MIDDLE bar in the centre of the boards was
entire, extending the whole length of the Tabernacle,
from end to end; beautifully suggestive of the widely
extended sphere of the labours of the EVANGELIST;

whose commission is, "Go ye into all the world, and preach the gospel to every creature."

The two bars near the top, represent the ministry of the PASTOR and TEACHER : the PASTOR watching over the souls of the converted, feeding the flock of God; the TEACHER leading the children of God onward and upward into further and higher acquaintance with divine truth, and of the love, person, and ways of the Lord Jesus.

THE OVERLAYING OF THE BOARDS WITH GOLD.

"And thou shalt overlay the boards with gold, and make their rings of gold for places for the bars; and thou shalt overlay the bars with gold " (v. 29).

It is remarkable that the direction for OVERLAYING the boards does not occur in the portion which treats of the BOARDS (*v* .15-25), but in connection with the BARS ; doubtless, this is significant. The boards were of shittim wood : representing believers, IN THEMSELVES partakers of HUMAN NATURE in its weakness and frailty. But overlaid with gold : signifying that, as one in Spirit with Jesus, believers are also partakers of the DIVINE NATURE (2 Peter i. 4). As we are by the grace of God—as seen by Him in the Son of His love—such we ought to be practically, experimentally, at all times ; especially when gathered in the Name of Jesus, under the searching eye of Him with whom we have to do; that as builded together for a habitation of God through the Spirit, there may be nothing to grieve or quench that Holy Spirit of God, or hinder the full flow of blessing from our God and Father. As the shittim wood in the Tabernacle was nowhere to be seen, so the flesh, or that which is merely natural, should never be manifest in the assembly of God's saints. But putting off the old man, and putting on the new, as the elect of God, holy and beloved, the divine nature should appear, and divine charity be ever in full exercise. The distinctions which cannot be over-looked with impunity in the outward walks of life, would disappear when believers are assembled in the Church; and all as children of God, members of Christ, dwelt in by the Spirit, would hold the faith of our Lord Jesus Christ, the Lord of glory, without respect of persons (James ii. 1). Whilst the gold glittered on the surface, the shittim wood existed with-in. So it becomes us to remember that, notwithstand-ing all that divine grace has made us in Christ, in our-selves we are nothing at all. The true circumcision, worshipping God in the Spirit, rejoicing in Christ Jesus, but having no confidence in the flesh. This is no excuse for sin or failure; the grace of God is sufficient; His strength is made perfect in weakness.

But why is this direction inserted here with the in-structions respecting the bars? Does it not intimate a connection between the exercising of the gifts for ministry, and the fuller realization and manifestation of the divine nature? Thus holding the Head, "all the body, BY JOINTS AND BANDS, having nourishment ministered, and knit together, increaseth WITH THE INCREASE OF GOD." Whilst God, according to His divine power, has given unto us all things that pertain unto life and godliness, whereby are given unto us exceeding great and precious promises, THAT BY THESE WE MIGHT BE PARTAKERS OF THE DIVINE NATURE—is it not through the exercise of the gifts of the Spirit, in the ministry of the Word, that individually and collectively these great and precious promises are realized and this growth in grace is experienced? (2 Pet. i. 3, 4).

THE GOLDEN RINGS.

"Rings of gold for places for the bars." There is a divinely given place for ministry in the exercise of the gifts of the Spirit in the Church of God.

There is a place appointed of God for each kind of ministry.

A place for the APOSTLES and PROPHETS, which none else can occupy : a place of authority and power.

A place for the EVANGELIST, a work of vast importance and responsibility; having to do with souls and eternity.

A place for the PASTOR and TEACHER, in watching over and instructing the souls of the redeemed, with which the saints' well-being, and the honour of the Lord Jesus is connected.

THE OVERLAYING OF THE BARS.

Real ministry is the exercise of a gift received from God through Jesus Christ, in the power of the Holy Ghost, according to the ability which God giveth, and for God's glory. "As every man hath received the gift, even so minister the same one to another, as good stewards of the manifold grace of God. If any man speak, let him speak as the oracles of God; if any man minister, let him do it as of the ability which God giveth : that God in all things may be glorified through Jesus Christ" (1 Peter. iv. 10-11).

To sum up these various figures of ministry. In the CHERUBIM on the mercy-seat in the holiest of all, we have set forth MINISTRY IN ITS HEAVENLY ORIGIN AND SOURCE.

In the golden LAMPSTAND in the holy place, over against the Table, by the Altar of incense, MINISTRY IN THE ASSEMBLY, IN CONNECTION WITH COMMUNION AND WORSHIP. In these BARS uniting the BOARDS, we see MINISTRY FOR THE BUILDING UP AND COMPACTING of the Church of God.

THE CHARGE.

"And thou shalt rear up the Tabernacle according to the fashion thereof, which was showed thee in the Mount " (v. 30).

Whether as to Church gathering and constitution, or as to ministry, God's pattern, and that alone, is to be followed; a pattern not earthly and human, but heavenly and divine.

God has condescended to arrange everything for us in His Word in type in the Old Testament, in example in the Gospels and the Acts, and in express directions in the inspired Epistles of the apostles. May we esteem all God's commandments concerning all things to be right : and hating every false way, be fully persuaded that His plans are the best, and that in keeping His commandments there is great reward.

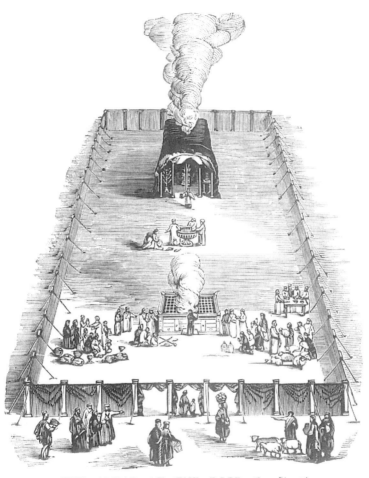

THE ALTAR AT THE DOOR (Lev. iv. 7)

To face page 96

The Vail.

Exodus xxvi. 31-33.

"And thou shalt make a vail of blue, and purple, and
scarlet [worm scarlet], and fine twined linen of cunning work; with cherubim shall IT be made " (v. 31).

THE spiritual signification of the vail is given us
by the apostle in the following words : "Having therefore, brethren, boldness to enter into
the holiest by the blood of Jesus, by a new [newly-
slain] and living way, which He hath consecrated for
us, through the vail, that is to say, His flesh" (Heb.
x. 19, 20). This vail represents the flesh of Jesus, and,
in connection with His atoning sacrifice, it shows Him
as the way of entrance, through the Spirit, by faith,
into the holiest of all. Before the death of Jesus, "the
priests went always into the first tabernacle, accomplishing the service of God. But into the second went
the high priest alone once every year, not without
blood, which he offered for himself, and for the errors
of the people : the Holy Ghost this signifying, that the
way into the holiest of all was not yet made manifest,
while as the first tabernacle was yet standing" (Heb.
ix. 6-8). But when Jesus expired on the cross at
Calvary, "The vail of the temple was rent in twain,
from the top to the bottom" (Matt. xxvii. 51). God
by this act distinctly intimating that the way of access
was clear—the glory could shine out, and the believer
in Jesus could enter in. God could be just, while He

justified—and manifest Himself as glorious in holiness, whilst the pardoned sinner was accepted and brought nigh by the blood of Jesus. The Lord Jesus told His disciples, "If I go not away, the Comforter will not come; but if I depart, I will send Him unto you" (John xvi. 7). The way was thus opened for the Comforter to come down from the ascended Christ, at Pentecost; and it is through Him, upborne by His eagle wings, we enter the Holiest, and draw near to God.

The word "new" in Heb. x. 20, is literally in the Greek "newly-slain," a beautiful illustration of which we get in the north gate of the temple of Ezekiel (ch. xl. 35-43), where there were eight stone tables on which the victims were slain, and the instruments were laid, and the flesh hung up on hooks on either side, so that the priests on entering passed through the flesh of the slaughtered victim, which was also the Eastern mode of ratifying a covenant (Gen. xv.).

THE MATERIALS OF THE VAIL.

We may trace in the materials, the various excellencies combined in the Person of Christ.

The "BLUE," His perfection as Man, and the heavenly beauty of His character, "the Son of Man which is in heaven."

"And PURPLE." The combination of the heavenly and earthly dignities in Him who was at once, Son of David and Son of God.

"And SCARLET." He was born "King of the Jews," and, though rejected of His own, He yet shall reign.

"And FINE TWINED LINEN." He was "that holy thing" born of the Virgin, and "separate from sinners" during His whole life and conversation here.

"Of CUNNING" or skilful "WORK." What beauteous blendings, what exquisite harmonies may be discovered in the character of Jesus! How each grace tempers the others, and enhances the glory of the whole.

The "CHERUBIM" on the vail represent the various kinds of service to God, which were seen in perfection in Jesus, who came down from heaven to do the will of the Father, and in whom the apostle and prophet, the evangelist, the pastor, and the teacher were combined and manifested in all their excellency.

THE PILLARS OF THE VAIL.

"And thou shalt hang IT upon four pillars of shittim wood overlaid with gold: their hooks shall be of gold, upon the four sockets of silver" (v. 32).

This beautiful and significant vail, representing the Incarnate Saviour, Immanuel, God with us, was to be suspended on four pillars of shittim wood, overlaid with gold. Can we be at a loss to ascertain the fact which answers to this foreshadowing?

Did not God employ FOUR individuals, men of like passions with ourselves, but divinely qualified by the inspiration of the Holy Ghost, to hold up to view the great mystery of godliness—God manifest in the flesh? In the four inspired records of the life and death of Jesus as given by the FOUR evangelists, the whole truth of His Person is exhibited as the Incarnate One.

Their HOOKS were to be of GOLD. The capacity to take hold of, to select, and to arrange, the various incidents in the life and death of the Man of sorrows, His words and teachings, so as to bring out the truth of His Person in all its fulness, was of God. So that those apparent discrepancies between the narratives of the four inspired historians which so puzzle the natural mind, and so often render futile the attempt to form a harmony of the FOUR GOSPELS—these seeming blemishes are, in fact, the marks and proofs of the handiwork of a Divine Editor.

Under His all-wise guidance and control—

MATTHEW selects and arranges those materials which present the Lord Jesus especially as Son of David and of Abraham, in connection with the kingdom, and with the promises made of God unto the fathers. This corresponds with the SCARLET.

MARK presents Him especially as the Son of God and Son of Man, in His untiring service. The PURPLE.

LUKE shows Him as the sociable Son of Man, in connection with mankind at large. The FINE TWINED LINEN.

And JOHN testifies to Him as the Divine and heavenly stranger, in all the perfection of His character and ways. Answering to the BLUE.

The full-length portrait—the perfection of the truth of the Person of our precious Immanuel, is the result of the whole combined.

These pillars stood on four SOCKETS OF SILVER.

For while the four inspired historians were employed and capacitated of God to exhibit the truth of the Person of Jesus, they themselves reposed on His redeeming work, and on His precious and atoning blood.

THE POSITION OF THE VAIL.

" And thou shalt hang up the vail under the taches [hooks], that thou mayest bring in thither within the vail the ark of the testimony: and the vail shall divide unto you between the holy place and the most holy " (v. 33).

These taches connected together the two larger curtains, composed of five smaller ones each, thus forming one Tabernacle (ch. xxvi. 3-6).

The vail was to be hung immediately beneath these taches, dividing the Tabernacle into two parts : twenty cubits for the holy place, and ten cubits for the most holy.

Into the first tabernacle, or the holy place, the priests went continually, accomplishing the service of God; setting forth the ordinary privilege of believers in their priestly service and worship.

But into the second, or most holy place, the high priest alone entered once every year. For while the first tabernacle was yet standing, the Holy Ghost signified that the way into the holiest was not made manifest.

The vail DIVIDED UNTO ISRAEL between the holy and most holy place. But the true light now shineth; the vail has been rent; the glory of God's grace has shone out; and the believer has boldness to enter in through faith in the blood of Jesus (Heb. x. 19-23).

Che Brazen Altar:

OR, THE ALTAR OF BURNT OFFERING.

Exodus xxvii. 1-8.

Verse 1. "And thou shalt make an altar [the altar]."

THE SIN OFFERING was burnt, or consumed, without the camp : the BURNT, or ASCENDING OFFERING, was converted into a sweet savour on the altar of burnt offering by the fire which came originally from God, and which was kept always burning in it.

In the SIN offering we see Jesus, who knew no sin, made sin for us, suffering without the gate, and putting sin away by the sacrifice of Himself.

In the other, Jesus, the spotless Victim, offering up Himself as a sweet savour unto God, and His acceptance manifested by His resurrection from the dead, and ascension to the right hand of the Father.

Outside the camp it is wrath CONSUMING, and for ever setting aside the sins which Jesus bore.

At the brazen altar it is justice and holiness, FEEDING with complacency on the excellency of the victim.

The altar of burnt offering, cleansed, anointed, santified—an altar most holy, on which the fire was always burning, and the sacrifice always consuming, was the place of communion between God and His people, and between the people and their God (see Exodus xxix. 36-46).

102

It sets forth Christ, through whom we draw nigh to God, and through whom God draws nigh to us, on the ground of His atoning work, and of His accepted sacrifice, by which every perfection of the Godhead is satisfied and glorified.

THE MATERIAL.
"Shittim wood."

In order that Jesus, through His atoning sacrifice, might furnish a meeting-place between God and the soul, it was requisite that He should become incarnate. This truth is set before us in the shittim wood. "Wherefore, when He cometh into the world, He saith . . . a body hast Thou prepared Me " (Heb. x. 5).

THE DIMENSIONS OF THE ALTAR.
" Five cubits long, and five cubits broad; the altar shall be foursquare: and the height thereof shall be three cubits."

Twice the length and height of the ark of the covenant. These dimensions were fixed by God Himself, who also prepared a body for Christ, every way adapted and adequate for His work and sufferings.

THE HORNS OF THE ALTAR.
Verse 2. "And thou shalt make the horns of it upon the four corners thereof: his horns shall be of the same: and thou shalt overlay it with brass."

The horn in Scripture is the emblem of power. "Bind the sacrifice with cords," says the psalmist, "even unto the horns of the altar" (Psalm cxviii. 27).

In the garden of Gethsemane we see this thought

strikingly exemplified. There we see Jesus, the BE-
LOVED Son of the Father, whose dwelling-place eternally was the Father's bosom; that HOLY One, who
knew no sin, and that blessed One, "God over all,
blessed for ever," drawing back from, and deprecating
the enduring of God's WRATH, the imputation of SIN,
and the infliction of the CURSE. Yet the cords of love
and obedience bound Him—love and obedience to the
Father, love and compassion to us. So that, in the
end, we see the willing Victim passing through the
three long hours of darkness, made SIN for us, and
nailed to the accursed tree.

This as to the VICTIM; then as to the SINNER, or the
WORSHIPPER. In 1 Kings i. 50 we read, "And Adonijah feared because of Solomon, and arose, and went,
and caught hold on the horns on the Altar." Again,
chapter ii. 28, "And Joab fled unto the Tabernacle of
Jehovah, and caught hold on the horns of the altar."
What strong consolation is provided for the poor sinner who flies for refuge, to lay hold on the hope set
before him in the Gospel, founded on the perfect and
accepted sacrifice of the sinner's Saviour, and the
sinner's Friend! And the believer, too, finds here a
refuge and a rest.

The SHITTIM WOOD and the BRASS—emblems of the
tender SYMPATHY and the Divine Almighty POWER of
the Saviour of the lost, and the Sustainer of the saved
—give faith its firm holdfast.

The WOOD and the BRASS—the SYMPATHY and the
POWER of Him who is thus set forth, giving faith its
grasp of undying tenacity. The sinner and the saint

find in Jesus, who is here set forth, one ABLE TO SYMPA-
THIZE and MIGHTY TO SAVE.

But what a solemn lesson is read out to us from
these horns of the brazen altar! In Exodus xxi. 14,
God says, "But if a man come presumptuously upon
his neighbour to slay him with guile, thou shalt take
him from mine altar, that he may die." For the PRE-
SUMPTUOUS sinner, and the hypocritical DECEIVER, the
atonement of Jesus itself provides no shelter, while he
continues such. It is of no avail for a person to say,
"I am trusting in the blood of Jesus," while presumptuously continuing in sin, or hypocritically professing
repentance. "Thou shalt take him from Mine altar,
that he may die," is the stern command of Divine in-
flexible justice. Solemn thought! How many a soul
has gone on for years, clinging with vain hope to a
mere profession of faith in Jesus, lulled into a false
peace, with a spirit unsanctified and a soul unsaved,
to perish at last. Thus was it in type with Adonijah.
"And Solomon said, "If he will show himself a worthy
man, there shall not a hair of him fall to the earth :
but if wickedness shall be found in him, he shall die"
(1 Kings i. 52). So it turned out. "King Solomon sent
by the hand of Benaiah the son of Jehoiada : and he
fell upon him that he died" (1 Kings ii. 25).

THE STAVES.

Verses 6, 7. "And thou shalt make staves for the altar,
staves of shittim wood, and overlay THEM with
brass. And the staves shall be put into the rings, and
the staves shall be upon the two sides of the altar, to
bear IT."

The staves adapted the brazen altar to the wilderness condition of God's people, so that the altar accompanied them in all their journeyings. Wherever the camp pitched, the altar rested; wherever the court was enclosed, the altar was placed at the entrance; wherever the tent of the congregation was set up, the altar stood at the door. The daily sacrifice on the altar of burnt offering, was the standing link of communion between God and His people typically. The taking away of the daily sacrifice was a national calamity. The fire was always burning in this altar, never permitted to go out. The victim always consuming on it day and night, the sweet savour of it was always ascending. Thus the ground of communion was at all times prepared, the way of communion at all times open. On this perpetual burnt offering, the other special sacrifices (as on the Sabbaths, new moons, etc.) were burnt, and the sin and trespass offerings presented. So now, though our God is a consuming fire (and the apprehension of this is ever to be kept alive in our hearts), the sacrifice of Jesus has met, and for ever satisfies, all the demands of holiness and justice on our behalf. On this account, "If we confess our sins, He (God) is faithful and just to forgive us our sins, and to cleanse us from all unrighteousness."

The ground of communion has been made good, the way of access is ever open, the fragrance of the sacrifice of Jesus is ever before God. Wherever we are, whatever our circumstances, communion with God may be maintained unbroken, our walk down here may be an Enoch walk—a walk with God.

The STAVES of the TABLE of shewbread were connected with the BORDER (chapter xxv. 27); for the guarding of COMMUNION is important in connection with our wilderness state. The STAVES of the GOLDEN ALTAR are connected with the GOLDEN CROWN; for it is a GLORIFIED CHRIST through whom we worship. The STAVES of the BRAZEN ALTAR are connected with the GRATE of BRASS; for it is a SUFFERING Saviour who laid the foundations of our constant communion with God.

THE DIVINE PATTERN.

Verse 8. "Hollow with boards shalt thou make IT: as it was shewed THEE in the mount, so shall they make it."

Jesus, though mighty to suffer, and Almighty to save, was the EMPTY and dependent One. "He was crucified through weakness."

How different is the appearance of Calvary, and of Him who suffered there, when seen on earth's low level, and with human thoughts and feelings, to what it is when looked at in the light of God—as God Himself reveals the marvellous scene! In spirit raised above surrounding things, and upon the MOUNT with God, looking down on Calvary's Cross! Thus are we to form our conceptions of it; thus shall we learn its mysteries and its uses, its value and its power; and thus shall our souls experience the blessing which God has provided. Communion with God on the ground of sacrifice must be according to God's order and thoughts, and not according to the plans and opinions of men.

The Court of the Tabernacle.

Exodus xxvii. 9.

Verse 9. "And thou shalt make the court of the tabernacle."

"WHATSOEVER things were written aforetime, were written for our learning," and "happened unto them for ensamples : and they are written for our admonition, upon whom the ends of the world are come" (1 Cor. x. 11). Thus the children of Israel, redeemed out of Egypt, are the types of the redeemed people of God. In the Scriptures we have Israel presented to us, in their history, and in the Divine arrangements respecting them, in various degrees of nearness to God.

First, we see them in Egypt, groaning under the bondage of Pharaoh. This is typical of the experience of the soul, under the first convictions of the Spirit, feeling the evil of sin, its bitter bondage, and heavy guilt, "labouring and heavy laden," from which deliverance is only obtained by taking shelter under the blood of the Lamb. "Christ our Passover sacrificed for us."

Secondly, we see them in the wilderness, having crossed the Red Sea, wherein all the power of the oppressor has been overwhelmed. Typical of the soul realising the triumph of the Cross. Principalities and powers spoilt and made a show of ; and death, and him that had the power of it, destroyed. And the believer, no longer at home in the world, but become a pilgrim and a stranger here.

Thirdly, we see them IN THE CAMP, occupying therein the various positions assigned them by God. Typical of believers in their different callings, ordinary occupations, and their social relationships. OUTSIDE the camp the sin-offering was consumed. OUTSIDE the camp the lepers and the defiled were obliged to remain. WITHIN the camp the people of God were required to be a holy people to the Lord their God, who walked up and down in their midst—to be holy in all manner of conversation, and in all the callings and relationships of life.

Fourthly, we see them assembled IN THE COURT OF THE TABERNACLE. Here the people of God are represented in their RELIGIOUS character. This is the especial subject of our present consideration.

Fifthly, the PRIESTS are seen entering daily through the door of the tent into the first tabernacle, or holy place, accomplishing the service of God. Typical of BELIEVERS in their PRIESTLY character and Church association, engaged in the worship and service of God.

Sixthly, the HIGH PRIEST is seen entering THROUGH THE VAIL into the Holy of Holies. Typical of JESUS, the HIGH PRIEST of our profession, entered for us into heaven itself ; and of the BELIEVER in Him having boldness to enter through the rent vail into the holiest of all (Hebrews x. 19-22).

Seventhly, we see Israel IN THE LAND, having crossed the Jordan. Typical of believers as in spirit raised up together, and made to sit together in Christ Jesus in the heavenly places (Eph. ii. 6).

1, Egypt; 2, the wilderness; 3, the camp; 4, the court; 5, the holy place; 6, the most holy; 7, the land.

Divided by—1, the blood of the Paschal Lamb; 2, the Red Sea; 3, the sin-offering; 4, the hanging of the court; 5, the door of the tent; 6, the vail; 7, the Jordan.

This is the Scriptural "Pilgrim's Progress," written "not in the words which man's wisdom teacheth, but which the Holy Ghost teacheth."

But to return to the court of the tabernacle. The children of Israel seen in this court represent the people of God in their RELIGIOUS character. Not as associated in Church fellowship—this is typified by the boards of the tabernacle—but in their general religious aspect. Not only seeking to maintain and to exhibit holiness in the assemblies of God's saints, and in Church relationship, but also in the wider sphere of ordinary and everyday life.

These curtains of fine-twined linen formed a court around the tabernacle, and kept it separate. As the table of shewbread has a border, so the tabernacle of God has a court—a court with hangings of fine-twined linen all around, marking separation to God in right-eousness and true holiness. Such is God's plan. As a TABLE without a BORDER is not according to God's pat-

tern, so a TABERNACLE without a COURT is contrary to
God's order. There must be consistency without, as
well as holiness and fellowship within; separation
from the world in daily life, as well as in Church
fellowship, and in the devotional exercises of the assembly. The COURT contained the ALTAR of burnt
offering and the LAVER, and had the tabernacle, or
dwelling-place of God in the midst. And the Israelites
collected there, and in the open space before it, represents believers, realising atonement and acceptance
through the sacrifice of Jesus, sanctification in Christ
Jesus, by the Holy Ghost, and walking and acting in
the presence of God.

The Hangings of the Court.

Exodus xxvii. 9.

Verse 9. "For the south side southward there shall be hangings for the court of fine-twined linen of a hundred cubits long for one side."

"THE FINE LINEN is the righteousness of saints" (Rev. xix. 8). " I counsel thee to buy of Me white raiment, that thou mayest be clothed," says Christ (Rev. iii. 18).

" Put ye on the Lord Jesus Christ," is the exhortation of the Apostle (Romans xiii. 14).

The COURT of the Tabernacle, surrounded by these hangings of fine-twined linen, represents believers in their ordinary Christian character and intercourse, walking in the presence of God in holiness and righteousness before Him, keeping their garments undefiled by sin, putting on and living out Christ, and exhibiting Him before men.

THE PILLARS AND SOCKETS.

Verse 10. "And the twenty pillars thereof and their twenty sockets shall be of brass."

Or, as expressed in chapter xxxviii. 10 : " Their pillars were twenty, and their brazen sockets twenty."

The PILLARS fixed in SOCKETS of BRASS, represent

THE COURT AND THE GATE

To face page 112

individual believers in their religious character, and their firm standing. There were twenty pillars on the north and south, corresponding with the twenty boards of the Tabernacle on those sides. The BOARDS representing believers associated in Church fellowship; and the PILLARS of the court, believers in their wider and ordinary Christian walk.

Each PILLAR stood firmly fixed in a SOCKET of brass, as expressing the firm and decided stand which is requisite in living out the Christian character. As united in Church fellowship, in the sight of God, we stand in redemption, like the boards of the Tabernacle on the sockets of silver. But as walking before God, and living before men, in our daily course, we need a holy decision of character, standing strong in the Lord, and in the power of His might, as the pillars of the court in their sockets of brass. "Having done all, to stand," says the Apostle. "Stand therefore" (Eph. vi. 13, 14).

If "the Church of the living God" is to be "the pillar and ground of the truth," individual believers in their Christian character and ordinary conduct should seek to maintain the truth, by walking in it with firmness and decision, like James, Cephas, and John, who seemed to be pillars in their day, and especially like the Apostle Paul.

THE HOOKS AND FILLETS.

Verse 10. "The hooks of the pillars and their fillets [connecting-rods] shall be of silver.

The HOOKS were to receive the FILLETS, and the fillets, as the Hebrew word for fillet implies, were

CONNECTING-RODS. These silver rods connected the pillars together, and formed the rods on which the linen curtains hung. The hooks and connecting-rods were to be of silver, and SILVER is typical of REDEMPTION; for the Atonement money was in silver (Exodus xxx. 11-16).

And SILVER is also typical of COMMUNION; for it was the ordinary medium for monetary transactions. And the hooks fixed in the pillars were always in readiness to receive the connecting-rods.

Thus these pillars, standing in the brazen sockets, with their hooks and connecting-rods of silver, sustaining the curtains of fine-twined linen, and forming together the COURT of the Tabernacle, most strikingly and beautifully represent the people of God, in their ordinary religious character, established and settled, walking in righteousness and holiness, always prepared for, and constantly maintaining communion together, on the ground of their common redemption by the Blood of the Lamb, in their intercourse one with another, and in the presence of God.

It is a sweet and happy thought, affording some consolation in the present state of things, that even now, in the outwardly divided conditions of the Church of God, when Church FELLOWSHIP with the majority of Christians may be sought in vain, we may still maintain communion and love in our intercourse one with another on the ground of our common redemption, by the same precious Blood, and of our agreement together in the same fundamental truths of salvation, as taught and united by the same Holy Spirit.

THE LENGTH OF THE COURT.

Verse 11. "And likewise for the north side in length there shall be hangings of a hundred cubits long, and his twenty pillars and their twenty sockets of brass; the hooks of the pillars and their fillets [connecting-rods] of silver."

One hundred cubits NORTH and SOUTH. "Awake, O north wind, and come, thou south," is the language of the Bride in the Song of Solomon (chap. iv. 16). Whether the chill north wind of adversity blows, or the genial south wind of prosperity breathes, there should be the same FIRM STANDING, and decided walk, the same maintenance of RIGHTEOUSNESS and holiness, the same manifestation of Christ, and the same readiness for FELLOWSHIP with all saints, on the ground of our common Christianity.

THE BREADTH OF THE COURT.

Verses 12-15. "And for the breadth of the court on the west side shall be hangings of fifty cubits: their pillars ten, and their sockets ten. And the breadth of the court on the east side eastward, shall be fifty cubits. The hangings of one side of the gate shall be fifteen cubits: their pillars three, and their sockets three. And on the other side shall be hangings fifteen cubits: their pillars three, and their sockets three."

In LENGTH—namely, one hundred cubits—the court of the TABERNACLE was one HALF the LENGTH of the INNER court of Ezekiel's TEMPLE, which will be two hundred cubits; and in BREADTH—namely, fifty cubits —HALF the BREADTH of the INNER court of the TEMPLE, which will be one hundred cubits.

THE GATE OF THE COURT.

Verse 16. " And for the gate of the court shall be a hanging of twenty cubits, of blue, and purple, and scarlet [worm scarlet], and fine-twined linen, wrought with needlework."

The hanging for the door of the tent and the vail, were both ten cubits by ten—one hundred cubits square; and the gate of the court twenty cubits by five in height—one hundred cubits square also; each representing CHRIST in different aspects. The GATE OF THE COURT being typical of CHRIST, by the faith of whom alone any really become Christians, and have a title to be regarded as such, and power in the Spirit for true fellowship in the Gospel.

THE DOOR OF THE TENT representing CHRIST, through whom alone there is access into the Church of God. And the VAIL representing Him as the way by whom only there is access by faith into the holiest of all.

THE PILLARS OF THE GATE.

Verse 16. "Their pillars shall be four, and their sockets four."

By these FOUR PILLARS, corresponding with the four pillars which sustain the vail, are represented, I believe, the four divinely inspired historians of the life of Jesus. There are some differences, however, which are significant.

The PILLARS of the VAIL have their HOOKS of GOLD, and their SOCKETS of SILVER; while the PILLARS of the GATE have their HOOKS of SILVER, and their SOCKETS of BRASS. The HOOKS of GOLD being significant of a

DIVINELY-given ability for laying HOLD on and exhibiting the perfection of Immanuel, as the way of access by faith into the Holiest; and the SOCKETS of SILVER significant of their STANDING in REDEMPTION.

The HOOKS of SILVER, and the silver connecting-rods of the PILLARS of the GATE, expressive of a capacity for communicating the truth of Christ; and the SOCKETS of BRASS, of decision and steadfastness.

It is interesting to trace in the four inspired histories of the "Word made flesh," the various beauties and perfections of Immanuel, as signified by the BLUE, PURPLE, SCARLET, and FINE-TWINED LINEN, composing the GATE OF THE COURT.

In JOHN's account, the BLUE, or HEAVENLY PERFECTION and glory of the Lord Jesus, is manifest.

In MARK, the PURPLE, or the combination of HEAVENLY PERFECTNESS with the EARTHLY GLORY. And hence it is worthy of notice, that, in Mark xv. 17, the robe in which, in mockery, Jesus was arrayed, is by the leading of the Spirit said to be of "PURPLE."

In MATTHEW, the EARTHLY DIGNITIES of the Son of David, as typified by the SCARLET, appear; and Matthew says, they "put on Him a scarlet robe" (xxvii. 28).

Whereas, in LUKE, the WHITE, or PURE and SPOTLESS, yet exquisitely beautiful humanity of the Son of Man is prominent, as typified by the FINE-TWINED LINEN. And Luke says, they "arrayed Him in a gorgeous robe." Gorgeous, *"Lampros,"* meaning also, shining, resplendent, dazzling, white. Compare Acts x. 30; Rev. xv. 6; xix. 8, in the Greek.

Verses 17-19. "All the pillars round about the court shall
be filleted with silver [connected with rods of silver]
their hooks shall be of silver, and their sockets of
brass. The length of the court shall be a hundred
cubits, and the breadth fifty everywhere, and the
height five cubits of fine-twined linen, and their sockets of brass. All the vessels of the tabernacle in all
the service thereof, and all the pins thereof, and all
the pins of the court, shall be of brass."

All the pillars of the court were connected together
by the SILVER RODS, and all were furnished with HOOKS
for attaching them; teaching us, that all believers
should maintain fellowship together in redemption,
truth, and brotherly love, and all be prepared for it
as occasion presents.

All the PILLARS stood on SOCKETS of BRASS; and all
believers have need of enduring strength in Jesus, by
the Spirit, to maintain, in such a world as this, their
religious character and standing; that strengthened by
God's Spirit in the inner man, Christ dwelling in the
heart by faith, they may be rooted and grounded in
love. (Eph. iii. 16, 17).

All the VESSELS of the Tabernacle for all the service
of it, and even the PINS of the tabernacle and court,
were to be of BRASS; for the same enduring spiritual
strength is needed for all manner of service, down to
the minutest particulars, in work connected with the
Name of Jesus, and the presence of God.

In Exodus xxxviii. 17, we read: "The overlaying of
their chapiters [tops or heads] of silver; and all the
pillars of the court were filleted with silver [connected
with rods of silver]," showing that the chapiters, or

heads of the pillars, and the fillets or connecting-rods, are distinct; though both were of silver, and all formed out of the redemption money. "And of the thousand seven hundred and seventy and five shekels, he made hooks for the pillars, and overlaid their chapiters, and filleted THEM" (Ex. xxxviii. 28).

The redemption which is in Christ Jesus, is not only the foundation of the Christian's FAITH, as shown by the silver sockets of the Tabernacle : it is also the ground of Christian LOVE and communion, as signified by the silver hooks and connecting-rods. And it is also the crown and joy of the Christian's HOPE, as signified by the silver chapiters, or crowns of the pillars. His faith, his love, and his hope, having each its ground and centre in Jesus, and in His mighty work.

The Golden Altar of Incense.

Exodus xxx. 1-9.

Verse 1. "And thou shalt make an altar to burn [burn as incense] incense upon: of shittim wood shalt thou make IT."

THERE were two altars, the brazen altar of burnt offering and the golden altar of incense. They are both typical of the Person and work of the Lord Jesus Christ, but in distinct aspects.

At the BRAZEN altar, we see Christ in death and resurrection, offering Himself without spot to God, and accepted in all the sweet savour of His perfect sacrifice —the ground of the believer's acceptance and communion with God.

At the GOLDEN altar, we see Christ in all the excellency of His character and ways before God, through whom the children of God draw near and worship with confidence and joy.

Both the brazen and the golden altar were made of shittim wood within, as showing that the Incarnation of Christ lies at the foundation of His whole work on behalf of His people; for the children being partakers of flesh and blood, He Himself likewise took part of the same.

THE DIMENSIONS.

Verse 2. "'A cubit shall be the length thereof, and a cubit the breadth thereof; four square shall it be: and two cubits shall be the height thereof."

The table of shewbread was two cubits in length, and one in breadth, and one cubit and a half in height. This altar was one cubit square, and two in height. The TABLE was on a level with the mercy-seat, and the brazen grate of the altar of burnt offering; for the table sets forth COMMUNION on the ground of atonement made, and in the remembrance of the death of Jesus. The GOLDEN ALTAR was half a cubit higher, because we draw nigh to God in the Name of Him who, though once humbled, is now risen and glorified.

THE HORNS OF THE ALTAR.

" The horns thereof shall be of the same."

The HORN is the emblem of strength; and there is power in Jesus, on which faith can lay hold in drawing nigh to God; while the human tenderness and sympathy of Jesus give sweet encouragement to faith.

THE OVERLAYING.

Verse 3. "And thou shalt overlay IT with pure gold, the top [roof] thereof, and the sides [walls] thereof round about, and the horns thereof."

The Divine glory and excellency of the Lord Jesus, as well as His humanity, and in combination with it, is thus set forth.

And the horns also are overlaid with gold; for **faith** not only apprehends the human sympathy, but also **the** Divine all-sufficiency of Jesus, through whom we worship.

THE GOLDEN CROWN.

"And thou shalt make unto it a crown of gold round about."

There was no crown to the brazen altar, for that sets forth Jesus in His humiliation, suffering, and death; the only crown He wore on earth was a crown of thorns. But there is a GOLDEN CROWN to the altar of incense, because it represents Him who, though once made a little lower than the angels for the suffering of death, is now "crowned with glory and honour."

THE RINGS AND THE STAVES.

Verses 4, 5. "And two golden rings shalt thou make **to** it under the crown of it, by the two corners [ribs] thereof, upon the two sides of it shalt thou make it; and they shall be for places for the staves to bear it withal. And thou shalt make the staves of shittim wood, and overlay THEM with gold."

The Hebrew word, translated in the text "corners," and in the margin "ribs," is the same word which occurs in chap. xxvii. 7, and which is there rendered "sides," "and the staves shall be upon the two sides of the altar to bear it," which gives the sense. Translating the word "corners," here and in chap. xxxvii "sides" is apt to mislead. It signifies a side, or, as in the present instance, an appendage to a side.

In the TABLE OF SHEWBREAD the rings and staves were connected with the BORDER (chap. xxv. 26, 27), to teach us that in travelling through a polluted world, separation from evil ought to characterise our communion. But in the GOLDEN ALTAR the rings and staves are connected with the CROWN OF GOLD, for, though strangers and pilgrims here, we worship in connection with an ascended and glorified Saviour. The rings and staves adapted the altar to the wilderness condition of Israel; they were "to bear it withal," that it might accompany them in their various journeyings. So Jesus, in the character in which He is presented to us by the GOLDEN ALTAR is ever present with us in Spirit, wherever two or three are gathered unto His Name. Both His humanity and His Deity adapt Him to our wilderness necessities.

THE POSITION OF THE GOLDEN ALTAR.

Verse 6. "And thou shalt put it before the vail that is by the ark of testimony, before the mercy-seat [propitiatory], that is over the testimony, where I will meet with thee."

In Hebrews ix. the golden altar in the holy place is omitted in the enumeration of the sacred vessels, and the GOLDEN CENSER in the holiest of all is inserted in its stead. The reason of this appears to be, that in Heb. ix., and in Heb. x., the High Priest is represented as on the day of Atonement, entered into the most holy place within the vail, with the golden censer, typical of Jesus entered into Heaven, now to appear in the presence of God for us.

But in the type before us, the same Saviour is represented as present in Spirit in the midst of His worshipping people on earth, by whom the sacrifice of praise
is offered up to God continually.   It is the vivid setting
forth of those invaluable words in Matt. xviii. 19, 20.

The altar stands before, not within the vail in the
holy place; for it tells of Jesus in the assembly, and yet
it stands before the ark and propitiatory, from whence
God holds fellowship with His servants.   And in Jesus
who is present in Spirit with us on earth, and present
in Person for us above, all the promises of God are
yea, and amen, to the glory of God by us.

All this is true to the believer individually, as well
as to the saints collectively.

THE PERPETUAL USE OF THE ALTAR

Verses 7, 8.   " And Aaron shall burn thereon sweet incense every morning: when he dresseth the lamps,
he shall burn incense upon it.   'And when Aaron
lighteth the lamps at even [between the two evenings]
he shall burn incense upon it, a perpetual incense
before Jehovah throughout your generations."

So Christ, the High Priest of our profession, ever
liveth to make intercession for us.

In John xvii. we have the reality and substance of
these Divine foreshadowings.   We there see Jesus on
earth, surrounded by His disciples; but in Spirit entering into the Holiest, His work finished, and the crown
of glory won.   In ACT it was the High Priest at the

golden altar—IN ANTICIPATION, the High Priest on the day of Atonement entering into the holiest.

Let us look at Him as at the golden altar, and listen to His words, "Father, I glorified Thee on the earth, I finished the work which Thou gavest Me to do." "I manifested Thy Name."

He thus presented before His Father, as sweet and fragrant incense, the memorial of what He had been in His character and life on earth; and then claiming for Himself the just recompense of reward, He obtains on behalf of His disciples, and of believers through their word, the richest, choicest, highest blessings. And these words He spake in the world, that we might have His joy fulfilled in ourselves, in being thus enabled to enter into His thoughts concerning us, through this magnificent specimen of His present and perpetual intercession, in the knowledge of the glory which He has, and which He will share with us.

THE TIME OF INCENSE.

We have considered the LAMPSTAND with its seven lamps, as the type of ministry or testimony in connection with Christ, and in the power of the Spirit. Christ Himself PREPARES His servants for this ministry in the Word, and He gives grace and power for its EXERCISE. Just as Aaron dressed the lamps in the morning; and caused the flame to ascend at even, or between the two evenings.

In Revelation i., ii., iii., the Lord Jesus is shown as one like unto the Son of Man in the midst of the seven

golden lampstands, giving and directing the testimony
which was to be borne in His Name.

Testimony to Christ is a sweet savour unto God, as
says the Apostle in 2 Cor. ii. 15, 16, "For we are unto
God a sweet savour of Christ, in them that are saved,
and in them that perish." This is not all : the type
before us beautifully and expressively shows, the connection between the preparation and exercise of ministry, in fellowship with Jesus, and the fragrance of His
own intercession. When the servant is preparing, or
being prepared for testimony, the intercession of Jesus
is ascending on his behalf ; and when he is giving his
testimony, the sweet savour of the Name of Jesus is
going up before God.

Verse 9. " Ye shall offer up no strange incense thereon,
    nor ascending-offering, nor gift-offering; neither shall
    ye pour drink-offering thereon."

Thus the altar of incense was kept perfectly distinct
from the altar of burnt or ascending-offering. We do
well to remember this in drawing nigh to God.

No strange incense was permitted, any more than
strange fire. Jesus pleads no other excellency than His
own, as the ground for the acceptance of our prayers
and praises.

The believer's priestly access to God is a progressive
thing. We go from strength to strength.

In the SIN-OFFERING consumed without the camp, we
see Jesus "delivered for our offences," and the question of sin settled.

At the BRAZEN ALTAR, we see Jesus "raised again for justification, and realise acceptance in Him, and the joy of God's salvation."

At the LAVER we recognise Christ as our SANCTIFICATION, through the Holy Ghost the Comforter sent down from heaven.

At the GOLDEN ALTAR He is presented as the High Priest of our profession, appearing in the presence of God for us, in all the value of His living service, personal excellency, and atoning work, which He pleads, and we plead for our acceptance before God.

As guilty sinners, we find acceptance at the brazen altar, through the accepted sacrifice of a crucified and risen Saviour.

At the laver we find provision made for our sanctification in Christ, through the Holy Ghost.

At the golden altar we have fellowship with God, and nearness of access to Him, in all the preciousness of the life and person of Jesus, as He was, and as He is.

In the ark of the covenant within the vail we see every promise of God yea and amen, to us in Christ, and full security for every blessing, for time and for eternity.

THE BLOOD ON THE HORNS OF THE ALTAR OF INCENSE.

Verse 10. "Aaron shall make an atonement upon the horns of it once a year, with the blood of the sin-offering of atonements: once in the year shall he make atonement upon it throughout your generations: it is most holy unto Jehovah."

The foundation of our acceptance is laid in atonement, and we know from Hebrews x. that this yearly act was a type of the one offering of Jesus, whereby He hath perfected for ever them that are sanctified. And this act of atonement was two-fold, for on the tenth day of the seventh month, Aaron entered within the vail; first, with the blood of the bullock for himself and for his house, typical of Christ and the Church (Heb. iii. 6); and then with the blood of the goat for all Israel and the sanctuary. At the same time he put the blood on the horns of the golden altar (Lev. xvi). And while no burnt sacrifice nor gift-offering was to be offered on this altar, yet the blood of atonement on the horns of it speaks of peace once made, and the remission of sins once for all, through the sacrifice of Christ.

THE CAMP AT REST

The Laver and His Foot.

Exodus xxx. 17-21.

Verses 17, 18. "And Jehovah spake unto Moses, saying, Thou shalt also make a laver of brass, and his foot [base] also of brass, to wash withal: and thou shalt put IT between the tabernacle [tent] of the congregation and between the altar, and thou shalt put water therein."

THESE Scriptures are "the Word of God;" this gives them their importance and authority. They are also "the testimony of Jesus Christ;" this gives them their interest to us as redeemed sinners, and their value to our souls, as containing God's testimony concerning His Son.

God's thoughts about Christ are embodied in type, and given us in the Scriptures, that we might have fellowship with the Father in His own estimate of His Son, through the Spirit.

In the laver and his foot, we have the divinely given figure or shadow of CHRIST as our SANCTIFICATION. "Who of God is made unto us wisdom, and righteousness, and sanctification, and redemption" (1 Cor. i. 30).

In this chapter in Exodus, typically the believer is regarded, first, REDEEMED BY THE BLOOD (verses 11-16); secondly, SANCTIFIED with the washing of WATER (verses 17-21); thirdly, ANOINTED with the OIL (verses

129

22-33); fourthly, ACCEPTED in the PERFUME (verses 34-38). "The Spirit, the water, and the blood" (1 John v. 6-8).

In Solomon's Temple there were TEN LAVERS, standing on their TEN BASES, and ONE MOLTEN SEA, standing on twelve oxen (1 Kings vii. 23-26).

In Ezekiel's Temple there will be no laver nor sea, but a RIVER, whose waters will issue out from under the threshold of the house eastward, deepening and widening as it flows.

In Revelation iv. 6, we read of a SEA OF GLASS like unto crystal before the throne, emblematical of the fixed purity which becomes the presence of God.

In Revelation xv. 2, of a SEA OF GLASS mingled with FIRE, indicative of the fiery trial through which those who come out of the great tribulation, will have passed.

In Revelation xxii. 1, of a PURE RIVER OF WATER OF LIFE, clear as crystal, proceeding out of the throne of God and of the Lamb.

All these are figures of Christ, and of the cleansing, sanctifying, life-giving, life-sustaining power of the Spirit of God.

The word "laver," in the Hebrew, signifies "like a river." The laver consisted of two parts, "the laver and his foot." The upper part or laver, being a large reservoir of water, from which, when required, the water poured down "like a river" into the foot or basin at its base. The lower part being alone used for bathing or washing, so that the water in the laver remained always pure and undefiled, reminding us of Titus iii.

5, 6, "The washing [literally laver] of regeneration, and renewing of the Holy Ghost; which He shed on us abundantly through Jesus Christ our Saviour." Also of "the supply of the Spirit of Jesus Christ," given for the ministry of the Word through the evangelist, pastor, and teacher, at the present time.

The laver presents Christ in two aspects; the FOOT, Christ in HUMILATION on earth; and the upper part, or laver proper, Christ in His exhaltation in heaven.

In His life on earth, Christ left us an example that we should follow in His steps.

On the Cross, from His pierced side came forth the water and the blood.

But it is from Christ crucified, risen, and exalted, that the Holy Ghost, the Comforter, the Spirit of purity and life, is now given. "In the last day, that great day of the feast, Jesus stood and cried, saying, If any man thirst, let him come unto Me and drink. He that believeth on Me, as the Scripture hath said, out of his belly shall flow rivers of living water. But this spake He of the Spirit, which they that believe on Him should receive; for the Holy Ghost was not yet given; because that Jesus was not yet glorified " (John vii. 37-39). We read in Ephesians v. 25, 26, " Christ loved the Church, and gave Himself for it, that He might sanctify and cleanse it with the washing of water by the Word." This is His present action, " that He might (ultimately) present it to Himself, a glorius Church, not having spot, or wrinkle, or any such thing " (Eph. v. 27).

ITS MATERIAL.

"A laver of brass, and his foot [base] also of brass."

Brass is the emblem of strength, and Christ, as our
sanctification, is the Strong One, mighty to sanctify as
well as "mighty to save." Many trust in Christ for
their salvation, but have recourse to their own efforts,
or to the law, for sanctification. Justification by faith
of Christ is the doctrine of the Reformation; but sanctification by the faith of Christ, how little apprehended!

There is POWER in the example of His life; constraining power in His dying and redeeming love;
power in looking unto Jesus glorified at God's right
hand above. Stephen found it so (Acts vii). Power
in the Spirit sent down from this ascended One. The
secret of power in the Christian experience is having
Christ " all " as our object, " and in all " as our life.

In Exodus xxxviii. 8, we read, " And he made the
laver of brass and the foot [base] of it of brass, of the
looking-glasses [brazen mirrors], of the women as-
sembling, which assembled at the door of the tent of
the congregation." This is significant, and intimates a
connection between self-examination and sanctification.
The Apostle James wrote, " But be ye doers of the
Word, and not hearers only, deceiving your own selves.
For if any be a hearer of the Word, and not a doer,
he is like unto a man beholding his natural face in a
glass; for he beholdeth himself, and goeth his way,
and straightway forgetteth what manner of man he
was. But whoso looketh into the perfect law of liberty, and continueth therein, he being not a forgetful

hearer, but a doer of the Word, this man shall be blessed in his deed" (James i. 22-25).

The foot of the laver was made of burnished brass.

Sanctification to the believer is especially and effectually connected with the contemplation of Christ, once crucified, but now risen and glorified, as exhibited in the mirror of the Word, through the power of the Holy Ghost sent down from heaven. This is real and divine photography. " Now the Lord is that Spirit : and where the Spirit of the Lord is, there is liberty. But we all, with open [unvailed] face beholding as in a glass [mirror] the glory of the Lord, are changed into the same image from glory to glory, even as by the Spirit of the Lord."

THE POSITION OF THE LAVER.

"And thou shalt put IT between the tabernacle [tent] of the congregation and between the altar."

The progress of the soul in drawing near to God is that set forth.

The soul first realising PARDON at the sin-offering without the camp.

Secondly, ACCEPTANCE at the brazen altar within the court.

Thirdly, SANCTIFICATION at the brazen laver.

Fourthly, NEARNESS IN WORSHIP at the golden altar.

Fifthly, ENTRANCE INTO THE HOLIEST through the value of the blood, and of the sweet incense from the golden censer, carried by the High Priest within the vail.

THE WATER.

Verse 18. **"And thou shalt put water therein."**

Christ loved the Church, and gave Himself for it, that He might sanctify and cleanse it with the washing of water by the Word" (Eph. v. 26). "Sanctify them through Thy truth; Thy Word is truth," is His prayer to the Father (John xvii. 17). "It is the Spirit that quickeneth; the flesh profiteth nothing : the words that I speak unto you, they are Spirit and they are life" (John vi. 63). Not the Word apart from the Spirit, nor the Spirit apart from the Word. It is the truth that sanctifies, and the Spirit is truth. But it is the truth of Christ, "as the truth is in Jesus."

The water which filled the laver in the wilderness came first from the smitten rock (Ex. xvii.) ; the type of Christ crucified, from whose pierced side flowed forth the water and the blood. For "that rock was Christ" (1 Cor. x. 4).

Secondly, it came from the rock which was to have been spoken to, at the end of the wilderness wanderings, in connection with the blooming, blossoming, and fruit-bearing rod (Numbers xx.). Typical of Christ glorified, and sending down the Spirit in answer to prayer (Acts ii.; John vii).

THE USE OF THE LAVER.

Verse 19. **"For Aaron and his sons shall wash their hands and their feet thereat [therefrom]."**

The laver sets forth Christ, made of God unto the believer SANCTIFICATION, practically (1 Cor. i. 30).

It is the action of the Lord Jesus in John xiii. embodied in type. The washing of the laver was twofold.

First, of the entire person, as at the consecration of the priests (Ex. xxix. 4), where it should be translated, "bathe them in water." This washing, or bathing in water, at their consecration was not repeated. To this the Lord refers John xiii. 10, "He that is washed [bathed] needeth not save to wash his feet, but is clean every whit." The signification of this bathing is given in Romans vi., Colossians ii. etc. It sets forth the death, burial, and resurrection of the believer with Christ, and faith's apprehension of it.

Secondly, this washing was partial, the washing of the hands and feet; and it is this which is here specially mentioned—its constant use. "Aaron and his sons" typify Christ and the Church in their priestly character (Heb. iii. 6). The sanctification is one : "For their sakes I sanctify Myself, that they also might be sanctified through the truth" (John xvii. 19). He is our sanctification.

The HANDS and FEET express the whole character of the believer's ACTION and CONDUCT. In John xiii. the feet only are mentioned, as including the whole course of the believer's walk.

"Thereat," literally, therefrom. It was not sufficient to wash elsewhere. It is the practical, conscious cleansing which flows from faith's apprehension of Christ, which fits for God's tent, and God's altar, and not that which comes from mere moral considerations or precepts.

Verse 20. "When they go into the Tabernacle [tent] of
   the congregation, they shall wash with water, that
   they die not; or when they come near to the altar to
   minister, to burn offering made by fire unto Jehovah."

This cleansing by the faith of Jesus, is essential to
living fellowship with the Father and the Son in the
Spirit, and to true fellowship with the saints. "Holiness becometh God's house for ever." "If I wash thee
not, thou hast no part with Me." Holiness becomes
God's service, as well as God's house. "Be ye clean
that bear the vessels of the Lord." " I will wash mine
hands in innocency; so will I compass Thine altar, O
Lord."

" That they die not," is repeated in verse 21. It may
be taken as a warning. " If ye live after the flesh ye
shall die." Spiritual deadness is the inevitable conse-
quence of the foot defiled, and sanctification through
personal intercourse with Christ neglected.

Verse 21. "So they shall wash their hands and their feet,
   that they die not: and it shall be a statute for ever for
   them, even to him and to his seed throughout their
   generations."

"It shall be a statute for ever;" a principle from
which God never departs. "Without holiness no man
shall see the Lord." Christ ever lives, the source of
life, holiness, and power, to all who draw nigh to God
by Him. Thus full provision is made in Christ, that
the blood-bought heirs of glory, and the royal priests
of our God, might ever worship Him in the beauties
of holiness, as well as in the confidence of faith and
love.

Directions for Setting Up the Tabernacle

Exodus xl. 1-8.

Verses 1, 2. "And Jehovah spake unto Moses, saying, On the first day of the first month shalt thou set up the tabernacle of the tent of the congregation."

THE first day of the first month is significant of a beginning, or beginning anew. A type of the commencement of the Christian dispensation at Pentecost. On the first day of the month the moon began to shine afresh on the earth with light reflected from the sun : so the Church, during the present night-time of the world, is appointed to shine in the light of an absent Christ. A dispensation altogether new; characterised by Messiah rejected, and the Comforter present, to communicate to the Church the truth of Christ, and to maintain His Lordship.

" The tabernacle of the tent of the congregation."

Both titles are here combined; the tabernacle being the type of a dwelling-place for God through the Spirit, and the tent of the congregation, typical of believers assembled in the Name of the Lord Jesus.

137

THE ARK.

Verse 3. "And thou shalt put therein the ark of the testimony, and cover the ark with the veil."

The ark is first mentioned, for it sets forth Jesus, God's centre of gathering to His own people, and in whom they are builded together for a habitation of God through the Spirit (Eph. ii. 22).

The veil was to be hung up before the ark, the Holy Ghost thus signifying that the way into the Holiest was not then made manifest; but to us since Calvary the veil is rent, and the way into the Holiest is open; for we gather to the name of a risen and glorified Christ.

It is here called "the Ark of the Testimony," for the purpose for which the Church is gathered is, that it should be a testimony to Him, and especially to the great "mystery of godliness, God manifested in flesh, justified in the Spirit, seen of angels, preached among the nations, believed on in the world, received up into glory."

THE TABLE.

Verse 4. "And thou shalt bring in the table, and set in order the things that are to be set in order upon it."

Where believers are gathered unto the Name of the Lord Jesus, and builded together for a habitation of God through the Spirit, there in God's presence, the sweet and sacred memorials of a Saviour's sufferings and death are to be observed.

It is remarkable that after the ark, the table is first

mentioned; and at Troas, on the first day of the week, the disciples came together to break bread (Acts xx. 7).

If the communion of saints in the presence of God, and in the remembrance of the sacrifice of Christ, is to be observed, it must be in God's *order.* "God is not the author of confusion." He has His order, and this must be maintained. The table is to be a pure table, and all things which are done in connection with it, must be done decently and in order, as in the presence and fear of God.

THE LAMPSTAND.

"And thou shalt bring in the lampstand, and light the lamps thereof."

Ministry, according to God, in the exercise of the gifts of the Spirit, and in testimony to the truth of Christ, has its place in connection with God's dwelling-place. It is to be brought in, and its light maintained. Ministry in the power of the Spirit of God, is to be in God's order, according to His mind and will; and the gifts of an ascended Saviour are "for the perfecting of the saints, for the work of the ministry, for the edifying of the Body of Christ."

THE ALTAR OF GOLD.

Verse 5. **"And thou shalt set the altar of gold for the incense before the ark of the testimony."**

Teaching us that the worship of the Father in the Spirit and in truth, is connected with Christ risen and glorified within the veil, through whom the believer has boldness and access with confidence by the faith of Him.

THE HANGING OF THE DOOR.

"And put the hanging of the door [entrance] to the tabernacle."

Christ said, "I am the door, by Me if any man enter in he shall be saved." Faith in, and confession of the name of Jesus, living, dying, risen and glorified, is the way, no mere ordinance, nor anything else, is to take the place of Christ.

THE ALTAR OF BURNT OFFERING.

Verse 6. "And thou shalt set the altar of the burnt offering [ascending offering] before the door [entrance] of the tabernacle of the tent of the congregation."

Christ, in death and resurrection, in His atoning and accepted sacrifice, is to be set forth as the only ground of communion and acceptance with God. And only through faith in Him can the communion of saints be enjoyed.

THE LAVER.

Verse 7. "And thou shalt set the laver between the tent of the congregation and the altar, and shall put water therein."

Christ is also to be set forth as made of God, SANCTIFICATION to the believer, as well as redemption; and the full provision of the Spirit of God for the sanctification of the believer through the truth, is to be testified to.

THE COURT AND THE GATE.

Verse 8. "And thou shalt set up the court round about, and hang up the hanging at the court gate."

Consistency of character and conduct with the confession of the name of Christ is to be maintained, and the exercise of fervent charity one towards another, with separation from the world, is to be manifested even when not assembled together in Church fellowship.

The Tabernacle Reared Up

Exodus xl. 9-19.

IN verses 9-16, we have the anointing of the Tabernacle and all therein, its vessels, the altar, and laver. Also the clothing and anointing of Aaron and his sons; but as we have had this subject previously, we now proceed at verse 17.

THE PERIOD WHEN THE TABERNACLE WAS REARED.

Verse 17. "And it came to pass in the first month in the second year, on the first day of the month, that the tabernacle was reared up."

The first day of the second year of Israel's experience as a redeemed people, was an important period in their history. On this day the Tabernacle was set up.

On the day of the SECOND month, in the second year after they were come out of the land of Egypt, the commandment was given for the numbering of the children of Israel from twenty years old and upward; all that were able to go forth to war in Israel (Numbers i. 1, 2).

And on the day that Moses had FULLY SET up the Tabernacle, and anointed it and sanctified it, and all the vessels thereof, the princes of Israel that were over them that were numbered, presented their offering to

142

Jehovah of six covered waggons, twelve oxen, with twelve silver chargers, and spoons of gold full of incense, with the ascending offerings, sin offerings, and peace offerings, and twelve days were occupied with the presentation (Numbers vii.).

During the FIRST year the lessons of the wilderness were learnt : What the wilderness was ; what the flesh was, both under grace (Ex. xix. 4-6), and under law ; and what God was in the various manifestations of His character.

With the SECOND year, Israel's experience in connection with the Tabernacle commences, and to this period the books of Leviticus and Numbers apply.

The FIRST year is typical of the Christian's individual experience ; the SECOND, of his experience in connection with the Church of God, and in association with others professing Christianity.

THE TABERNACLE SET UP. "And Moses reared up the Tabernacle." The Tabernacle is first mentioned before the tent of the congregation ; for the first thought in the mind of the Spirit is a habitation for God, before that which represents the assembly of God's saints is spoken of.

"And fastened his sockets." The sockets of silver composed of the redemption money of the children of Israel. Thus, typically, the foundations of God's Tabernacle are laid in redemption.

"And set up the boards thereof." Typical of those believers who are gathered together to the confession of the name of Jesus, individually, standing firm on redemption, and collectively forming God's Tabernacle or dwelling-place (Eph. ii. 22).

"And put in the bars thereof." For the compacting and establishment of the whole. Like the joints and bands, the gifts of the Spirit for the edifying of the Body of Christ (Eph. iv.).

"And reared up his pillars." The four pillars which held up the vail, corresponding with the four inspired historians of the life and death of Jesus; and the five pillars which supported the hanging of the door; answering to the apostles and prophets, the evangelists, pastors, and teachers, who exhibit Jesus as the way of entrance into the Tabernacle of God. And thus the Church becomes not only the house of God, and Church of the living God, but also the pillar and ground of the truth, for the manifestation and maintenance of the truth of God in the world.

THE TENT OF THE CONGREGATION SPREAD.

Verse 19. "And he spread abroad the tent over the Tabernacle, and put the covering of the tent above upon it; as Jehovah commanded Moses."

The tent over the Tabernacle, or the tent of the Congregation, represents the assembly of believers, meeting in the Name of Jesus, who, in Spirit also, compose the habitation of God.

The covering of the tent was twofold.

First, the covering of ram's skins dyed red, typical

of the atoning work of the Lord Jesus, under the shelter of which the Church is seen by God.

Secondly, the covering of badger's skins, above and over all, significant of the external lowly form and pilgrim character of the Church on earth.

All done according to the Will and Word of God.

The Overshadowing Cloud and the Indwelling Glory.

Exodus xi. 34, 35.

MOSES having set up the ARK in the most holy place, and brought the ALTAR OF INCENSE, the LAMP-STAND, and the TABLE into the sanctuary or holy place; and having reared up the COURT, and brought in the LAVER, and the BRAZEN ALTAR, "as Jehovah commanded Moses."

Verse 34. "Then the cloud covered the tent of the congregation, and the glory of Jehovah filled the Tabernacle."

The EXTERNAL and INTERNAL manifestation of the Divine presence, protection and glory; Divine and almighty protection above, and Divine glory within. For "he that dwelleth in the secret place of the Most High, shall abide under the shadow of the Almighty." God Himself is "a wall of fire round about His people, and the glory in the midst." "The Spirit of glory and of God resteth upon them." "The eternal God is their refuge, and underneath are the everlasting arms."

This overshadowing cloud and this indwelling glory was a prefiguring of what took place at Pentecost,

when the Church of God first commenced its history
and its course, and when believers were first builded
together for a habitation of God, through the Spirit.
" And when the day of Pentecost was fully come, they
were all with one accord in one place. And suddenly
there came a sound from heaven as of a rushing
mighty wind, and it filled all the house where they
were sitting. And there appeared unto them cloven
tongues like as of fire, and it sat upon each one of
them. And they were all filled with the Holy Ghost,
and began to speak with other tongues, as the Spirit
gave them utterance."

See also the inspired prayer of the Apostle in Eph.
iii., that being strengthened by God's Spirit in the
inner man, Christ dwelling in the heart by faith, believers might be filled into all the fulness of God.

Seven times the Word of God testified that Moses
had done each particular as Jehovah commanded.
Then, and not till then, the cloud covered the tent, and
the glory filled the Tabernacle.

There is a principle of the utmost importance which
throws a Divine light on many a perplexing question.
Jude said unto the Lord, " How is it that Thou wilt
manifest Thyself unto us, and not unto the world?
Jesus answered and said unto him, If a man love Me
he will keep My Words : and My Father will love him,
and We will come unto him, and make Our abode
with him " (John xiv. 22, 23).

So when Solomon had finished the house of Jehovah,
according to the Divine will and pattern, then " the

cloud filled the house of Jehovah, so that the priests could not stand to minister because of the cloud, for the glory of Jehovah had filled the house of Jehovah " (1 Kings viii. 10, 11).

Isaiah prophesies of the future blessing to Israel, when " Jehovah will create upon every dwelling-place of Mount Zion, and upon her assemblies, a cloud and smoke by day, and the shining of a flaming fire by night; for upon all the glory shall be a defence " (Isaiah iv. 5).

Ezekiel, who saw in a vision the glory taking its gradual departure from the first Temple (Ezek. x., xi), afterwards also in a vision saw the glory returning to the millennial Temple. " And, behold, the glory of Jehovah filled the house of Jehovah " (Ezekiel xliv. 4).

John, in the apocalyptic vision of the Church's future blessedness, as the Bride of the Lamb, saw that great city, the holy Jerusalem, but " saw no Temple therein, for Jehovah, God Almighty and the Lamb are the temple of it. And the city had no need of the sun, neither of the moon to shine in it, for the glory of God did lighten it, and the Lamb is the lamp thereof " (Rev. xxi. 22, 23).

> There no Temple rose before him,
>   There no glory shone above;
> All was Temple, all was glory,
>   All in all was God and love.

The saints in glory will dwell in God, and God in them. His glory is their overshadowing cloud; His presence is their indwelling glory.

Verse 35. "And Moses was not able to enter into the tent of the congregation, because the cloud abode thereon, and the glory of Jehova filled the Tabernacle."

And so on the Mount of Transfiguration, when Moses and Elijah appeared with Jesus in glory, there came a bright cloud and overshadowed them, and the disciples feared as they entered into the cloud. And there came a voice out of the cloud, saying, " This is My beloved Son, hear Him." And when the voice was past, Jesus was found alone (Luke ix. 34-36). Thus, whether it be Moses the servant of God, or the priests in Solomon's Temple in their priestly ministry, or the two men on the Mount of Transfiguration, all give place to the glory of God and of the Lamb.

THE GUIDANCE OF THE CLOUD.

Exodus xl. 36-38. "And when the cloud was taken up from over the Tabernacle, the children of Israel went onward in all their journeys; but if the cloud were not taken up, then they journeyed not till the day that it was taken up. For the cloud of Jehovah was upon the Tabernacle by day, and fire was on it by night, in the sight of all the House of Israel throughout all their journeys."

The people of God are a journeying people, yet He will never leave them nor forsake them. The great thing is to walk with God, so as ever to enjoy the light and guidance of His presence. Moses said, "If Thy presence go not *with us*, carry us not up hence" (Ex. xxxiii. 15). Who that values that presence, but will often be presenting the same petition? The PRESENCE

OF GOD with us—How seasonable! How suitable!
Shade in sunshine! Light in darkness! Abiding with
us while we tarry! Going before us when we move.

There is one thing of all-importance taught us here.
God's guidance of His people, and the manifestation of
His presence with them, is connected with the Tabernacle, His dwelling-place among them. It was "when
the cloud was taken up FROM OVER THE TABERNACLE,
the children of Israel went onward." Their individual
movements were controlled by God's acting in connection with the Tabernacle. So with us, if our individual
actions are not influenced by the manifestation of
God's presence and actings with the assembly, no wonder if we miss His guidance, and walk in darkness.

Not only were the children of Israel to pitch round
about the Tabernacle, having it as their centre, the
very place of their tents being regulated by the position
of the Tabernacle, because it was God's dwelling-
place; but their every movement was to harmonise
with God's movements in connection with it.

Oh, for grace ever to remember and to act on this!
We are so prone to make self our centre, and our individual interests and comforts, temporal or spiritual,
the guides of our actions, that we need every now and
then to be broken off from them, and to be brought
back to God, and to the things of God.

May we value the presence of God with us, and the
unclouded sunshine of His smile in our individual

pathway. But may we also seek the manifestation of His presence in the assembly of His saints, so as ever to see His power and His glory as we have seen it in the sanctuary.

May the chill and the darkness, occasioned by the loss of His smile, be to us a warning of our wandering, if we turn aside to the right hand or to the left; whether it be in our individual course, or in our Church associations. May we walk, O God, in the light of Thy countenance, the confident language of our hearts being this, "Thou shalt guide us with Thy council, and afterward receive us to glory."

SOLOMON'S TEMPLE
AND ITS TEACHING

Solomon's Temple on Moriah

Interior of Solomon's Temple

Solomon's Temple and its Teaching

THOMAS NEWBERRY

CONTENTS

Solomon's Temple and its Teaching

INTRODUCTION

WHEN the Lord God—Jehovah-Elohim, the Triune God—had planted the garden of Eden, and filled it with everything that could delight the senses, he placed man there. Adam and Eve having sinned, and hearing the voice of God, walking in the garden in the cool of the day, they hid themselves from His presence amongst the trees. God asked, "Adam, where art thou?" And he said, "I heard Thy voice . . . and I was afraid" (Gen. iii., 10).

Concerning Enoch, the seventh from Adam, it is recorded that "he walked with God" (Gen. v., 21-24). The word is the same as is used of Jehovah *walking* in the garden. It is implied that before the Fall, God walked with man and man with God. "Enoch walked with God." When he struck out on that path he was not the inventor of it. God had set the example. He desires companionship with us more than we do with Him. The walk begun in Eden, broken off by sin, was renewed with Enoch, amid the evils of a fallen world, continued with Noah and all the children of faith onward to the Cross. A Sunday-school teacher, explaining the translation of Enoch to her class, thus expressed herself:—"God was in the habit of taking long walks with Enoch, and one evening, when they had gone far and talked so long, it was too late for Enoch to go back to his home, so God took him home with Him." Thus shall it be with all who walk with God. That walk begun in Paradise before the Fall, renewed in grace, taken up in resurrection by the Lord Jesus, will be continued in the Paradise of God through eternity, in that eternal day which knows no shadow and no evening. "In a moment, in the twinkling of an eye" the Lord will come and take His pilgrim people who walk with Him down here to be for ever with Himself at home up there. (1 Thess. iv., 16. 17) "The Lamb which is in the midst of the throne shall feed them and shall lead them" (Rev. vii., 17). According to His own words, "I go to prepare a place for you. . . . I come again, and will receive you unto Myself" (John xiv., 2, 3).

CHAPTER ONE

GOD'S EARTHLY DWELLING-PLACES

THERE are three structures mentioned in the Word of which God was pleased to give patterns and particular instructions:—First, the Tabernacle in the Wilderness; next, the Temple of Solomon, on Mount Moriah; and, thirdly—yet in the future—the Temple spoken of by Ezekiel—the Millennial Temple.

God, in the condescendence of His grace, has caused His Word to be written, so that His children may not be ignorant. He has given His Spirit also to guide them into all the truth. The Word of God is an illustrated Book, full of object-lessons conveying spiritual truths. Of these the chief are the Tabernacle and the Temple. Creation has its voice to man. "The heavens declare the glory of God, and the firmament showeth His handiwork" (Psalm xix., 1), so that men are without excuse (Rom. i., 20) as to the acknowledgment of His eternal power and Godhead. In the two structures of which He is the designer and the architect, "every whit speaks His glory" (Psalm xxix., 9). This makes them of eternal interest to us.

THE TABERNACLE IN THE WILDERNESS

When the children of Israel were brought out from

11

Egypt under shelter of the blood of the paschal lamb, on their way to Canaan, God could speak to them, as a redeemed people, concerning a sanctuary for Himself —God's dwelling-place with man on earth. He gave Moses a pattern of the Tabernacle; He revealed to him upon Mount Sinai His own thoughts about it, and directed him to make all things according to the pattern shown him (Ex. xxv., 8, 9). The Tabernacle in the wilderness, which was thus made in accordance with God's command, is an appropriate and expressive type of the Church of God in its *present* wilderness condition during this dispensation—the dwelling-place of God in His redeemed, according to the Word—"I will dwell in them and walk with them; and I will be their God, and they shall be My people" (2 Cor. vi., 16). "But will God in very deed dwell with men on the earth? Behold, heaven and the heaven of heavens cannot contain Him" (2 Chron. vi., 18). What a vivid idea Solomon gives us of the infinitude of God in that expression! All created things are finite, unlimited as the spaces occupied by them may appear to us—heavens stretching beyond heavens in apparently interminable succession, but, in the nature of things, limited. Not so God; He is infinite. The Apostle John writes of the holy Jerusalem: "I saw no temple therein: for Jehovah God Almighty and the Lamb are the temple of it" (Rev. xxi., 22). When the Lord Jesus was on earth, He was God's dwelling-place (John i., 14). The redeemed are God's temple in which He dwells (Eph. ii., 22); but God

Himself is the temple in which they worship. Creation cannot contain His fulness; but those who love Him and abide in Him are filled INTO all the fulness of God (Eph. iii., 19). God says, "Heaven is My throne, and earth is My footstool." "I dwell in the high and holy place, with him also that is of a contrite and humble spirit" (Isa. lvii., 15; lxvi., 1, 2). Marvellous condescension of Divine and infinite love! God seeking the companionship of men! He desired to renew it with Israel, and, through them, with the rest of mankind. Broken by sin, He longed to renew it and this He has done through redemption, as is here set forth in type. No sooner was the sanctuary provided, and everything accomplished according to God's word, than "the glory of Jehovah filled the tabernacle" (Ex. xl., 34).

CHAPTER TWO

THE TEMPLES OF SCRIPTURE

THERE are five temples mentioned in Scripture. The FIRST is the Temple of Solomon, built on Mount Moriah, connected with Israel in the land, a type of all the redeemed who have part in the first resurrection—not alone the saints of the present dispensation, but including all from Adam and Eve and Abel, on to the coming of our Lord Jesus Christ, and our gathering together to Him, the true King of kings. The Temple of Solomon, because of the transgression of the children of Israel, was given over into the hands of their enemies. It was destroyed by the Chaldeans because Israel had defiled it, and the holy vessels were carried away to Babylon.

The SECOND is the Temple of Ezra. When Israel had completed the seventy years of captivity, God in fulfilment of His promise, stirred up Cyrus to give commandment for the rebuilding of the Temple on its ancient site (Ezra i., 1-6), God using His prophets Haggai and Zechariah to strengthen the hands of the children of Israel who returned from the Babylonish captivity. Though this temple was inferior to that of Solomon, it was built on the same site, and God was pleased to own it with the manifestations of His presence.

The THIRD Temple was that of Herod the Great,

14

the Idumean king, which was forty-six years in building; and whilst, no doubt, it retained some portions of the original structure, it differed from both Solomon's and Ezra's, especially in the arrangement of the courts. From the account given by Josephus, it seems to have been larger than Solomon's, and was built according to his own taste, much being added. There were added the Court of the Gentiles and the Court of the Women, of which the Word of God says nothing. This is the Temple which was in existence when our Lord was upon earth. There is much confusion in the minds of some as to the place where our Lord and His disciples worshipped. They could not enter the Courts of the Priests or draw near to the altar. When we read of the Lord and His disciples going up to the Temple, we are not to suppose that they entered beyond the exterior courts. The Holy Ghost has employed two distinct words in the original Greek of the New Testament in speaking of the Temple: one is *Hieron* (from *hieros*, sacred or priestly), which refers to the whole Temple, its courts and other buildings—the external structure. The other word, *Naos* (from *nais*, to dwell) signifies the inner building, embracing the porch, the holy and most holy places—the sanctuary. It was into the external courts our Lord went, for, not being of the tribe of Levi, He could not enter the inner Temple. "Christ is not entered into holy places made with hands" (Heb. ix., 24). Into the holy place the priests entered to trim the lamps in the morning and light them in the evening; to burn incense, morning and evening, on the golden altar; and to arrange, once a week, the shewbread on the tables. Consequently, Zacharias (Luke i., 8-10) was alone in the Temple, while the people prayed without, at time of incense.

This Temple of Herod was destroyed by the Roman army under Titus, Anno Domini 70. The destruction was foretold by our Lord Himself when He said to His disciples that not one stone should be left upon another (Matt. xxiv., 1, 2). It had also been foretold by the Spirit of God through the prophet Daniel in that wondrous vision of the seventy weeks of years (Dan. ix., 24-27). The Jews reckoned years by periods of weeks (from *shebang*, seven) as well as days. In Dan. x., 2 it is weeks of days. The angel Gabriel informed Daniel, "Seventy weeks (of years) are determined (cut out) upon thy people and upon thy holy city." These seventy weeks commenced "from the going forth of the commandment to restore and build Jerusalem" (Neh. ii.)—from the date of that commandment from Artaxerxes "unto Messiah the Prince" (not the Sacrifice, thus taking in the whole period) "shall be seven weeks" (that is, forty-nine years), during which the wall and the street shall be built "in troublous times." After the "threescore and two weeks" (making up, with the previous seven weeks, sixty-nine weeks—four hundred and eighty-three years) "shall Messiah be cut off," mark "but not for Himself"—literally, "and nothing to Him," or, as some render it "He shall have nothing." Thus sixty-nine weeks are accounted for. The seventieth week is in abeyance. The present dispensation fills up the gap—that period during which Israel is in rejection because she rejected the Messiah—a time of mercy to the Gentiles, for God is taking out of them a people for His name, and a remnant of Israel according to the election of grace. As Daniel foretold, after the cutting off of Messiah, "the *people* of the prince that shall come shall destroy the city and the sanctuary." The "prince that shall come" is Antichrist, the Lawless One, the Man of Sin, the head of the Roman Empire in its final form. The Romans were "the people of the prince." The cutting off of Messiah was to be a preliminary fact to the destruction of the city and Temple. All this has come to pass as God had said.

Now we come to the FOURTH Temple mentioned in the Sacred Scriptures. Read Daniel ix., 26, 27, xii., 11; Matt. xxiv., 15-22; 2 Thess. ii., 1-8; Rev. xi., 1, 2. Our Lord says Jerusalem shall be trodden down of the Gentiles till the times of the Gentiles are fulfilled (Luke xxi., 24). Israel had been carried away and scattered among the nations. There is no temple of God, no earthly house in which He has placed His name now, but, in order that the Word of God may be fulfilled, there will be a temple on earth called by His name in which the Antichrist will appear. At the time of the end the prince shall come, of whom our Lord foretells, "Another shall come in his own name; him ye will receive." When he comes he will make a covenant with the Jews of "one week" (seven years). Here we get the missing week of years, thus completing the seventy. The prince, the head of the Roman Empire, in the midst of the week, according to another prophecy, breaks the covenant, and takes away the daily sacrifice. The "abomination of desolation" is to be set up in the Holy Place, as we read in 2 Thessalonians ii., 4, "He as God sitteth in the temple of God, showing himself that he is God." The moment that sign appears, the Lord warns His people to flee, and in His tender grace to pray that their flight may not be in the winter nor on the Sabbath Day. There must be a temple of God (Rev. xi.) in which Antichrist is to show himself thus, an altar recognised as an "altar of God," a daily sacrifice which can be taken away, a Sabbath Day observed. Thus we have the last week of Daniel divided into two portions, three and a half years from the time the covenant begins until the taking away of the daily sacrifice. Then comes the time of great tribulation (Matt. xxiv., 21).

The Mosque of Omar or "Dome of the Rock" stands on that marble platform which was the firm foundation of the former temples, on the spot which David bought of Araunah the Jebusite, and where Abraham offered up his son Isaac. For centuries it has been kept sacred in the hands of the Mohammedans, and thus preserved from the idolatries of the Romish and the Greek Church.

The FIFTH will be the Millennial Temple, as fully described in the last nine chapters of the Prophet Ezekiel. It will be built in the land of Israel during the millennial period, and will be the centre of worship for Israel and all the inhabitants of the earth. According to Isaiah lxvi., 23, and lvi., 7, "My house shall be called a house of prayer for all nations." "All nations shall flow into it" (Isaiah ii., 2). This temple will be erected in the midst of the priests' portion of the holy oblation (Ezekiel xlv., 1-5).

CHAPTER THREE

PREPARATIONS FOR THE TEMPLE

DAVID'S FIRST THOUGHT

AFTER David had been established on the throne and his kingdom at peace, he set his heart on building a house for Jehovah. That which at first led David to think of building the Temple, doubtless under Divine guidance, was a desire to provide a suitable resting-place for the Ark of the Covenant, as connected with the manifestation of God's presence with Israel. "David said to Nathan the prophet, Lo, I dwell in a house of cedars, but the Ark of the Covenant of Jehovah remaineth under curtains" (1 Chron. xvii., 1. See also Psalm cxxxii). But Jehovah told David that Solomon his son was to build the house to His name.

THE RANSOM MONEY

We read in Exodus xxx. God's commandment concerning the numbering of the children of Israel in the wilderness, that, when the people were taken account of, from twenty years old and upwards, each one numbered among the people of God was to bring a ransom for his soul, a bekah or twenty gerahs, the half shekel of the sanctuary (the

20

didrachma of the New Testament, value about fifteen pence) (see Matt. xvii., 24-27), "that there might be no plague"; the ransom price being paid into the treasury of God, they were numbered as a ransomed or redeemed people. In Exodus xxxviii., we find it amounted to one hundred talents and one thousand seven hundred and seventy-five shekels of silver, each talent being about 114 lbs. of our weight, or £343 3s. 9d. in value. Of these, one hundred talents of silver were cast for the sockets of the tabernacle, ninety-six for the sockets of the boards, and four for the pillars of the veil; the remainder of the silver was for the hooks, chapiters, and connecting rods of the pillars. What was all this a type of? The Spirit of God through the Apostle Peter throws the light of Heaven on this subject, in the words, "Ye were not redeemed with corruptible things, as silver or gold, . . . but with the precious blood of Christ" (1 Peter i., 18, 19). This is "the redemption which is in Christ Jesus." "It is the blood that maketh atonement for the soul" (Romans iii., 2). This typical tabernacle of God in the wilderness, pitched on the sands of the desert, each board of shittim wood fixed in their sockets of silver, was founded on the redemption, foreshadowing the redemption price of God's own spotless Lamb, on which alone our souls can rest, as builded together for a habitation of God through the Spirit.

DAVID'S TEMPTATION

God permitted Satan to tempt David, and David, acting under the instigation of the adversary, requested Joab to number the children of Israel, for, it would appear, his own gratification, "that I may know the number of the people." They were not numbered as God's redeemed, but as the people of David, consequently judgment followed. There is no mention of the redemption price having been paid. The angel of God went forth in judgment, and seventy thousand in Israel in three days fell. On David's confession of his sin, God, in His tender mercy and longsuffering, abundant in goodness, as well as in truth, commanded by the prophet Gad that David should build an altar to Jehovah on the threshing-floor of Ornan (or Araunah) the Jebusite. David obeyed. He purchased the threshing-floor for fifty shekels of SILVER, with the oxen and implements (2 Samuel xxiv., 24), paying its full value, the legal price; but he GAVE for the surrounding place, or land, six hundred shekels of GOLD, a place for the courts of Jehovah's house, a site for the Temple. David there erected an altar, offered sacrifice, a burnt or ascending offering, and a peace offering, and God showed His acceptance by answering David by fire from Heaven, accepting the sacrifice as a savour of rest to Himself. SILVER is the emblem of redemption; therefore for the site on which atonement was made silver was paid. GOLD is the emblem of Divine glory, and gold was given for the site of the Temple. Christ redeemed us from the curse of the law, having been made a curse for us, thus satisfying justice to the full, but He has redeemed us TO everlasting glory; and the glory which the Father gives Him He shares with His people (John xvii., 22). The demands of law have been met, and the atonement price fully paid in the blood of the Lamb; but, over and above all this, glory has been GIVEN in the riches of Divine grace. In Matt. xiii., the FIELD was purchased for the sake of the TREASURE hid in it; the PEARL for its own preciousness and beauty.

DAVID'S PROVISION FOR THE TEMPLE

David, "in his trouble," "before his death," prepared abundantly for the house of his God (1 Chron. xxii). He considered that the house to be built to Jehovah should be "exceeding magnifical of fame and of glory throughout all countries," and he made provision accordingly. He provided "a hundred thousand talents of gold." A talent of gold is considered to be of about 114 lb. weight, and is computed to be worth £5,475 of English money. Thus a hundred thousand talents would amount to five hundred and forty-seven millions five hundred thousand pounds sterling. And he also provided "a thousand thousand talents of silver." This, at £342 the talent, amounts to three hundred and forty-two millions of pounds. These together, GOLD and SILVER, eight hundred and eighty-nine million five hundred thousand pounds sterling! He provided also of brass and iron without weight, for it was in abundance, and timber and stone also, all manner of precious stones and marble stones! Moreover, "because he had set his affection to the house of his God," he gave of his own proper good, over and above what he had prepared, "three thousand talents of gold of the gold of Ophir," amounting in value to £16,425,000, "and seven thousand talents of refined silver," amounting to £2,394,000, "to overlay [plaster] the walls of the houses withal" (1 Chron. xxix., 3, 4). David in the first instance (1 Chron. xxii.) provides with all his MIGHT, in the second instance (1 Chron. xxix., 1-4) because he had set his AFFECTION on the house of his God; the former we may say was a work of faith, the latter a labour of love. Faith works with all its might, Love impoverishes itself to enrich its object, provides its utmost and its best. David, not content with emptying the exchequer of his kingdom, so to speak, throws in his own private property over and above, not only gold, but gold of Ophir; not only silver, but refined silver; reminding us of Him who, though He was rich, yet for our sakes became poor (2 Cor. viii., 9).

In addition to this, the chiefs, princes, and captains of Israel contributed five thousand talents of gold and ten thousand drams, ten thousand talents of silver, eighteen thousand talents of brass, and one hundred thousand talents of iron. "And they with whom precious stones were found gave them to the treasure of the house of Jehovah." "Then the people rejoiced, for that they offered willingly." This was a matter of joy. "David the king also rejoiced with great joy" (1 Chron. xxix., 6-22). In noticing the contributions, we may observe that the Spirit of God not only mentions the talents but the drams; so, whatever is done for God in the name of the Lord Jesus, be it ever so little in man's estimation, has a value set upon it. Even a cup of cold water is not overlooked.

The magnificence of the house consisted, not so much in its size as in its structure and material. God was its architect, so planning it that it might be a pattern of spiritual and heavenly realities; and its materials were designed to be emblematical of excellencies and glories which are spiritual, heavenly, and divine. When we consider the enormous value of the gold and silver contributed for the Temple, unbelieving atheism may ask, "To what purpose was this waste?" But that which was expended on the house of God and devoted to His glory was not wasted. There is such a thing as laying up "treasures in heaven, where neither moth nor rust doth corrupt, and where thieves do not break through nor steal."

SOLOMON'S PREPARATION

"Solomon determined to build a house for the name of Jehovah" (2 Chron. ii., 1). DAVID may be regarded especially as a type of Jesus in His humiliation and sufferings on earth; SOLOMON of Christ in resurrection and heavenly glory. Solomon sends to Huram or Hiram, king of Tyre, informing him of his design, in these remarkable words, "Behold, I build a house to the name of Jehovah my God, to dedicate it to Him." "And the house which I build is great; for great is our God above all gods. But who is able to build Him a house, seeing the heaven and heaven of heavens cannot contain Him? Who am I, then,

that should build Him a house, save only to burn
sacrifice [incense] before Him?" (2 Chron. ii.). And
reminding Hiram that he had sent cedars to David his
father, Solomon requests him to send a skilled workman, cedar trees, fir or cypress trees, and algum trees
out of Lebanon. To this Hiram consents, promising
to send the cedar and fir trees by floats to Jaffa; and
Solomon was to give to the workmen wheat and oil
(1 Kings vi., 1-12; 2 Chron. ii).

SOLOMON'S WORKMEN

He raised a levy out of Israel of thirty thousand,
whom he sent to Lebanon: ten thousand a month by
courses, so that they were a month in Lebanon and
two months at home. Adoniram was over this levy.
And of the strangers that were in Israel he sent seventy
thousand to be bearers of burdens, eighty thousand to
be hewers in the mountains, and three thousand and
six hundred officers and overseers (2 Chron. ii., 2, 17,
18). It was under Solomon that we see this remarkable combination of JEW and GENTILE in the work;
so it is CHRIST JESUS, risen and glorified, of whom
Solomon was a type, who builds the Temple of God,
and having reconciled both Jew and Gentile unto God
in one body by the Cross, employs those who are His
own, called out from both, in His service.

Christ incarnate was God's living Temple while
He was on earth. When He spake of the Temple of
God, it was "the temple of His body" (John ii., 19-21).
But Christ, risen and glorified, is the chief corner-
stone of the heavenly Temple, uniting JEW AND

GENTILE in Himself, "in WHOM all the building, fitly framed together, groweth unto a holy Temple in the Lord" (Eph. ii., 20, 21). When the present dispensation is past, Jew and Gentile will again be recognised and dealt with separately by God; but all such distinctions are unknown in the Church, which is His body and His temple.

CHAPTER FOUR

THE FOUNDATION PLATFORM

IN order to raise the surrounding ground to a level with the threshing floor, the place of the altar on its summit, a foundation platform of stupendous structure was built. It was to form this foundation platform that the Lord gave commandment, as we read in 1 Kings v., 17, "And the king commanded, and they brought great stones, costly stones, *and* hewed stones, to lay the foundation of the house." This broad platform, level and secure, was for the erection of the Temple, its courts, and other buildings. "And the foundation was of costly stones, even great stones, stones of ten cubits, and stones of eight cubits" (1 Kings vii., 10)—in plain language, about twenty feet and sixteen feet in length. These firm foundation stones remain intact beneath the surface to the present day. One of the great services which the Palestine Exploration Fund Committee has rendered to the Church of God is the investigation which they have so skilfully carried on in respect to this foundation platform. It is an oblong structure, in round numbers about one thousand five hundred feet long, and about one thousand feet in breadth; it is known as the *Haram-esh-Sherref*, or Noble Sanctuary of the

Mohammedans. The surface is nearly level, carpeted with grass; cypresses are found there, and oratories and mosques. About the centre of the enclosure rises a platform nearly square, about sixteen feet in height, formed in part of masonry, in part of the native rock, and paved with stone slabs, on which stands that which is now known as the Mosque of Omar, which the Mohammedans call *Kubbet-es-Sakhra*, or "Dome of the Rock." Above the surface of this platform time has done its work; siege after siege has committed ravages; but below the surface, to a depth of sixty, seventy, or one hundred and twenty feet, there have been discovered those vast stones of which we read in the Sacred Record, so closely joined that scarcely a pen-knife could be put between the joints; without cement, firm and immovable. On some of them may be seen the marks of the builders, in red vermilion.

FOUNDATION TRUTHS

This foundation platform is built upon Mount Moriah—Moriah, the vision or manifestation of Jah or Jehovah; as it was said, "In the mount of Jehovah it shall be seen." In that wondrous twenty-second chapter of Genesis, we have not only foretold God's own Lamb which He has provided, but we have there the mount of Jehovah—JEHOVAH JIREH. Solomon as a wise master-builder, went deep, and laid the foundations upon a rock: hence their security. Let us learn from it afresh the lesson of our Lord in the seventh chapter of Matthew, that, however "well builded," however skilfully erected, our house may be, if built on sand, when the hour of trial comes and the overwhelming scourge passes through, it must come down. When God lays judgment to the line and justice to the plummet, He will sweep away every "refuge of lies." It is on GOD that the firm foundations of our faith for time and for eternity must rest. If our faith is in Christ, it must be in THE CHRIST OF GOD, founded upon the character, the perfections, and the attributes of the unchanging, eternal God. "Trust ye in Jehovah for ever: for in Jah (Jehovah) is the Rock of Ages" (Isa. xxvi., 4). *Jah*—the title of God in the eternity of His existence, "inhabiting eternity," to whom past, present, and to come is one eternal NOW. *Jehovah*—the title of God as the everlasting one, "that is, and was, and is to come." God's PUR- POSES and PLANS connected with the ransom of man in time, and the monument of His eternal glory to be erected thereupon in eternity, were laid deep in the counsels of eternity; the work was according to the eternal purpose, the purpose of the ages, which He purposed in our Lord Jesus Christ (Eph. iii., 11). The FATHER in eternity laid the stupendous plan. The SON laid down His life to accomplish it. The eternal SPIRIT renders the work effectual in each believing soul. "Other foundation can no man lay than that is laid, which is Jesus Christ" (1 Cor. iii., 9-11). "This is the stone which was set at nought of [by] you builders, which is become the head of the corner. Neither is there salvation in any other: for there is none other name under heaven given among men whereby we can be saved" (Acts iv., 11, 12). If faith is to be steadfast and secure, it is not to be for ever laying and relaying the foundation. "Not laying again the foundation of repentance from dead works, and of faith toward God, of the doctrine of baptisms, and of laying on of hands, and of resurrection of the dead, and of eternal judgment" (Heb. vi., 1, 2). Let these vast truths be taught as the rudiments and foundations of our knowledge of Divine things—unchanging, immovable. There can be no glory to God, no salvation to men, where there is no Divine foundation. It is no building of God, no habitation of God through the Spirit, if the DIVINITY *of Christ is denied.* The rock foundation of our faith must be "God manifest in the flesh." As the Apostle says, "To whom coming, as unto a living stone, disallowed indeed of men, but chosen of God, and precious, ye also as lively [living] stones, are built up a spiritual house. . . . Wherefore also it is contained in the Scripture, Behold, I lay in Sion a chief corner-stone, elect, precious; and he that believeth on Him shall not be confounded [ashamed]" (1 Peter ii., 4-8). Christ Himself, in His person and work, is the chief corner-stone of the whole. The ROCK is the truth of God which He reveals to the soul, as in the case of Peter (see Matt. xvi., 15-18), when he confessed, "THOU art the Christ, the Son of the living God." And Jesus answered and said unto him, "Blessed art thou, Simon Bar-jona: for flesh and blood hath not revealed it unto thee, but My Father which is in heaven. And I say unto thee,

That THOU art Peter [a stone], and upon this rock I will build My church." Then we also read, "built upon the foundation of the apostles and prophets, Jesus Christ Himself being the chief corner" [foundation corner] (Eph. ii., 20). The apostles and prophets of the New Testament dispensation, through whom the truth of God was revealed and given to us, built upon those great and grand foundation truths contained in the inspired Scriptures of the New Testament in full confirmation, dovetailed in, and builded together with the massive truths of the Old; resting upon the same foundation. Every doctrine of revealed truth is truth as it is in Jesus—all centering in His blessed person, all in harmony with His work, accomplished at no less a cost than the incarnation, sufferings, and death of the Son of God.

Then, again, where there is no DIVINE, ETERNAL SPIRIT, there can be no Christ. Who is the Christ? The *Christos* in the Greek, which means the ANOINTED—"The Spirit of Jehovah is upon Me, because He hath anointed Me" (see Luke iv., 16-21)—is the answer. You cannot have Christianity without Christ; you cannot have Christ without the Spirit; you cannot have the Son without the Father, nor the Father apart from the Son. To take away or deny one of these foundation truths is to disturb the whole, for these things, like those great massive stones of the Temple foundation, are embedded together.

CHAPTER FIVE

THE MEASUREMENTS AND STRUCTURE

IT is by combining the statements in 1 Kings vi., 2 Chron. iii., and Ezekiel xl., xli., etc., that we ascertain the dimensions and details of the Temple and its courts; some particulars being given in one place, some in another; but, wherever the measurements are repeated in the different books, they perfectly coincide, or differ only in a manner which helps to ascertain the truth. In general the INTERNAL measurements are given rather than the external. The measure generally employed is that of the CUBIT or forearm, respecting the exact length of which there is diversity of opinion. According to some, eighteen inches, to others twenty-one, while others make it 21.888 inches, or nearly one foot ten, and some even twenty-five inches. It will be generally sufficient, in order to form an idea of the various dimensions, to adopt some easy measurement, say one foot ten, or two feet. The cubit of Ezekiel is one-sixth larger, being a cubit and a handbreadth (Ezek. xl., 5), the handbreadth being reckoned as one-sixth of the ordinary cubit. Ezekiel's REED of six GREAT cubits is therefore equal to seven ordinary cubits. But when the SCALE is larger, the number of cubits where the measurements coincide is the same. SEVEN being the Scriptural number for completeness or perfection, it is interesting to observe that the measurements of the Temple of Ezekiel, or the MILLENNIAL Temple, are thus brought up to the scale of perfectness.

THE MEASUREMENTS OF THE HOLY AND MOST HOLY PLACE

The length (of the house) by cubits, after the first measure (that is, as I understand it, after the ordinary cubit), was threescore cubits, and the breadth twenty cubits (1 Kings vi., 2, 17; 2 Chron. iii., 3). This is internal measurement, and inclusive both of the Holy and Most Holy places. This is distinctly stated in Ezekiel xli., 2, 4. "He measured the length thereof, forty cubits: and the breadth, twenty cubits" (verse 2), that is, of the Holy Place. "So he measured the length thereof, twenty cubits; and the breadth, twenty cubits, before the Temple: and he said unto me 'This is the most holy' [holy of the holies]."

"The height thereof thirty cubits" (1 Kings vi., 2), the internal height of the wall of the Holy Place, while the height of the Oracle, or Most Holy Place, was twenty cubits (1 Kings vi., 20).

THE PORCH

The Porch BEFORE THE HOUSE in internal measurement was twenty cubits in length, ten cubits in breadth, twenty cubits in height (1 Kings vi., 3). It is well to remember that in the Tabernacle in the Wilderness the Holy Place was twenty cubits long by ten cubits broad, but TEN cubits internal HEIGHT. In 2

Chron. iii., 4 the Porch is described as a hundred and twenty cubits HIGH, but this is acknowledged to be a mistake arising from a transposition of letters; the Alexandrian copy of the Septuagint reads "twenty cubits." In Ezek. xl., 49 the breadth is from the door of the Holy Place one cubit deeper, eleven cubits.

THE WINDOWS

"Windows of narrow lights" [broad within, narrow without] (see 1 Kings vi., 4, margin). These appear to be for the Holy Place; whilst in Ezek. xli., 26 we read, "And there were narrow windows and palm trees [artificial palms] on the one side and on the other side, on the sides of the porch, and upon the side-chambers of the house." These last were the windows of the porch and of the side-chambers on either side.

THE FLOORS, CHAMBERS, AND GALLERIES

"And against the walls of the house he built chambers [floors or stories] round about" [on either side] (1 Kings vi., 5). The Hebrew word *sahbib* rendered "round about" is to be interpreted according to the connection. Sometimes it means "on either side," as in Ex. vii., 24, where it first occurs; and sometimes "round about." These FLOORS were formed of rafters of cedar, in three storeys, on which the side-chambers and galleries were, and they extended the whole length of the house.

"And he made chambers [side-chambers] round about: the nethermost chamber [floor or storey] was five cubits broad." The word is FLOOR, but it is true

both of the floors and chambers. Compare Ezek. xli., 7. "The middle was six cubits broad, and the third was seven cubits broad: for without in the wall of the house he made narrow-rests [narrowings or rebatements] round about [on either side], that the beams should not be fastened in the walls of the house" (1 Kings vi., 6, 10). This is further explained in Ezek. xli., 5-8. The wall of the house, at the foundation of the side-chambers, was six cubits; the thickness of the wall for the LOWER side-chamber was five cubits (verse 9); as the side-chambers of the second and third storeys enlarged one cubit each, the wall decreased in proportion. The side-chambers were in three storeys, fifteen on either side in each storey, making ninety in all, four cubits broad each (Ezek. xli., 5), five cubits high (1 Kings vi., 10). They seem hinted at in 1 Chron. xxviii., 11. David gave to Solomon the pattern of the TREASURIES, probably the side-chambers on the first floor; and of the UPPER CHAMBERS, or the second and third storeys; and of the INNER PARLOURS, or the innermost side-chambers toward the west.

It appears there was but one door of entrance from the galleries, on each side of the Temple, so that the passage was from one to another into the innermost (1 Kings vi., 8; Ezek. xli., 11). And from the whole building being said to be seventy cubits broad (Ezek. xli., 12), these galleries appear to have extended ten cubits on either side; for the width of the house was fifty cubits. I might suggest that the chambers

reached by ascending stairs were for the use of the
priests and Levites, who day and night served in the
Temple, watch by watch, that they might wait on God
continually.

THE TYPICAL IMPORT

We read in 2 Cor. xii., 2 of the third heaven, im-
plying a first and second; so the threefold division of
the Temple, the Porch, the Holy Place, and the Holiest
of all, may be figures of these three heavens; while
the side-chambers in three storeys, becoming larger as
they ascend, and leading one into another from east
to west, and still ascending higher and higher, is
strikingly suggestive of thoughts of enlargement and
progress in heavenly glory, of higher heights, of fuller
conformity to God and fellowship with Him. Not only
do these chambers ascend higher and grow larger, but
there is a progress from east to west, from one
chamber to another, until the innermost chamber is
reached, the nearest to "the Holiest of all," the nearest
to the manifested glory of God. Thus shall the saints
have increasing capacity to enjoy and serve God in the
countless ages of eternity to come. Their progress
also from the sun-rising towards the Holiest of all is
suggestive of thoughts of that eternal day, having a
morning without clouds, "a sacred, high, eternal noon,"
without an evening or night, still—

"Nearer, our God, to Thee,
Nearer to Thee."

The variety and number bring forcibly to our remembrance the words of Jesus to His disciples, "In My

Father's house are many mansions" (John xiv., 2). The GALLERIES in front of the side-chambers, on their three storeys, afford a wider range, an increasingly higher and more extensive prospect. We can scarcely imagine that a million ages spent in the presence and service of God will leave us the same at the end as we were at the beginning. Surely we shall rise higher and higher, and yet higher in our enjoyment, our acquaintance, and communion with God in that eternal day. As we rise in our apprehension of God, our capacities for knowing Him will proportionately expand. What heart can conceive, what tongue can tell, what God and the Lamb have in reserve for the redeemed in glory in the ages to come, which stretch onward before us in ever-widening and brightening anticipation! There to be nearer and yet nearer, to worship, admire, adore. No standing still, but an ever-growing acquaintance with God, and an ever-increasing capacity for the enjoyment of, and communion with, Him whom we adore.

CHAPTER SIX

THE STONES OF THE TEMPLE

"AND Solomon's builders and Hiram's builders did hew [them], and the stonesquarers: so [and] they prepared timber and stones to build the house" (1 Kings v., 18). "And the house, when it was in building, was built of stone made ready [perfect] before it was brought thither: so that there was neither hammer nor axe, nor any tool of iron heard in the house, while it was in building" (1 Kings vi., 7). Stone placed upon stone, each fitted into its appointed place, and all these white marble stones were polished after the similitude of a palace—

"Like some tall palm the noiseless fabric sprung."

In 1 Chron. xxix., 2, we read that David provided "marble stones in abundance." The Hebrew word employed shows that the marble was WHITE. These stones were doubtless used for the paving of the court, for the structure of the wall, and for the building of the Temple, "according to the measures of hewed stones" (1 Kings vii., 9, 11). The Spirit of God interprets in one portion of the Scriptures the figures He uses in another. The Apostle Peter says, "Ye also, as living stones, are built up a spiritual house"

39

(1 Peter ii., 5). Each stone represents the individual believer, once dead in trespasses and sins, but now quickened by the Spirit of the living God; hence we are called upon to "look unto the rock whence ye are hewn" (Isaiah li., 1). The EVANGELIST is God's quarryman, used by Him to detach these stones from the world in which they are embedded according to nature. This is often hard work, requiring great skill. Then follows the work of the PASTOR, leading them to a deeper experience of Divine truth, bringing them into the communion of saints below, preparatory to their being built by the true Solomon in resurrection glory into an everlasting habitation for God. Then these stones must be "polished after the similitude of a palace." This is the work of the TEACHER, who unfolds the mysteries of God, and leads souls upward, onward, Godward, into closer conformity to Christ. The present world is God's workyard, in which there is fellowship of labour. The Lord Jesus is not only making use of the gifts of the Spirit, but also of the trials and temptations which come upon Christians; for all things are under His skilful hand, therefore "all things work together for good to them that love God." Well may the Apostle Paul write that the sufferings of this present time are not worthy to be compared with the glory that shall be revealed, that "our light affliction, which is but for a moment, worketh for us a far more exceeding and eternal weight of glory" (2 Cor. iv., 17). Being thus polished and MADE READY, "the spirits of just men made perfect" (Heb. xii., 23)

are waiting for the time when they shall be presented "faultless before the presence of His glory." There the sound of the hammer shall no more be heard, for there shall be no sorrow nor sighing, only the sound of thanksgiving and blessing; glory, honour, praise, and power unto Him that sitteth on the throne, and to the Lamb for ever and ever.

THE ROOFS

"So he built the house and finished it; and covered [ceiled] the house with beams [vault-beams] and boards [ceiling boards] of cedar" (1 Kings vi., 9). "And the greater house he ceiled with [covered above with] fir [cypress] tree" (2 Chron. iii., 5). These vault-beams, as the Hebrew word informs us (*gelbim* from *gab*, an arch), were semi-circular, thus forming a DOME for the covering. The vault-beams and the ceiling boards (probably the internal rafters) were of cedar, both for the Holy and Most Holy house; while the greater house, constituting the Holy Place and side-chambers, was covered again externally with fir (or cypress, as Hesenius considers, as being exceedingly firm and durable, and employed where strength and durability were especially required). These domed roofs covered with cedar and cypress, in contrast with the shittim wood and flat badgers'-skin covering of the Tabernacle, are in keeping with the heavenly character of the Temple—the Tabernacle in the Wilderness being the type of the Church of God on earth, the Temple the type of the redeemed, as called with a heavenly calling and perfected in heavenly glory.

The Woodwork and the Temple

The whole of the Temple was covered within and without with wood. The walls within were wainscotted with cedar, and all the exterior was covered with cedar or cypress, including the galleries (see 1 Kings vi., 15, 16, 18; Ezek. xli., 16, 17, 25, 26); the floor of the Holy Place with planks of cypress; and cedar covered the whole of the Most Holy Place.

Four kinds of wood are mentioned in the Word in connection with Jehovah's dwelling-places:—Shittim Wood, of which the Ark of the Covenant was constructed, an emblem of humanity. In the Ark it set forth the sinless humanity of the Lord Jesus Christ.

Cedar, being from its incorruptible nature an emblem of the incorruptible resurrection body. A piece of worm-eaten cedar was never seen. The sap of the cedar is death to the worm; so that, instead of the worm destroying the cedar, the cedar destroys the worm.

Fir or Cypress, employed where strength and durability were required, typical of resurrection strength.

Olive, or oily wood, is emblematic of resurrection spirituality, or the "spiritual body." All these seem to be dealt with in that wonderful passage, 1 Cor. xv., 42, 44, 53, where the resurrection bodies of the saints are so fully described. "It is sown a natural body (the shittim wood), it is raised a spiritual body (the olive or oily wood); it is sown in corruption, it is raised in incorruption (the cedar); it is sown in weakness, it is raised in power" (the cypress). "For this corruptible must put on incorruption, and this mortal must put on immortality."

THE CARVINGS

The cedar was carved with knops [gourds] and open flowers, cherubim and palm trees, similar to the carving on the doors (1 Kings vi., 18, 29; Ezek. xli., 18-20). Christ says of Himself, "I am the Door." The cedar boards, being carved in conformity with the doors, represents the bodies of saints conformed in resurrection glory to the glorified body of the great Redeemer; for, "as we have borne the image of the earthly, we shall also bear the image of the heavenly" (1 Cor. xv., 49). He shall change the body of our humiliation, that it may be fashioned like unto the body of His glory (Phil. iv., 21). "When He shall appear, we shall be like Him" (1 John iii., 2). As melted wax takes the impress of the seal, so, the moment the saints are caught up to meet the Lord in the air, these bodies will take the impress of His glorious body; thus we shall be conformed to the glorious pattern of the Divine Redeemer. Capacities for service may be typified by the CHERUBIM; dignity, fruitfulness, and triumph by the PALM TREES; the germs and unfoldings of every spiritual grace by the SEED VESSELS and OPEN FLOWERS. All these were seen in their beauty and excellency in Jesus, and the risen saints will be conformed to Him in resurrection glory.

THE OVERLAYING WITH SILVER AND GOLD

The reason given for David's contribution of silver, in 1 Chron. xxix., 4, was to overlay—literally, to PLASTER—the walls of the house. It would appear that the stone walls were first plastered with SILVER, then covered with CEDAR, and afterwards overlaid with GOLD—the whole house within and without, including the roof, walls, floor, doors (1 Kings vi., 20-22, 30, 32, 35; 2 Chron. iii., 5-9)—not gilded, but covered with gold, fitted upon the carved work, bringing the whole into surpassing splendour. SILVER is the emblem of atonement, for the typical redemption price was paid in silver (Ex. xxx., 11-16). GOLD, the most precious of metals, appears to be the emblem of that which is Divine—divinely excellent and glorious, a faint foreshadowing of the glory of God which the redeemed will for ever share. So also the Holy City, New Jerusalem, the emblem of the Church as the Bride of the Lamb (Rev. xxi., 11, 18), was seen of John in vision as "pure gold," "having the glory of God." "The glory which Thou hast given Me," says Jesus, "I have given them" (John xvii., 22). The bodies of the saints, sown in dishonour, will be raised in glory (1 Cor. xv., 43). As the gold fitted on the carved work did not obliterate, but added perfection to the carvings of the cedar, so the Divine glory put upon the redeemed will display more fully those excellencies of the Redeemer which they will reflect, into whose image they will have been transformed. The weight of gold is enormous, reminding us of that expression, "our light affliction which is but for a moment," these chisellings and carvings so painful now, "worketh for us a far more exceeding and eternal weight of glory" (2 Cor. iv., 17). Not only will glory given to them press upon the spirits of the redeemed, constraining to gratitude and praise, but redemption wrought for them will press with still heavier burden. Oh, for more of that faith which is the substance of things hoped for in eternity, to bring the pressure of these obligations to bear on our hearts in time! These afflictions will soon be past, these clouds shall give place to one unclouded day, encircling with perpetual spring the everlasting year.

THE PRECIOUS STONES

David provided for the house of his God "onyx stones and stones to be set, glistering stones, and of divers colours, and all manner of precious stones" (1 Chron. xxix., 2, 8). Solomon "garnished the house with precious stones for beauty" (2 Chron. iii., 6). So also the light of the Holy Jerusalem, seen of John in vision, "was like unto a stone most precious, even like a jasper stone, clear as crystal" [crystallising] (Rev. xxi., 11). Paul appears to have had these things in his mind when he wrote, "If any man build upon this foundation gold, silver, precious stones." For he is speaking of believers as being God's Temple, in which the Spirit of God dwelt (1 Cor. iii., 12, 16, 17). These precious stones aptly set forth those spiritual excellencies and perfections which will be conspicuous in the redeemed in glory, the workmanship of the ETERNAL SPIRIT, those GRACES of the Spirit of God which will be there in full bloom—"open flowers," not simply graces in the bud and embryo, but in growth and perfection, which shall there appear in the clear radiance of the Divine presence in all their spiritual beauty.

CHAPTER SEVEN

THE DOORS AND VAIL

FIRST, of the MOST HOLY PLACE.—"For the entering of the oracle [speaking-place] he made doors of olive tree [oil trees]: the lintel and side-posts were a fifth part," that is, of the width of the house. The Most Holy Place, being twenty cubits wide, a fifth part is four cubits. "The two doors also were of olive tree [oil trees]; and he carved upon them carvings of cherubim and palm trees and open flowers [openings of flowers], and overlaid them with gold, and spread gold upon the cherubim, and upon the palm trees" (1 Kings vi., 31, 32; Ezek. xli., 23-25).

Second, of the TEMPLE, or HOLY PLACE.—"So also made he for the door of the Temple side-posts of oil trees, from the fourth part" (1 Kings vi., 33 [Hebrew]). The fourth part of the width of the house is five cubits. The posts of the door of oil tree two cubits, and the door six cubits (Ezek. xli., 3). "And the two doors were of fir [cypress] tree: the two leaves of the one door were folding, and the two leaves of the other door were folding. And he carved thereon cherubim and palm trees and open flowers [openings of flowers]: and covered them with gold fitted upon the carved work" (1 Kings vi., 34, 35). The doors

47

were divided in the centre into two folding leaves, reminding us of the rent vail—Christ crucified. They appear to be typical of Christ Jesus, by whom we draw near to God; and through Him, by faith in Him, we have boldness of access, not only into the Holy Place but also into the Holiest of all (Heb. x., 19-22). The one of OIL tree, type of Christ risen in His SPIRITUAL body; the other of fir or CYPRESS, in His resurrection STRENGTH; while the carvings and the gold set forth the various perfections and Divine glory.

THE VAIL

There are significant variations in the colour and materials of the vails of the Tabernacle and Temple. In the vail of the Tabernacle it is SCARLET (*tolahath-shanee*), which means "the splendour of a worm"), typical of the royal dignity of the Son of Man, as born King of the Jews. In the Temple it is CRIMSON (Heb. Carmel), the emblem of fruitfulness and excellency (see Isa. xxxv., 2), and of the glory of Christ in resurrection. In the vail of the Tabernacle FINE LINEN is *Sheesh*, white, the emblem of pure human nature; in that of the Temple it is another Hebrew word, *Butz*, white and glistening, as the raiment of Christ was on the Transfiguration Mount.

It was the vail of Herod's Temple that was rent in twain at the death of Christ. "Having therefore, brethren, boldness to enter into the holiest by the blood of Jesus, by a new [newly-slain] and living way, which He hath consecrated [or inaugurated] for us, through the vail, that is to say, His flesh" (Heb. x., 19).

In the Tabernacle there was only a vail between the Holy and Most Holy Place; in Solomon's Temple there was a two-leaved, olivewood, gold-covered door as well as a vail. In the Temple of Ezekiel there is no vail, only a turning door, divided in the centre, making manifest the way into the Holiest. The Tabernacle vail is typical of the spotless humanity of the Lord Jesus—"The Word made flesh, who tabernacled among us." The vail of the Temple is the type of the same humanity in resurrection dignity, fruitfulness, and glory. Not only was Jesus the Son of David, but also the Son of God: not only the heir of David's throne, but the One who has sat down on the right hand of the throne of the Majesty on high.

CHAPTER EIGHT

THE CHERUBIM

THE word "cherub" is of doubtful interpretation; it probably signifies "like the majesty." The plural is "cherubim"—I believe emblematic of those whom God employs to communicate His mind or to perform His will. We first read of the cherubim in Gen. iii., 24—"He placed at the east of the garden of Eden cherubim . . . to keep the way of the tree of life"—here evidently emblematic of ANGELIC ministry. Next they are seen on the mercy-seat of the Ark of the Covenant (Ex. xxv., 20), of pure GOLD, a continuation of the golden propitiatory, therefore Divine—an emblem of the Eternal Spirit. The Mercy-seat, or Propitiatory, represents the mercy or loving-kindness of God, which is from everlasting to everlasting. The cherubim were beaten out of the two ends of the mercy-seat, and their wings, meeting above, formed a complete circle. Their faces were towards the mercy-seat, setting forth the fact that the atoning work of Christ was the centre purpose of God, the Eternal Spirit foretelling and foreshadowing it before its accomplishment, and keeping up the remembrance of it throughout eternity.

50

In Incarnation the Spirit of Jehovah rested on the Man Christ Jesus, fitting Him for His earthly service; and "through the Eternal Spirit He offered Himself without spot to God" (Heb. ix., 14). Then, as the Priest in resurrection, He received the anointing of the Holy Spirit for His priestly and eternal service in Heaven.

The various emblems used in Scripture to describe the operations of the Spirit of God are exceedingly beautiful and significant.

First, there is the overshadowing or fluttering wing —"The Spirit of God moved (or fluttered) upon the face of the waters" (Gen. i., 2). "As an eagle stirreth up her nest, fluttereth over her young, spreadeth abroad her wings, taketh them, beareth them on her wings" (Deut. xxxii., 11). When the Spirit descended on Christ at His baptism, it was in the form of a dove (Luke iii., 22). Christ risen and exalted has received the gifts of the Spirit, which He has distributed for the work of the ministry and for the edifying of His body (Eph. iv., 11, 12).

DIVINE AND SPIRITUAL AGENCY

The Cherubim again figure largely, and are minutely described, in the prophecy of Ezekiel, as the LIVING CREATURES of the vision. Here they appear to symbolise the various characteristics of PROPHETIC ministry—the face of a MAN, showing sympathy and intelligence; the ox, patient perseverance; the keen eye, lofty flight, strong wing of the EAGLE; the LION emblem of boldness and courage.

The four beasts, or LIVING ONES, in Rev. iv., 6-8, represent the CHURCH in resurrection glory, as God's agency for earth and Heaven, for time and for Eternity.

When John was caught up into Heaven, in fulfilment of the word of the Lord in John xxi., 22, he saw a throne and One seated on it. Four-and-twenty elders were seated round about the throne, representing those of a former dispensation, who, having died in Christ, rise first when Jesus comes: all who have departed in the faith of Christ from Abel downwards, previous to the Pentecostal dispensation.

Then we read—"In the midst of the throne and round about the throne were four living ones." In chapter five, the Lamb as it had been slain is seen standing in the midst of the throne, and these four living ones are connected with Him. They are symbolic of the Church of the Firstborn, written in Heaven—those who by the Pentecostal Spirit are baptised into one body, one spirit with the Lord. When to these we add the multitude that no man can number, we see the whole of those who share the first resurrection.

The TWO LARGE cherubim in the Holiest of the Temple of Solomon (1 Kings vi., 23-28; 2 Chron. iii., 10-13) represent, I believe, the ministry of ALL THE REDEEMED in its heavenly exercise. They were of olive tree or OILY wood, type of the spiritual body, serving in the power of the SPIRIT of God; of image work, as conformed to the image of the risen CHRIST.

Overlaid with GOLD, as partakers of a glory which is Divine; their height, ten cubits; the WINGS reach from wall to wall, meeting in the centre, over the mercy-seat of the Lord. The ministry of the redeemed in glory will be extensive, having the mystery of redeeming love in Christ Jesus for its centre, filling all Heaven, and continuing through all eternity.

THE CHARIOT OF THE CHERUBIM

David gave to Solomon "gold for the pattern of the chariot of the cherubim, that spread out their wings, and covered the Ark of the Covenant of Jehovah" (1 Chron. xxviii., 18). Psalm lxviii., 17, appears to throw light on this subject—"The chariot (singular) of God is twenty thousand [two myriads], even thousands of angels [or changed ones]: the Lord [*Adonahy*] is among them, as in Sinai, in the holy place." We may compare with this Deut. xxxiii., 2—"Jehovah came from Sinai, and rose up from Seir unto them; He shined forth from Mount Paran, and He came with ten thousands of saints" [holy myriads]. Also in Jude 14, the prophecy of Enoch—"Behold, the Lord cometh with ten thousand [myriads] of His saints" [holy ones].

The CHARIOT OF THE CHERUBIM and the two cherubim in the Most Holy Place appear to be the same, and to represent those holy ones whom God employs as the vehicle of His visitation to His creatures, the ministers of His will, and the manifesters of His glory. The whole illimitable universe of God will be filled with the manifestation of Divine grace and glory, and God will make His redeemed ones the especial ˌministers of this manifestation. For God will "head up together all things in Christ, both which are in the heavens and which are on the earth"; and the Church is the fulness of Him that filleth all in all (Eph. i., 9, 10, 21, 22).

CHAPTER NINE

THE ARK OF THE COVENANT

AT the dedication of the Temple it was brought up out of the city of David, and carried into the oracle of the house, the Most Holy Place, even under the wings of the cherubim (2 Chron. v., 7-10). This was the Ark which was in the Tent of the Congregation in the Wilderness (Ex. xxv., 10-17). It is a complete type of the Lord Jesus Christ—a full-length representation of Immanuel—of His INCARNATION, as typified by the shittim wood (John i., 14), of His DIVINE nature by the gold (1 Tim. iii., 16), of His PERFECT OBEDIENCE by the unbroken tables of the law within (Psalm xl., 8), His atoning DEATH, the foundation of God's merciful actions, by the BLOOD-stained mercy-seat (Ex. xii., 13), His RISEN glory by the crown of gold round about (Heb. ii., 9), and the FULNESS of the SPIRIT received in ascension by the cherubim on the mercy-seat (Acts ii., 33). There were RINGS of GOLD and STAVES of SHITTIM WOOD overlaid with GOLD. These staves were put into the rings, never to be taken out so long as Israel continued a wandering people (Ex. xxv., 12-15), reminding us of the promise, "Lo, I am with you always, even unto the end of the age," never leaving, never forsaking. "Where two or

55

three are gathered together in My name, there am I in the midst of them" (Matt. xviii., 20). There He is, in the tenderness of His humanity and the glorious perfection of His Godhead—shittim wood overlaid with pure gold.

When that Ark was brought to its resting-place under the shadow of the larger cherubim, these staves were drawn out of the rings and placed behind the Ark, so that the heads of the staves were seen from before the oracle; the staves were hidden behind the Ark; wilderness wanderings will soon be over, but God will have His abiding presence with His people to be kept in everlasting remembrance. We shall look back with thanksgiving and praise to Him who was always with us here below.

The Crown of Gold

"And thou shalt make upon it a CROWN OF GOLD round about." Beautiful type of the exaltation of the Lord Jesus in resurrection and ascension; in the presence of God "crowned with glory and honour," the sufferings of death for ever past.

The Tables of the Law

In the Ark were placed the two unbroken tables of the law on which God wrote with His own finger when Moses went up to the mount a second time. The first tables were provided by God Himself, but broken by Moses owing to Israel's transgression. These tables were typical of the covenant of works, by which no man can be justified before God. The second tables, having been prepared by Moses and written again by God, were deposited in the Ark, and are typical of the New Covenant in Christ Jesus. They also remind us of the words of Him who said, "In the volume of the Book it is written of Me, I delight to do Thy will, O My God. Yea, Thy law is within My heart" (Psalm xl., 8). The Lord Jesus, made of a woman, made under the law, in His life of perfect obedience, doing the will of God, magnified the law, and made it honourable.

THE PROPITIATORY

Above the two tables was the Propitiatory, upon which the blood of atonement was sprinkled by the high priest once a year, when he entered into the holiest. First, with incense beaten small, which he put on the censer, from which a cloud covered the Propitiatory, a type of Christ entering the Holiest in the memorial of His life and character and walk and work on earth.

Then the high priest dipped his finger in the blood of the bullock, which had been slain without, and sprinkled it on the mercy-seat eastward. Why eastward? Because that was the line in which the worshippers must draw nigh as they entered. When God sees that blood of atonement, the way is clear for the worshippers to draw near. It seems to say, "Though your sins be as scarlet, they shall be white as snow; though they be red like crimson, they shall be as wool" (Isa. i., 18). Scarlet seen through crimson appears white to view; so God looks upon the approaching worshipper through the crimson light of Christ's atoning blood. Having sprinkled the blood ONCE eastward beneath the eye of God, the priest sprinkles it SEVEN TIMES before the mercy-seat, for the eye of the worshipper drawing near. Thus we come right with God in full assurance of faith, knowing that we are welcome through the way of redemption there. The Propitiatory, therefore, sets forth Christ in His atoning death, as the tables in the Ark tell of His perfect life of obedience.

CHAPTER TEN

THE ALTAR OF INCENSE

DAVID provided "for the altar of incense refined gold by weight." And with this the whole altar of cedar was overlaid (1 Kings vi., 20, 22; 1 Chron. xxviii., 18). The altar stood before the vail. CEDAR is the type of the Lord Jesus Christ in resurrection, overlaid with GOLD, setting forth the Divine glory of His person, the One in whose name we worship, who said, "Hitherto have ye asked nothing in My name; ask, and ye shall receive, that your joy may be full" (John xvi., 24). Not only is He the one Mediator between God and man in time, but He is the One through whom throughout eternity all praise, honour, and glory, in the power of the Holy Ghost, will be given to God the Father. "God also hath highly exalted Him, and given Him a name which is above every name: that at [in] the name of Jesus every knee should bow, of things in heaven, and things in [on] earth, and things under the earth; and that every tongue should confess that Jesus Christ is Lord, to the glory of God the Father" (Phil. ii., 9-11). Worship in the ages past was paid direct to the Triune God, as in Isa. vi., where the thrice holy, Three in One, Jehovah, is the object of adoration. But now there is One to whom a Name has been given above every name, and IN that Name every knee must bow. From that time a new order of worship has been established in the universe; and throughout the countless ages of eternity the hosts of Heaven will render all thanksgiving, glory, honour, and power to the Triune God in the name of Jesus Christ. This is what the Golden Altar in the sanctuary of God signifies.

All these varied types are shadows, the substance of which is to be found in the Person, Work, and Offices of the Lord Jesus Christ. It was God who gave the commandment, "Thou shalt make." They are the embodiment of Divine thought concerning His beloved Son.

CHAPTER ELEVEN

THE TABLES OF SHEWBREAD

IN the Tabernacle in the wilderness there was one
table of shittim wood overlaid with gold, representing God's provision for His ransomed people in
this dispensation. The twelve loaves upon that table
tell of full provision for the whole family of God
throughout all their wilderness days.

The table sets forth the Lord Jesus as the centre
and ground of communion with God, in the power of
the Spirit, for the redeemed while here on earth.

In the Temple of Solomon there were TEN TABLES
OF GOLD, five on the one side and five on the other
(1 Kings vii., 48; 2 Chron. iv., 8). The TABLE is a type
of the Lord Jesus Christ as the centre and ground of
COMMUNION in the power of the Holy Ghost. The
BREAD thereon is God's provision in Christ for all His
ransomed ones when safely brought home to glory.
He is the true bread which endureth unto everlasting
life (John vi., 32-58).

THE TABLES OF SILVER

"Silver for the tables of silver" (1 Chron. xxviii.,
16). The silver tables were probably in use in the

61

side-chambers of the Temple and elsewhere. SILVER is not only a type of REDEMPTION, but of COMMUNION on the ground of redemption, for it was the chief circulating medium.

CHAPTER TWELVE

THE GOLDEN LAMPSTANDS

"AND the candlesticks [lampstands] of pure gold, five on the right side, and five on the left, before the oracle [speaking-place] with the flowers, and the lamps, and the tongs of gold, and the bowls, and the snuffers, and the basons, and the spoons, and the censers [fire-pans or snuff-dishes] of pure gold" (1 Kings vii., 49, 50; 2 Chron. iv., 7, 20-22).

In the Temple there were TEN GOLDEN LAMP-STANDS, with their SEVENTY LAMPS. The word is generally rendered "candlestick," but the word "candle" never occurs in the sacred Scriptures, neither in the Hebrew nor in the Greek; it is always "lamp" and "lampstand." The LAMPSTAND is a type of the Lord Jesus Christ as the centre, source, and subject of testimony in the power of the Holy Ghost. The CENTRE SHAFT is typical of His own personal ministry; the BRANCHES of ministry in the Church by the evangelist, pastor, teacher. The candle is self-sufficient and self-continuing; you have only to light it, and it burns from beginning to end. Not so the lamp, which is dependent on the OIL, typical of the HOLY SPIRIT. There lies the difference between that ministry which is in the words which the Holy Ghost

63

teacheth, and that ministry which is the result of man's wisdom and intellect. Real ministry is dependent on the presence and power of the HOLY SPIRIT, who has come to testify of Jesus, to take of the things of Christ in the glory of the Father, and reveal them to us, and to show us things to come. In Rev. xxi., 23, we read, "And the city had no need of the sun, neither of the moon, to shine in it: for the glory of God did lighten it, and the Lamb is the light [lamp] thereof." Christ is not only the centre and source and subject of truth in the present time, but He will continue to be so throughout eternity; light in the glory tenfold; in beauty, splendour, and truth revealed, there we shall bask in His full light.

THE SILVER LAMPSTANDS

"And for the candlesticks [lampstands] of silver by weight" (1 Chron. xxviii., 15). The SILVER lampstands were probably for the use of the priests in the side-chambers of the sanctuary, and express spiritual truth held in the COMMUNION of saints, by the teaching of the Spirit of God.

CHAPTER THIRTEEN

THE GOLDEN AND SILVER VESSELS

" ALSO pure gold for the flesh-hooks, and the bowls, and the cups: and for the golden basons he gave gold by weight for every bason; likewise silver by weight for every bason of silver" (1 Chron. xxviii., 17; 1 Kings vii., 48, 50; 2 Chron. iv., 8, 11, 19). In the flesh-hooks, bowls, and covered bowls, some precious thoughts are suggested by the roots of the Hebrew words. These vessels of gold and silver were probably among the treasures of the House of God, laid up in the lower side-chambers of the Temple. Even so, God's holy priesthood are stewards of sacred mysteries, the antitypes of these, to be the themes of adoring wonder and grateful praise to countless myriads throughout all eternity above. What more precious to be saints on earth or to the redeemed in glory than thoughts of the sufferings of Christ, His precious blood, His complete atonement! These are some of the things set forth by these instruments and vessels.

The root of the Hebrew word for FLESH-HOOK is "to draw out"—suggestive of the thought of the blood-shedding of Immanuel.

"The very spear that pierced His side,
Drew forth the blood to save."

The root of the word for BOWL is "to sprinkle." These bowls or basons were probably employed in carrying the blood into the Holiest when the blood of atonement was SPRINKLED there. It is the blood of Jesus which gives boldness of access within the vail.

"That rich atoning blood
Which, sprinkled round, we see
Provides for all who come to God
An all-prevailing plea."

The root of the word CUP—or, more properly, "cover"—is "to be hard," and, when repeated, is employed to express the scales of a fish and scale armour, giving the thought of security and defence. What a shelter for the soul is the precious blood of Jesus! Over the blood-sprinkled habitations in Egypt the destroying angel passed. What an impenetrable scale armour it affords, combining freedom of action with perfect security.

The word rendered BASONS here properly signifies "covered bowls." The root of the word is "to cover, to expiate, to make atonement." This suggests ATONEMENT fully made. What treasures for the treasuries of God! What memorials for eternity! What things for angels to look into! to be explained and unfolded by those who have been the subjects of redeeming grace in the ages of eternity to come.

CHAPTER FOURTEEN

THE TWO PILLARS: JACHIN AND BOAZ

THE pillars of brass which stood by the porch of the Temple, one on either side, are mentioned in seven places in the Scriptures—1 Kings vii., 13-22, 41-46; 2 Kings xxv., 16, 17; 2 Chron. iii., 15-17; 2 Chron. iv., 12, 13; Jer. lii., 20-23; Ezekiel xl., 49. On the surface these accounts appear to vary; it requires prayerful waiting upon God, and pondering His Holy Word, to harmonise the whole. It has been found with this as with other apparent discrepancies of Scripture, that they are, in fact, Divine perfections, and the seeming diversities tend to the elucidation of the truth.

> "Blind unbelief is sure to err,
> And scan His work in vain;
> God is His own interpreter,
> And He will make it plain."

THE HEIGHT

In two or three places the height is given as EIGHTEEN cubits apiece, the chapter on the top of each pillar was FIVE cubits, making the entire height twenty-three cubits. In 2 Chron. iii., 15, we read, "He made before the house two pillars of THIRTY and

FIVE cubits high." In the margin you will find the Hebrew word rendered "high" should be "long": the Hebrew word used for "pillar" signifies "round pillar"; the length of the round shaft was seventeen and a half cubits each pillar, the two together making THIRTY-FIVE cubits long; if we add half a cubit for the pedestal we have eighteen as the height of each.

With regard to the POSITION of the pillars, the word which in 1 Kings is rendered "in" signifies "by"—"He set up the pillars by the porch of the Temple"; and this corresponds with 2 Chron. iii., 17, "He reared up the pillars before the Temple." They were cast "in the clay ground between Succoth and Zarthan (1 Kings vii., 46); they were hollow, and the thickness of the brass was four fingers" (Jer. lii., 21). BRASS is the emblem of strength; HOLLOW expresses emptiness. Those skilled in these questions say that the proportions of thickness and size here given are those whereby the greatest amount of strength is secured with the smallest quantity of metal. That is just like God in His perfect wisdom.

THE CHAPITERS, OR CROWNS

In 1 Kings vii., 16, the chapiters—or crowns, as the Hebrew word *Cotharoth* signifies—are said to be five cubits high; in verse 19 the lily work is said to be four cubits; and in 2 Kings xxv., 17, "the height of the chapiter was three cubits." The truth is, I apprehend, that each of these chapiters consisted of four parts—(1) a square ledge on the top, half a cubit thick, on which were the pomegranates;

(2) a similar ledge at the bottom; (3) a bowl of pommel of one cubit deep (1 Kings vii., 41); and (4) a belly of protuberance of three cubits (1 Kings vii., 20); the two last together, covered with LILY WORK, would make the FOUR cubits, and two ledges would complete the height of FIVE cubits. The chapiters also were covered with a NETWORK or CHEQUER work, expressive of TEMPERANCE and SELF-CONTROL (1 Kings vii., 17, 18).

THE POMEGRANATES

The number is variously given; the pomegranates were in two rows, TWELVE in a row, TWENTY-FOUR on the upper ledge of each pillar, and TWENTY-FOUR on the lower ledge, fronting the four winds (Jer. lii., 23)—that is, fronting the east, west, north, and south—forty-eight on each pillar, ninety-six together, one pomegranate at each corner of the ledges, making ONE HUNDRED round about on each ledge, two hundred on EACH pillar. The number on the two pillars was four hundred. The pomegranates and lily work speak of the FRUITS and GRACES of the SPIRIT.

THE CHAINS

The SEVEN CHAINS of WREATHEN work on each pillar tell of entire subjection, and that which it results in, fulness of honour. In the English translation there is a constant confusion between the network or chequer work and the chain work or wreaths—seven chains suspended on each pillar. The confusion is not in the Hebrew Scriptures, which are perfectly clear and distinct—but in the translation. It is only from the Hebrew originals it is possible to harmonise these various discrepancies.

POSITION AND NAMES

Solomon reared up the pillars before the Temple, one on the right hand, and the other on the left; and called the name of that on the right hand Jachin ['He will establish'], and the name of that on the left Boaz ['In Him is strength'] (2 Chron. iii., 17). They are silent but eloquent testimony-bearers of the great truths of ESTABLISHMENT BY GOD and STRENGTH IN CHRIST. The truths thus declared are expressed by the Holy Ghost in 2 Cor. 1., 21—"Now He which stablisheth us with you in Christ, and hath anointed us, is God; who hath also sealed us, and given the earnest of the Spirit in our hearts."

We learn from the sacred Scriptures that God foresaw that the creature could not stand in its own strength, could not sustain itself by its own strength, and for this He made provision from all eternity. As He foresaw, so it came to pass. Angels, and one evidently of the mightiest order, fell and kept not their first estate. Man, placed at the head of the lower creation, made in the image of God, tempted by Satan, likewise fell. Thus corruption and defilement entered the creation of God, through angels into its height, and through man into its depth. It is in this sense that, as we read in Job xv., 15, "The heavens are not clean in His sight." The same infinite wisdom which foresaw all this provided a remedy in the Son of God.

Incarnation, redemption, resurrection, the gift of the Holy Spirit received by Christ in ascension, and bestowed on men, are God's means. This is a chain linking time with eternity and God with man.

The first wondrous link we find in the INCARNATION, God manifest in flesh. On that emptied and dependent One the Holy Ghost rested, the Spirit of Jehovah was poured without measure.

In Heaven there is a throne set, and One sitteth on the throne. Man lost Paradise by having a will of his own. In Gethsemane we see the surrender of the will of the Perfect Man, who said, "Not My will, but Thine be done" (Matt. xxvi., 36-44). So, as sin entered by man having a will of his own, God counteracted it by a perfect and surrendered will. "It pleased the Father that in Him should all fulness dwell; and, having made peace through the blood of His cross, by Him to reconcile all things unto Himself; through Him, I say, whether they be things in earth or things in heaven" (Col. i., 19, 20). Thus a link has been formed, by the atoning work of Christ, between the reconciled creature and the Creator. He "became obedient unto death, even the death of the cross; wherefore God also hath highly exalted Him, and given Him a name above every name; that in the name of Jesus every knee should bow" (Phil. ii., 9-11). Henceforth every ascription of honour and glory and power must be given to the Father through the Son, IN (Greek) His name must every knee bow. Since Jesus Christ has been constituted the Head of the creation of God, and is the firstborn from among the dead, the security of the universe is headed up in Christ, the second Man, the Lord from Heaven (see Eph. i., 9, 10). Here is at once the foundation Corner-stone and the Head-stone of universal security. It is laid deep, low in Bethlehem's manger, deeper still at Calvary's cross and Joseph's new tomb. In the finished work of Christ is laid the deep foundation of the security of the creation of God; and in a risen and glorified Christ is seen the keystone of the arch—God the Father establishing in Christ the Son, and crowning the whole with the graces, gifts, and perfections of the Divine Eternal Spirit.

CHAPTER FIFTEEN

THE BRAZEN SEA

THE Brazen Sea in the court of the Temple took the place of the Laver of the Tabernacle. All these vessels are the embodiment of Divine thought connected with the person and work of the Lord Jesus Christ. As in the altar we see Christ as our redemption, so in the Laver we have Christ as our sanctification. One beautiful title by which God is made known in the Old Testament is *Jehovah-Mekaddesham*, which means, "I am Jehovah that doth sanctify you." How does Jehovah sanctify? In Christ Jesus through the truth (John xvii., 17). The Word of God is the means, and the Word is effectually applied by the Spirit. This is the truth set forth in the Tabernacle Laver.

The larger reservoir, the Brazen Sea, suggests the idea of a greater fulness and more abundant supply. It was thirty cubits in circumference, ten in diameter, five in height, a handbreadth in thickness. It was constructed to hold three thousand baths; it generally contained two thousand (1 Kings vii., 23-26; 2 Chron. iv., 2-5, 10, 15)—each bath being calculated to be equal to seven gallons and four pints of our measure. It stood upon twelve oxen, three looking

toward the north, three toward the west, three toward
the south, three toward the east, their hinder parts
inward. The Brazen Sea made by Hiram for Solomon,
standing by the Temple of God, reminds us of the
words of the Psalmist, "With Thee is the fountain of
life." It is said concerning the Laver—"Aaron and his
sons shall wash their hands and their feet thereat"
(Ex. xxx., 19). The Hebrew expression is "there
from," teaching that the water was drawn from it; the
water IN the Laver remained uncontaminated. The
same explanation will apply to the Brazen Sea: it was
for the use of the priests; they could not reach up to
dip their hands into it. In some old drawings water is
represented as flowing from the mouths of the oxen;
the oxen were probably hollow. The brim was
wrought like the brim of a cup, with flowers of lilies,
and knops or gourds in two rows, ten knops to a cubit.
This Brazen Sea, with its vast collection of water, presents to us the idea of unlimited supply; it is emblematic of Jesus in resurrection and in ascended
glory, in whom dwells all fulness of spiritual life,
power, and blessing. The water is typical of the
Spirit as given from the risen and glorified Christ. In
John vii., 37, 38, we read, "In the last day, that great
day of the feast, Jesus stood and cried, saying If any
man thirst, let him come unto Me and drink. He that
believeth in Me, as the Scripture hath said, out of his
belly shall flow rivers of living water." Then follows
the interpretation, "But this spake He of the Spirit
which they that believe in Him should receive," when

He was glorified. God the Father, the Source of all, is the Fountain-head. But "it pleased the Father that in Him (the Son) should all fulness dwell." He is the vast Reservoir; the Father the Source. In Christ all fulness dwelleth; and the fulness of the Father which is in the Son is communicated to us by the Holy Spirit sent from a glorified Christ. The water in the Brazen Sea, as interpreted by the Lord Jesus, signifies the Holy Spirit descending from a glorified Christ, as at Pentecost, remaining in the Church until that Church as the body and bride of Christ, is made meet for Him to come and receive her to Himself.

THE TWELVE OXEN

We have a beautiful embodiment of Divine thought connected with ministry, of which the ox in Scripture is the emblem of patient, laborious service. This figure is applied by the Apostle Paul to those who minister the Word—"Thou shalt not muzzle the mouth of the ox that treadeth out the corn." The ox treading out the corn for the household represents that servant whom his Lord has set over His household, to give them their portion of meat in due season, and who, by going over the Sacred page with unmuzzled mouth, feeds as he treads it out for others. The oxen through which the water flowed may be typical of those who, abiding in Christ, and drawing out of His fulness, minister the Spirit to others, according to that word, "He that ministereth to you the Spirit" (Gal. iii., 5). This is true ministry—drinking into the Spirit of Christ, receiving out of His fulness, speaking out of the abundance of the heart, ministering the Spirit, so ministering grace unto the hearers.

LIVING WATERS

In the Temple of Ezekiel neither laver nor brazen sea are mentioned; the waters that issue from under the threshold take their place. They flow down eastward, at the south side of the altar (Ezek. xlvii.). These waters are emblematic of life in the Spirit: small in its commencement in the new birth, it goes on deepening and widening as it flows, leading to purity of WALK, as symbolised in the water reaching to the "ancles." A patient continuance in holy walking leads to a spirit of WORSHIP; this is indicated by the waters reaching to the "knees." The prophet was conducted from the SOUTH side—the side of loving-kindness and grace—back to the NORTH—the side of righteousness and judgment—a further progress, that of "worshipping God in the Spirit," realising the holiness of Him whom we worship. "Our Father which art in the heavens, hallowed be Thy name." The waters now reach unto the "loins," for worship leads to SERVICE. the bent knee to the girded loins, occupied with the service of the Master in the hope of His return, "Waters to swim in." Patience continuance in well-doing leads the soul into a richer and fuller acquaintance with God, the enjoyment of His manifested presence, and the communion of the Holy Ghost. Strengthened with might by God's Spirit in the inner man, Christ dwelling in the heart by faith, rooted and grounded in love, the believer is led to comprehend, with all the saints, what is the length and breadth and depth and height of love Divine; and, knowing the love of Christ which passeth knowledge, the soul is "filled into all the fulness of God" (Eph. iii., 19—an ocean of boundless blessedness, without a bottom and without a shore. "God is love; and he that dwelleth in love dwelleth in God, and God in him"—like a fish in ocean depths, drinking in from the boundless fulness which surrounds it, and enjoying unlimited freedom in the activity of its happy existence—"a river that could not be passed over."

THE RIVER FROM THE THRONE OF GOD AND OF THE LAMB

The river in Rev. xxii. is traced up to its source in God, the fountain of living waters, and reveals the sovereignty of His grace, founded on the atoning work of His beloved SON.

Ezekiel xlvii. gives the literal and earthly view, Revelation xxii. the spiritual and heavenly; while both are millennial.

THE BASES AND LAVERS

There were ten bases and lavers of brass (1 Kings vii., 27, 38), five placed on the south or right side or shoulder of the Temple, and five on the north or left side (1 Kings vii., 39). The BASES were SQUARE, four cubits wide, three cubits high, with ledges, borders, or sides, and certain additions, and undersetters or supports for the laver. They stood on wheels, one and a half cubits high, and had gravings of lions, oxen, and cherubim. There are two Hebrew words both ren-

dered "base" in 1 Kings vii. A base under the laver —
keen, the word rendered "foot" in connection with
the laver in the Tabernacle; and the larger base,
meconah, of four cubits by three. The LAVERS were
CIRCULAR, four cubits in diameter; each one contained forty baths (1 Kings vii., 38). Altogether they
appear to have stood about eight cubits in height
"Such things as they offered for the burnt [ascending]
offering they washed in them" (2 Chron. iv., 6). The
inward and legs of the burnt offerings were washed;
thus they became typical of Him whose inward
thoughts, feelings, purposes, and desires were ever
pure and holy; whose walk and ways were blameless
and undefiled, and who "offered Himself without spot
to God."

"The pots, and the shovels, and the basons: and
all these vessels, which Hiram made to King Solomon
for the house of the Lord, were of bright brass" (1
Kings vii., 45).

CHAPTER SIXTEEN

THE BRAZEN ALTAR

IT was twenty cubits square, ten cubits in height (2 Chron. iv.), commensurate in length and breadth with the Holiest of all (the ATONEMENT IS CO-EXTENSIVE with the HOLINESS of God), equal in height to the cherubim, which stood ten cubits high, whose wings met over the propitiatory. The fire was to be ever burning (Lev. i., 7-13; vi., 12, 13). Upon this the daily lamb was to be laid in order (Ex. xxix., 39). The other sacrifices were laid upon the burnt offering (Num. xxviii.). The immense size of Solomon's altar, the orderly disposition of the wood and sacrifices, would render it necessary that the approach should be on the four sides. In connection with the altar of Ezekiel, steps or stairs are mentioned (Ezek. xliii., 17). The prohibition of steps in Exod. xx., 26, refers to the primitive altar of EARTH or of UNHEWN STONE, concerning which it was also said that the lifting up of a tool upon it would pollute it. The priestly garments afterwards provided obviated the need of the prohibition (Exod. xxviii., 42).

The vast number of sacrifices at the dedication of the altar of Solomon was an ineffectual attempt to give expression to faith's apprehension of the infinite value of the one atoning sacrifice of Immanuel. The various offerings* were a foreshadowing of those realities of which Christ Himself is the substance.

The Altar of Ezekiel

It is intermediate in size between that of the Tabernacle and that of the Temple of Solomon (Ezek. xliii.). The "bottom," bosom, or ashpit, on the ground, is a square of sixteen cubits, and one cubit high. The lesser settle or ledge is fourteen cubits square, and two cubits in height; the altar itself twelve cubits square, four cubits high. The sacrifices offered PREVIOUS to Christ's offering of Himself were FORESHADOWINGS of the work accomplished on the cross; the only thing which in the Christian Church takes their place is the Lord's Supper, COMMEMORATIVE of His broken body and shed blood. Sacrifices will come again into observance during the last week of Daniel's seventy weeks, and in the millennium (Ezek. xliii., 18), with significant alterations. In the MILLENNIAL period there is no mention of the evening lamb, only of the morning (Ezek. xlvi., 13). The evening sacrifice has received its accomplishment in the Cross of Calvary; the morning lamb is the memorial, or the bringing to remembrance, of the same. Neither any mention of the Feast of Weeks, or Pentecost; it has received its accomplishment in the present Church dispensation. Neither of the Day of Atonement; the High Priest

* A full exposition of these will be found in "Types of the Levitical Offerings," by the same author.

of our profession is now in the Holiest, presenting in ANTITYPE the blood of the bullock on behalf of Himself and the Church, His house. The sacrifice on behalf of Israel is foreshadowed by Aaron going the second time into the Holiest with the blood of the goat. The sacrifices to be offered on the millennial altar will be commemorative remembrances of the ONE great sacrifice offered ONCE FOR ALL, complete and perfect for eternity.

CHAPTER SEVENTEEN

THE COURTS AND GATES

THE Courts of the Temple were three in number, as follows:—

First, the Great or Outer Court, five hundred cubits square, where the people assembled to worship God. It was open to all.

Second, the Court of the Priests, three hundred cubits square. It was for the priests and their servants, the Levites, alone.

Third, the Court of the Altar, one hundred cubits square, with the altar of burnt offering in its centre.

The Separate Place, whereon the Temple stood, one hundred cubits square. The Court of the Altar and the Separate Place formed what was named the Inner Court, which was surrounded by a wall five cubits thick, built of three rows of hewn stones, with cedar beams on the top.

The Outer Court was elevated above the surrounding ground by flights of seven steps in front of the three gates, and the Court of the Priests was elevated above the Outer Court by flights of eight steps.

The walls of the Outer Court and Court of the Priests were six cubits broad and six cubits high.

There were three gates to the Outer Court—the North Gate, the East Gate, and the South Gate. There was no gate to the west. There were three gates to the Court of the Priests, over against and corresponding to the three gates of the Outer Court. These gates had two porches each.

THE TYPICAL TEACHING OF THE COURTS

These courts are only mentioned in 1 Kings vi., 36, and 2 Chron. iv., 9; their dimensions are fully given in Ezekiel, chapter xl. The Court of the Gentiles and the Court of the Women, said to have been connected with Herod's Temple, were an innovation of Herod himself. There is nothing said about them in the Word of God.

The Outer Court, with its flight of seven steps, may be regarded as a type of earthly and millennial rest.

The Court of the Priests and the Inner Court, ascended by flights of eight steps, we may regard as typical of resurrection and heavenly rest.

The arrangement of the courts also affords much valuable instruction regarding our approach to God and our nearness of communion with Him.

As WORSHIPPERS in the Outer Court, we simply know and realise ourselves as belonging to the people of God, the redeemed of the Lord.

As MINISTERING in the Court of the Priests, the believer is reminded of his heavenly calling, his priestly standing and privileges, by virtue of his anointing by the Spirit.

The **Court** of the Altar, with its ever-ascending **sacrifices,** reminds him of the ground of his acceptance **with, and** access to, God.

While the Separate Place, with the sanctuary **erected** upon it, teaches the necessity of separation **from** evil, and of the need of that holiness which be**cometh** God's house for ever, in all who draw near to **commune** with a holy God, in whose sight evil cannot **dwell.**

THE COOKING PLACES

The prophet is shown a place in the priests' **court,** on the "two sides westward" or "hinder part," **where** the priests are to boil the trespass and sin**offering** and bake the meat-offering [gift offering]. **He is** next brought into the outer court, in each of the **four corners** of which he is shown a smaller court, forty **cubits** long by thirty broad, in which were places for **boiling** the sacrifices of the people (Ezek. xlvi., 19-24). Sometimes the word "joined" or "attached-**chamber**" is rendered "parlour," as when Samuel took **Saul into** the parlour and gave him the portion set for **him** (1 Sam. ix., 22). These attached-chambers of the **outer court** are for the use of those who come up to **worship,** either for retirement, prayer, conference, or **as a** place in which to partake of the peace offering. **In the peace** offering, God accepted a part, "the food **of the offering** made by fire unto Jehovah" (Lev. iii., 11). All the fat that covered the inwards was burnt **as incense** on the altar; this was God's portion. The **priest who** sprinkled the blood, and who is typical of

Christ, has his portion out of the accompanying meat
or gift offering; the wave breast, emblematic of sympathy and affection, and the heave shoulder, the
emblem of strength and service, were given to Aaron
and his sons, from off the sacrifices of the peace offerings, by a perpetual covenant (Lev. vii., 28-34). The
remainder is the portion of the worshipper who offers
his sacrifice of peace offering unto Jehovah. Thus we
get a beautiful type of fellowship with the Father and
with His Son Jesus Christ, and with the whole priestly
family, in the one offering of Him who hath made
peace through His blood.

GALLERY AGAINST GALLERY IN THREE STOREYS

In the outer court, probably on the west, behind
the Temple, Ezekiel was shown in vision a building
consisting of attached-chambers, in three storeys, with
galleries in front (Ezek. xlii., 1-8). These galleries, it
appears, were over against, and corresponding with,
the galleries of the Temple on the north and south
sides. The attached, or joined, chambers were entered
from one into another, from north to south. The
breadth of the Temple on the west, including the
sanctuary and the side chambers on the north and
south, was fifty cubits. The length of the walls of this
structure, including the attached-chambers, was also
fifty cubits (verse 7). Before the side-chambers of the
Temple, on either side, were galleries in three storeys,
extending outward ten cubits north and south.
Similarly, before the attached-chambers of this building, north and south, were galleries in three storeys,

extending outward ten cubits on either side. Thus the galleries of the building, in three storeys, were over against the galleries in three storeys of the Temple. The expression GALLERY AGAINST GALLERY in three storeys (Ezek. xlii., 3) may thus be explained. The attached-chambers connected with this building in the outer court, in CONTRAST with the side-chambers of the Temple, DECREASED in size as they ascended, being probably seven, six, and five cubits respectively. The doors leading into them, from one to another, faced the north—the galleries taking out a cubit from the attached-chambers on each storey, similar to the way in which each storey of the side-chambers took out a cubit from the walls of the Temple. These attached-chambers, proceeding from north to south, from the side emblematic of justice and judgment to that of mercy and loving-kindness, and diminishing in size as they ascend upward, teach us that, in proportion to deeper views of Divine love, and higher contemplation of Heavenly glories, self, and the space occupied by self, will diminish in equal proportion.

THE PRIESTS

"The priests, the Levites, the sons of Zadok, that kept the charge of My sanctuary when the children of Israel went astray from Me, THEY shall come near to Me to minister unto Me, and they shall stand before

Me to offer [bring near] unto Me the fat and the blood, saith the Lord God [Sovereign-Lord Jehovah]: THEY shall enter into My sanctuary, and THEY shall come near to My table, to minister unto Me, and they shall keep My charge" (Ezek. xliv., 15, 16). These priests appear to be typical of those who believe in Jesus in the present dispensation, when Israel as a nation have gone astray from God.

"When they enter in at the gates of the inner court, they shall be clothed with linen garments" (verses 17, 18). In all their ministrations, whether at the altar or within the sanctuary, nothing of woollen is to come upon them. In the worship and service of the sanctuary above, there will be the absence of all that is carnal or exciting; all will be spiritual and holy. "And when they go forth into the utter [outer] court, even into the utter court to the people, they shall put off their garments wherein THEY ministered, and lay THEM in the holy chambers [attached-chambers], and they shall put on other garments" (verse 19). As those who ministered in the court of the priests were required to change their apparel when they went out to the people in the outer court, even so the risen saints, the heavenly priesthood, in their intercourse with earth during the millennial period, will not be seen in the same glory in which they minister in the heavenly courts above. No high priest is mentioned; the prince (not a king) takes a prominent part in providing the sacrifices (Ezek. xlv., xlvi.). The Lord

Jesus will unite the Kingship and High Priesthood in His own Melchisedec office.

CHAPTER EIGHTEEN

THE HOLY PORTION OF THE LAND

"THE land is Mine, and ye are strangers and so-journers with Me," saith Jehovah to Israel (Lev. xxv., 23). "Moreover, when he shall divide by lot the land for inheritance, ye shall offer an oblation unto Jehovah, a holy portion of the land" (Ezek. xlv. 1). This holy portion is twenty-five thousand reeds square, or about sixty miles; and is divided into THREE parts.

FOR THE PRIESTS AND SANCTUARY

The first portion, towards the north, is about sixty miles long and twenty-four miles broad. "It shall be for the priests, the ministers of the sanctuary, which shall come near to minister unto Jehovah: and it shall be a place for their houses, and a holy place for the sanctuary" (Ezek. xlv. 2-4).

FOR THE LEVITES

Adjoining this portion is that of "the Levites, the ministers of the house," about sixty miles by twenty-four (verse 5).

FOR THE PRINCE

On either side of this oblation for the priests, the Levites, and the City, the PRINCE has his portion, east

and west, extending as far as the portions for the tribes
extend.

THE MILLENNIAL DIVISION OF THE LAND
Ezekiel xlvii., xlviii.

In the division of the land among the twelve tribes,
Levi has no part; he has his inheritance in the holy
oblation belonging to Jehovah. The Levites are
saints, and of the household of God, heirs of God, and
joint-heirs with Christ. Seven of the tribes of Israel—
Dan, Asher, Naphtali, Manasseh, Ephraim ("Joseph
shall have two portions" [chap. xlvii. 13] Reuben,
and Judah—have their portions on the north of the
holy oblation; and five tribes on the south—namely,
Benjamin, Simeon, Issachar, Zebulon, and Gad. The
sanctuary is thus in the very centre of Immanuel's land.
Reckoning from the north seven tribes, the portion for
the priests with the SANCTUARY IN THE MIDST is
the eighth; reckoning from the south five tribes, which
with the City portion and that of the Levites make
seven, the priests' portion is again the eighth. In the
very centre of the sanctuary portion is the altar of
burnt offering. When, in the millennial age, the mountain of Jehovah's house shall be established upon the
top of the mountains (Isa. ii. 2, 3; lxvi. 23; Zech.
xiv. 16), and exalted above the hills, and all nations
shall flow into it, then the altar in the midst of the land
shall not only be God's centre for Israel, but His
centre for worship for the whole earth; THE LAMB
ON THE THRONE is, and ever will be, God's centre for
Heaven and the universe.

God will cause the Gentiles to bring from all parts gold, silver, etc., to make the place of His feet glorious (Isa. lx., 9-14).

THE CITY PORTION

Next to the portion of the Levites towards the south is the possession for the City, about twelve miles in breadth and sixty miles in length; the suburbs enlarge the City to a square of five thousand reeds. In the City of David, where Solomon had his royal palace, will probably be the residence of the prince who will be the earthly representative of Messiah the King; Mount Zion, in Jerusalem, the centre of government and rule. "For the law shall go forth of Zion, and the word of Jehovah from Jerusalem" (Micah iv. 2). The GATES of the City are called after the names of the tribes of Israel—three gates northward, and three at the east, the south, and the west sides (Ezek. xlviii., 30-35)—twelve gates. This city is literal; it may be instructive to compare with the symbolic city of the Revelation, the holy Jerusalem, the emblem of the Church in resurrection glory.

The City of Ezekiel formed a square of four thousand five hundred reeds; the City of Revelation is described as foursquare, the length, breadth, and height equal; it, too, was measured by the reed, but the reed of Revelation is a golden one, the emblem of an estimate which is Divine. Also twelve gates, according to the twelve tribes of Israel (Rev. xxi., 9-22). Concerning the earthly City it is said, "The name of the city from that day shall be "The LORD *is* there"

[Jehovah Shammah] (Ezek. xlviii., 35). So, also, of the holy Jerusalem of Revelation it is said, "The throne of God and of the Lamb shall be in it; and His servants shall serve Him: and they shall see His face; and His name shall be on their foreheads. And they shall reign for ever and ever."

CHAPTER NINETEEN

THE TEMPLE OF SOLOMON
FILLED WITH GLORY

WHEN God had planted Israel in the land which He had promised, and settled them there, David desired to find a Tabernacle for the God of Jacob. But Solomon built Him a house. No sooner was the house built and prepared according to the pattern, than the glory of Jehovah filled the house of God (1 Kings viii. 10-13; 2 Chron. v. 11-14; vii. 1-4).

There are three particulars to notice in connection with the glory filling the Temple:—First, the bringing in of the ARK into its place in the Holy of Holies, and under the shadowing wings of the larger cherubim. In the Ark we have seen a beautiful type of the person of our Immanuel. God has given to His beloved Son a central place of authority and glory. For Him there was no place in His own world, or on the throne of His father David; but there was a place for him on high. To Him God the Father said, "Sit Thou on My right hand, until I make Thine enemies Thy footstool." When the Ark of the Covenant was brought into its proper place, "the cloud filled the house of Jehovah, so that the priests could not stand to minister because of the cloud: for the glory of Jehovah had

filled the house of Jehovah." When the Lord Jesus
came, after His resurrection, into the midst of the
disciples—the doors being shut for fear of the Jews—
He stood in their midst. On the first Lord's Day
evening, and on the second Lord's Day evening, He
takes His own proper place IN THE MIDST. Let us
give the Lord Jesus Christ His proper place, gathering
unto His name and around Him now. Secondly, when
Solomon had prayed, and the sacrifices were offered
"the fire came down from heaven, and consumed the
burnt offering and the sacrifices; and the glory of
Jehovah filled the house. And when all the children
of Israel saw how the fire came down, and the glory of
Jehovah upon the house, they bowed themselves with
their faces to the ground upon the pavement, and worshipped, and praised Jehovah, saying, For He is
good; for His mercy [loving-kindness] endureth for
ever." The value and acceptability of the sacrifice
upon the altar was attested by the fire descending and
consuming it.

So Christ, having presented Himself as an offering
and sacrifice to God, for a sweet-smelling savour, God
the Father showed His acceptance thereof by raising
Him from the dead and setting Him at His own right
hand, and also by the descent of the Holy Spirit, filling
the Church of God with the glory of His presence
(Acts ii., 1-4).

Thirdly, after the Ark was in its place, and the
sacrifices had ascended as a sweet savour unto God
then, when the priests were come out of the Holy

Place, "it came even to pass, as the trumpeters and singers were as one, to make one sound to be heard in praising and thanking Jehovah . . . the priest could not stand to minister by reason of the cloud: for the glory of Jehovah had filled the house of God."

So now, if we would have the house of God filled with the glory of God, we must observe the lessons here taught us; for these things are foundation principles. A crucified, risen, and glorified Christ; a Christ having His own proper place of authority, in gathering and rule; the hearts of His people as one in rendering thanksgiving, praise, and blessing—then shall the glory of the presence of the Lord be known amongst us.

The first disciples (Acts i. 2) had been gathered around His person; they were one in heart and mind, perfectly joined together, determined to give the Lord Jesus Christ His own place (as David's servants were of one heart to make David king). Then we read, "There came a sound from heaven as of a rushing mighty wind, and it filled all the house where they were sitting." The glory of Jehovah and His presence was manifested when the Divine Eternal Spirit came into the midst of the gathered disciples, filling all the house, and resting in tongues of fire upon each of them.

Is not He "the same yesterday, to-day, and for ever"? Is not He who sought of old the companionship of man still desirous of renewing His Edenic walks with man? Will He not walk with every Enoch

who seeks to please God? If we make for Him a
sanctuary, a holy habitation, will He not dwell with
us? If we are of one mind and one heart to make
Jesus King, to accept His authority, and give Him the
glory due unto His name, will He not fulfil His own
promise, and manifest Himself to us? What we want
in our assemblies is the realised presence of God in
Christ; the glory of the Father in the person of the
Son, manifested by the ungrieved Holy Spirit, as the
quickener of dead souls and sanctifier of the believer
unto increasing meetness for the glory yet to be revealed. Three things are essential to the manifested
presence of God. The first is that we are all ready to
HEAR and OBEY; able to say, "Now, therefore, are we
all here present before God, to hear all things that are
commanded thee of God" (Acts x. 33), to hear God's
voice speaking to us from off the mercy-seat, out of the
Holiest of all. Are we listening for the voice of God,
desiring communion with God, who has said to the
scattered ones, "I will be to them as a little sanctuary
in the countries whither they shall come" (Ezek. xi.,
16). We may find the presence of God wherever we
are—

"Where'er we seek Him He is found,
And every place is holy ground."

The next essential is JESUS IN THE MIDST, the
supreme authority of the Lord Jesus Christ in His own
Church. Do we recognise the Lordship of Christ?
Further, there must be the unhindered power of the

Holy Ghost. Is our ministry carried on, not in the words which man's wisdom teacheth, but in the words which the Holy Ghost teacheth? God is waiting to come in; Christ is willing to occupy His proper place. The Spirit of God has not lost His majesty and might; He is as ready as ever to take of the things of Christ, in the glory of the Father, and reveal them unto us.

When the Temple of God shall be erected in the millennial reign; when the mountain of Jehovah's house shall be established in the top of the mountains, exalted above the hills, and all nations shall flow into it; then shall the glory of God once more fill the house. Jehovah shall be in His holy Temple; His glory shall be revealed: and all flesh shall see it together.

When we, as living stones, are builded together in resurrection perfectness a holy house for God, a habitation of God through the Spirit, then shall the presence of God and of the Lamb and of the Eternal Spirit fill it with everlasting glory. Turn to Rev. xxi., 22, to that wondrous description of the Holy City, the New Jerusalem, the Church, the Bride, the Lamb's Wife—"I saw no temple therein; for Jehovah God Almighty and the Lamb are the temple of it. And the city had no need of the sun, neither of the moon, to shine in it: for the glory of God did lighten it, and the Lamb is the light [lamp] thereof." LAMP is the word used in the original by the Spirit of God. The word "lamp" reminds us of those lamps which, supplied with oil, illuminated the sanctuary of old with brilliancy and light. So the glory of God will for ever be seen in the face of Jesus Christ, manifested and made known by the Eternal Spirit of our God.

The presence of the Holy Ghost here on earth is a constant witness of the exaltation and glory of Jesus Christ at the right hand of the Majesty on high (John xiv., 16-20). By the Pentecostal Spirit were all believers baptised into one body, and made to drink into one Spirit in union with the Head in glory, one Spirit with the risen Lord. O to realise this according to the prayer of the Apostle in Eph. iii., 14-19—"For this cause I bow my knees unto the Father of our Lord Jesus Christ, of whom the whole [every] family in heaven and upon earth is named, that He would grant you, according to the riches of His glory, to be strengthened with might by His Spirit in the inner man; that Christ may dwell in your hearts by faith; that ye, being rooted and grounded in love, may be able to comprehend with all saints what is the breadth, and length, and depth, and height; and to know the love of Christ which passeth knowledge, that ye might be filled with [into] all the fulness of God"! O wondrous word! Can we be so filled? Filled INTO all His infinite, eternal, boundless love, like some tiny shell in ocean's depths, or like a little fish swimming in a boundless ocean. Blessed with all spiritual blessings in heavenly places in Christ; upheld by the power of Omnipotence; supplied by the bounty of Him whose fulness is inexhaustible, and whose love is shed abroad in our hearts by the Holy Ghost given unto us. "God is love; and he that dwelleth in love dwelleth in **God,** and God in him."

ANSWERS TO QUESTIONS

ON POINTS OF INTEREST CONNECTED WITH
THE TEMPLES OF SOLOMON AND EZEKIEL

Given by Mr. Newberry in connection with his Lectures

Is there a difference between the "threshing-floor" (2 Sam. xxiv., 24) *and "the place"* (1 Chron. xxi., 25)? *The price is said to be "fifty shekels of silver" in the one case and "six hundred shekels of gold" in the other?*

The threshing-floor and OXEN were BOUGHT for fifty shekels of silver—the ransom-money of a hundred souls (see Exod. xxx., 13)—their full legal value, meeting the requirements of law. This was the place for the altar, according to 2 Sam. xxiv. 25. But we further learn from 1 Chron. xxi., 25 that David GAVE for the whole place or field six hundred talents of gold by weight. This was the site of the Temple. SILVER, the emblem of REDEMPTION, was PAID for the threshing-floor connected with the altar and sacrifice.

100

GOLD, the emblem of GLORY, was GIVEN for the field connected with the Temple and the glory.

What would the value in English money be, of the enormous quantities of gold and silver prepared by David (1 Chron. xxii., 14)?

One hundred thousand talents of gold at £5,475 the talent of 114 lb. - £547,500,000; and a thousand thousand talents of silver at £342 the talent equals £342,000,000: together £889,500,000. Part of this silver and gold was used for the gold and silver vessels of the sanctuary; but by far the greater portion was employed, as we are informed in 1 Chron. xxix., 4, to overlay (literally, to plaster) the walls of the houses, the stones being encased in solid silver, then overlaid with cedar or cypress, and afterwards overlaid with gold. The whole building, including the porch, roof (2 Chron. iii., 4), walls, floor, posts, beams, and doors (1 Kings vi., 21, 22, 30), was not gilded, but COVERED with gold, the gold being fitted upon the carved work (1 Kings vi., 35), thus—not obliterating—but setting forth the exquisite carving on the wood in surpassing splendour.

The silver plastering of the stones tells of RE-DEMPTION, the living stones of the spiritual house being redeemed by the blood of the Lamb; while the gold covering all faintly foreshadows the GLORY of God which the redeemed will for ever share. In Rev. xxi., 11 the New Jerusalem is seen in resurrection per-fectness and glory, having the GLORY OF GOD: "the city itself was pure gold, like unto transparent glass."

Did the Temple built by Herod stand on the site of Solomon's Temple?

When the Idumean king came to the kingdom, he found the Temple erected in Ezra's time after the fashion and on the site of Solomon's Temple, but inferior in splendour and glory. This did not meet his taste. He took it down, and on its site erected another Temple, which was forty-six years in building. This was the Temple which was in existence at the time of our Lord. It was made after his own design; and while, no doubt, he retained some parts of the original structure, as a whole it was entirely different from the Temple of Solomon. If we are to accept the testimony of Josephus and other writers, the Temple of Herod seems to have been built on a much larger scale and higher than the original. The stones of which it was built were white and wonderfully great: some say twenty-five cubits by twelve cubits. Whether we may take this as correct or not, it is certain, from the expression used by the disciples in Mark xiii., 1, that the stones used were conspicuous for their size.

When it is said that Peter and John went up to the Temple at the hour of prayer (Acts iii.), are we to understand that they entered as worshippers there?

There is confusion in the minds of some regarding the place where our Lord and His disciples prayed and taught. Not being of the tribe of Levi, they could not enter into the court of the priests, nor draw near to the altar, nor enter the Holy Place. The Holy Ghost, in speaking of the Temple, uses two distinct words in the original Greek. One is *Hieron* (from *hieros*, sacred), which refers to the entire Temple, its courts and other buildings, the whole *external* structure. The other word is *Naos* (from *naio*, to dwell), and signifies the inner building, the Holy and Most Holy Places, the sanctuary. Where our Lord and His apostles prayed and taught was in *Hieron*, the external courts alone.

What Temple is referred to in 2 Thessalonians ii., 6, and there called the Temple of God?

The fourth Temple which will be built and in use, according to Dan. ix., 26, 27; xii., 11; Matt. xxiv., 15-22; 2 Thess. ii., 1-8; Rev. xi., 1, 2. There will be a Temple acknowledged as the Temple of God on earth, and daily sacrifices offered on its altar, during the first three and a half years of Daniel's seventieth week, The prince who is the head of the Roman Empire of that time will confirm a covenant for one week, or seven years with the people of Israel; but in the midst of the week—at the end of three and a half years—according to the prophecy, he breaks the covenant, takes away the daily sacrifice, and sets up the abomination of desolation in the Holy Place. There is, therefore, a "temple of God" which is known in Rev. xi., 1, and measured by John, and also an altar, recognised as the Temple and Altar of God, with a daily sacrifice which can be taken away. The Antichrist occupies the place of God, and "showing himself that he is God," and claiming all worship to himself. Then commences that period of unparalleled woe called "the great tribulation," such as never before has been on earth.

Wherein do the types of the Temple differ from those of the Tabernacle?

In comparing the Tabernacle with the Temple, we learn from the New Testament application that the Tabernacle in the Wilderness is a type of the Church in the present dispensation. During the period of our Lord's sojourn on earth, He was the dwelling-place of God with man. "The Word was made flesh, and TABERNACLED among us." But that will not exhaust the full significance of the Tabernacle type. It is further explained to us by that Word—"In whom (Christ) ye also are builded together an habitation of God through the Spirit" (Eph. ii., 22). Thus, the Church on earth, in its wilderness condition, becomes a habitation of God, a sanctuary wherein He may dwell.

The Temple is another type of God's presence with His redeemed people. "Ye are the temple of God, and the Spirit of God dwelleth in you" (1 Cor. iii.). And again, "In whom all the building fitly framed together groweth into an holy temple in the Lord" (Eph. ii., 21). I take the Temple, therefore, to be a type of the whole of the redeemed going on growing; living stones being added from time to time to the holy temple of the Lord—living stones, built up a spiritual house. And this not only in its present wilderness condition, but of all the redeemed as associated with the risen Christ in resurrection and heavenly glory, clothed upon with their house from Heaven, the eternal glory of the redeemed, monuments erected to the praise of God's redeeming grace and love.

The Temple described in Ezekiel will be an earthly reflection of all the redeemed in heavenly glory. The Holy Jerusalem of Revelation xxi. is an emblem of the Church as the Bride of the Lamb in resurrection and heavenly glory, the earthly reflection of which will be the literal, earthly Jerusalem under the new covenant in the millennial rest.

From whence was the water derived that was used in the Temple?

The laborious investigations of the persons employed by the Palestine Exploration Committee have discovered many extensive cisterns, series of arches, and watercourses under the vast Temple platform upon which it stood. A special exploration of one about 45 feet deep, 63 feet long, and 57 feet broad, has been made. Full investigation would, doubtless, throw much light on the arrangements for the supply of water for the brazen sea, the lavers, and other uses of the Temple.

If the present time is the period of preparation, when will the building of the spiritual temple take place?

The whole work of preparation belongs to the present time and scene. The time of the erection of the heavenly Temple will be at the first resurrection when the Lord comes, when the dead in Christ, from Abel downward, shall rise first, and the living ones shall be changed and caught up, and all will together be built up as an everlasting monument of redeeming grace and love.

What was the position of the two Pillars, Jachin and Boaz?

It is said in 1 Kings vii., 21—"He set up the pillars in the porch of the temple"; but this should be rendered "BY the porch." In harmony with this we read, in 2 Chron. iii., 17—"He reared up the pillars before the temple, one on the right hand and the other on the left." In Ezek. xl., 49, we read—"There were pillars by the posts (of the porch), one on this side, and another on that." Thus all these Scriptures are found to be in harmony.

What is the significance of the absence of the Brazen Sea and Lavers in the description of the Temple as given by Ezekiel?

In connection with the Temple of Ezekiel, neither Brazen Sea nor Brazen Laver are mentioned: the waters that issue from under the threshold take their place. These waters flow eastward from the right side of the house, at the south side of the altar, the exact position occupied by the Brazen Sea in Solomon's Temple. These waters are emblematical of life in the Spirit, in its origin and progress, deepening and widening as it flows, carrying with it and diffusing healing and life, verdure and fertility. This life, having its source in God, is spiritually and divinely pure, and needs no cleansing such as is typified by the Laver or the Brazen Sea. The pure river of water of life proceeding from the throne of God and the Lamb (Rev.

xxii., 1) is a figure corresponding to that of Ezek. xlvii. Its LOWLY and HOLY origin is set forth in its issuing from the THRESHOLD of the SANCTUARY; the SOVEREIGNTY of God's GRACE, founded on the atoning work of Christ, is revealed in its proceeding from the THRONE of God and of the LAMB. Ezekiel xlvii. gives the LITERAL and EARTHLY view of it; Revelation xxii. gives the SPIRITUAL and HEAVENLY; and both are millennial.

What is to be learned from the varied degrees of value of the materials used in making the vessels?

All the vessels of the Holy Places within were of GOLD. The lampstands and tables for use in the side-chambers were of SILVER. The vessels in the inner and outer courts were of BRASS. The IRON was used to make nails for the doors and for the joinings; and the brazen vessels were cast in CLAY (2 Chron. iv., 17). Thus we see a gradual decrease of value in order from within: gold, silver, brass, iron, clay. With this we may contrast the great image shown to King Nebuchadnezzar (Dan. ii., 31-35)—head of GOLD, breast of SILVER, thighs of BRASS, legs of IRON, feet of iron and CLAY. In the decreasing value of the materials in the image we see the DECLENSION of authority originally received from God downward; while in the Temple vessels we perceive the INCREASE of the value and glory of the worship and service rendered as the worshippers draw nearer and yet nearer into the presence of God.

What is the virtue of the sacrifices to be offered in connection with Ezekiel's Temple, and of what are the feasts to be kept symbolic?

As all the sacrifices offered previous to Christ's offering of Himself were FORESHADOWINGS of the work to be accomplished on the Cross, even so will all the sacrifices to be offered on the millennial altar be COMMEMORATIVE remembrances of His one great sacrifice offered once for all, complete and perfect for eternity. In connection with Ezekiel's altar there is no mention of the evening sacrifice, that having been accomplished when Christ offered Himself on Calvary; nor is there any mention of the Day of Atonement being observed in the future, that having had its answer when Christ entered into the Holiest with "His own blood," once for all.

Likewise are the feasts remembrances of grace and glory. The PASSOVER is the memorial of Israel's deliverance from Egypt (Exod. xii.); it is also a memorial remembrance of Christ, our passover sacrifice for us, as the Lord's Supper is in this dispensation. The FEAST OF TABERNACLES, or booths, was a memorial of Israel's wilderness wanderings (Lev. xxiii., 39-43); it is also named the "feast of ingathering" at the year's end (Exod. xxxiv., 22), and was a foreshadowing type of millennial rest and restoration which Israel will be then enjoying.

It is specially worthy of notice that there is no mention made of Pentecost or the FEAST OF WEEKS, which is typical of the present dispensation and having its fulfilment now.

Who is "the prince" mentioned in Ezekiel xlvi., 11-12, who prepares a voluntary burnt offering?

The prince is evidently a lineal descendant of the royal house of David, in whom the promises concerning the Kingdom will be literally fulfilled. He is not said to be the King. Messiah is King, and the prince appears to be His earthly representative. He is permitted to sit in the porch of the outer east gate, and to eat bread before Jehovah (Ezek. xliv., 3). The priests prepare His burnt offering and peace offering: he being of the royal and not the priestly line, though he worships at the threshold, does not enter into the court of the priests as a worshipper there.

Is the New Jerusalem as seen by John in Rev. xxi., a figure of Heaven, or of the earthly Jerusalem during the Millennium?

It is necessary to a right understanding of Scripture to distinguish between FIGURATIVE and EMBLEMATIC or symbolic language. The language used by the Apostle in Heb. xi., 10; xii., 22, is FIGURATIVE, whereas the structure of the Book of Revelation is EMBLEMATIC. The truth is made known, as we are told in chap. i., 1, by signs or symbols.

The CITY which Abraham looked for, and which we too are expecting, is a figurative representation for a fixed HEAVENLY habitation, a contrast to the pilgrim, earthly condition.

The Holy Jerusalem of Revelation, chap. xxi., is an EMBLEM of the Bride, the Lamb's wife. The resurrection body of the saint is compared to "a HOUSE not made with hands, eternal in the heavens." A city is a collection of houses; and as the many members of Christ form one body, what more appropriate emblem of the Bride, the Lamb's wife, can we conceive, when each individual member will be clothed upon with his house from heaven, than that here employed?

The city described in Ezekiel is the EARTHLY Jerusalem, the metropolis of the nation of Israel, when brought into possession of the land, during the Millennium. This city is LITERAL, and not SYMBOLIC, as the city of Revelation, xxi.

The Temple of Ezekiel is situated in the midst of the priests' portion, which is distinct from the city; while of the Holy Jerusalem it is said, "I saw no temple therein, for the Lord God Almighty and the Lamb are the temple of it." The redeemed in glory dwell in God, and God dwells in them.